COUSINEAU · TIM FOX · EDDIE GEORGE ISH

IE GRIFFIN · JOHN HICKS · JIM HOUSTO PE

NSON · MARCUS MAREK · JIM MARSHALL · TOM MATTE · M

BAUGH · CHRIS SPIELMAN · JIM STILLWAGON · PAUL WARFI

TH BYARS · JIM OTIS · TOM SKLADANY · CORNELIUS GREEN

N BASCHNAGEL · CRIS CARTER · HOWARD "HOPALONG" CASSA

COUSINEAU · TIM FOX · EDDIE GEORGE · RANDY GRADISH

IE GRIFFIN · JOHN HICKS · JIM HOUSTON · REX KERN · PE

NSON · MARCUS MAREK · JIM MARSHALL · TOM MATTE · M

BAUGH · CHRIS SPIELMAN · JIM STILLWAGON · PAUL WARFI

TH BYARS · JIM OTIS · TOM SKLADANY · CORNELIUS GREEN

N BASCHNAGEL · CRIS CARTER · HOWARD "HOPALONG" CASSA

COUSINEAU · TIM FOX · EDDIE GEORGE · RANDY GRADISH

IE GRIFFIN · JOHN HICKS · JIM HOUSTON · REX KERN · PE

NSON · MARCUS MAREK · JIM MARSHALL · TOM MATTE · M

BAUGH · CHRIS SPIELMAN · JIM STILLWAGON · PAUL WARFI

TH BYARS · JIM OTIS · TOM SKLADANY · CORNELIUS GREEN

N BASCHNAGEL · CRIS CARTER · HOWARD "HOPALONG" CASSA

WHAT IT MEANS TO
BE A BUCKEYE

JIM TRESSEL

AND OHIO STATE'S GREATEST PLAYERS

EDITED BY JEFF SNOOK

TRIUMPH
BOOKS
CHICAGO

Library of Congress Cataloging-in-Publication Data available upon request.

This book is available in quantity at special discounts for your group or organization. For further information, contact:

Triumph Books
601 South LaSalle Street
Suite 500
Chicago, Illinois 60605
(312) 939-3330
Fax (312) 663-3557

Printed in the United States of America
ISBN 1-57243-602-6
Interior design by Nick Panos
All photos courtesy of Chance Brockway or Chance Brockway Jr. unless indicated otherwise.

CONTENTS

Ken Fritz, Randy Gradishar, Cornelius Greene, Archie Griffin,
John Hicks, Vic Koegel, Ken Kuhn, Jeff Logan, Calvin
Murray, Lou Pietrini, Doug Plank, Bruce Ruhl, Vince Skillings,
Tom Skladany, Chris Ward

FOREWORD

What It Means to Be a Buckeye

IT WAS MY FATHER'S DREAM TO PLAY FOOTBALL for the Ohio State Buckeyes. Lee Tressel was the high school Player of the Year in Ohio in 1942, and he was recruited by the great Paul Brown to come to Ohio State. He played that spring of '43, throwing a touchdown pass to Les Horvath and running for two more touchdowns. After that spring, he enlisted in the U.S. Navy, giving up his dream of being a Buckeye so he could serve his country.

Dad was sent to Cleveland for training, and the school he was allowed to attend while there was Baldwin-Wallace, and that's how he ended up there. He later got a master's degree from Ohio State, and he remained a very loyal Buckeyes fan, so naturally, so were we.

So I was definitely a Buckeyes fan. When Rex Kern led Ohio State to the Rose Bowl and the national championship, I was a high school quarterback and Rex was my idol. I always had to know what Rex was doing. Rex Kern was pictured on the cover of the Cleveland *Plain Dealer* holding his Rose Bowl MVP football and his Bible. I thought maybe I ought to be reading the Bible because if Rex was doing it, that's what I ought to do. That's the way I felt about Rex, Woody Hayes, and Ohio State.

Throughout Dad's coaching career at Baldwin-Wallace, his season would end before the Ohio State–Michigan game would be played. We didn't get to sit down with him much during the season, but it was our tradition to sit down and watch the Ohio State–Michigan game together as a family. My dad loved Woody Hayes. He did many things while coaching at Baldwin-Wallace that Woody did at Ohio State. If Woody watered down the AstroTurf, so did my dad. If Woody ran a certain play this way, so did my dad.

Jim Tressel addresses the media following Ohio State's win at Northwestern on October 5, 2002.

I met Woody Hayes for the first time in 1976 when I came down to study coaching the quarterbacks with George Chaump, then the quarterbacks' coach at Ohio State. But most of my impressions of him were from afar. I read his book *Hotline to Victory*, and I studied him. In 1981, when my dad was on his deathbed, Woody found out and drove straight to Cleveland to be with him for all hours of the night. It was a few years after he had been released at Ohio State, but Woody was still being Woody.

He cared about people.

As a head coach, you study people who are successful, and you hope you learn from them and pick up some things from them, and it is natural to do some of the things those people did—but you have to develop some of your own beliefs, too. I have been blessed with a great background, because I got to watch a coach every day of my life. My dad was one of the greatest coaches, because he cared about every one of his players. He realized that the most important thing a player would ask was, "Do you really care about me?"

I know he did. I know Woody Hayes did, too. The times have changed since Woody Hayes coached at Ohio State. The rules have changed. The game has changed, but the fundamental beliefs haven't. It is still about blocking and tackling, and it is still about developing as a well-rounded person. Woody believed in those things; so did my dad, and so do I.

Coach Tressel yells encouragement from the sideline during the Buckeyes' win at Cincinnati on September 21, 2002.

After the Fiesta Bowl, it was hard not to think of my dad because I know what Ohio State meant to him. My brother Dick is on our staff, and I know we both thought of our parents after the game that night. Some of our family members came up to us and mentioned how proud they would be. I know it would have meant so much to them.

Football happens to be what we like, or what we love, but it is not all that we are going to do in life. We want to make it clear to our young players that they are here at Ohio State to learn and to do a bunch of other things. Some guys who think the NFL will be their sole provider end up being mistaken, so we work hard to make them believe that football will not be the sole provider for them. Each player is always one play away from never going to the NFL, from never playing another down again.

That is why we created "The Block 'O' of Life." We put this concept together at Youngstown State and we asked ourselves, "Where are the areas that we can help these young kids grow?"

With it, we have established a goal sheet that is given to each of our players.

Football is the easy part of it for these players. One of the most valuable things our players will take away from here will be the memories and experiences of this football family. It will mean more and more to them for every day of their lives.

For football/family, the goal sheet statement is: "I am part of one of the greatest families known to man. I count on my teammates, and they are counting on me. I will achieve great things for the family." The other parts of the goal sheet are spiritual/moral, personal/family, academics/career, strength/fitness, and caring/giving.

The spiritual, moral, and ethical part has to be at the top. We make it clear to them that no matter what they accomplish in life, no matter what they achieve, if they don't do it in an ethical or moral manner, they won't be fulfilled.

For spiritual/moral, our goal sheet statement reads: "Above all else, I realize that my spiritual beliefs and my ethical values will shape my life. I will do what is right!"

For personal/family: "The family is the basic social unit of our society. My family is very important to me in many, many ways."

For academics/career: "One of the primary reasons I am at Ohio State is to achieve academically, obtain a valuable degree and begin a profitable career. My degree will give me choices."

We also have a strength/fitness area. We want our people to be in great shape, which involves great health habits as well. There are many people in this world who would give everything back if they had their health.

For strength/fitness: "One of the greatest gifts we have is our health. My physical conditioning is a controllable commodity. My conditioning will win for me in the fourth quarter. I will develop lifetime habits."

At the bottom of "The Block 'O' of Life" are the caring and giving areas. We must be in the community to help others, to care about other people. As coach Hayes used to say, you "pay forward." We want our players to pay forward.

Coach Tressel patrols the field during warm-ups before the 2002 game at Northwestern.

The man in the middle: coach Tressel organizes a sideline meeting during the 25–7 win over Washington State on September 14, 2002.

For caring/giving, our goal sheet statement is: "My development does not end in the classroom or on the football field. How I function as a total person in society is important. I will give back to my community."

We try not to set the goals for the players—they set goals for themselves. We just want their goals to be comprehensive. Players who say they want to do only enough to remain academically eligible to play in college and then go on to the NFL are selling themselves short. What we have been trying to preach to our players is that this time is not a gap between high school and the NFL. This is life! This is what will fulfill you! This is the experience you need to treasure and learn from.

When it comes to Ohio State tradition, my firsthand experience began a day or two before Christmas in 1982 when Earle Bruce called me. At that time, I was coaching the quarterbacks at Syracuse and I was still recruiting Ohio, and he was looking for an assistant. I still remember meeting him at the Holiday Inn in Berea, at the corner of I-71 and Bagley Road. He was very focused, and he knew what he was looking for. I had to hold my breath for a week or so, but he called back and offered me the job. He said, "Get here as soon as you can."

Those two years at Syracuse are the only two years I have ever spent outside the state of Ohio.

I started working at Ohio State in early January of 1983, as quarterbacks and receivers coach. It was two years after my father had passed away, and I knew what Ohio State had meant him. My father loved it so much, so I felt as if I was coming back home.

Those three seasons at Ohio State provided so many good memories: the Fiesta Bowl win over Pitt when we scored late in the game—that was the first bowl game I had ever coached and it was a big thrill; the big comeback win over Illinois in 1984 when Keith Byars lost his shoe but kept running for that long touchdown; and beating Michigan that year.

When I was touring campus the week I was hired in January 2001, three words came to mind everywhere I went: *tradition, people, excellence.*

I believe that when you take a job and you are working somewhere, you should do your research and know about the foundation and tradition of what came before you. I didn't attend Ohio State, so I wasn't aware of "Carmen, Ohio," the Buckeye Grove, and the Victory Bell until I came to work here as an assistant and I studied it. Those three years were fundamental to me in learning about the Ohio State tradition, and that is what makes Ohio State so special. If you are not from Ohio, you do not know deep down inside what makes Ohio State special.

And that is why I believe it is important to expose these traditions to our players.

For example, I had always heard about the Best Damn Band's skull session at St. John Arena before games, but I had never experienced it. When I got here, I asked, "If this is such a great tradition, how come many players and coaches don't know about it?" We all looked at each other, and nobody had an answer. So we arranged to go over there and let the players see what it was all about. They loved it.

When you first tell young people about something new, they are less than ecstatic about it. When you talk about conditioning and you put them through it, they hate it—until they realize they are in better shape than the other team at the end of the game, and then they love it. When I got here as head coach, I didn't know what the players knew or didn't know. I didn't know if they knew "Carmen, Ohio" or didn't know it. But I knew I was going to give them the chance to know it, and learn it, and love it.

One thing is sure, as the years go by, those things mean more to you, and the passing of time brings everything into perspective. That's why "Carmen, Ohio" means so much to people. When we are singing it after each game and I look into that crowd of scarlet and gray, I see tears running down faces. It means so much to people. Ohio State is important to them. Ohio State is important to us. If kids come in here as freshmen and they don't know what it should be like, they will know it by the time they leave.

The Ohio State–Michigan game is one of the most prestigious, most important games not only in football but in all of sports. It is an honor for our players and coaches to be a part of it. And as I have said before, I want our fans and alumni to be proud of our players when we play that game and proud of our coaches when we coach that game.

On the sideline at the Fiesta Bowl, I looked around and saw so many Buckeyes from years past. They were so pumped up and so fired up, and by the end of the game, I had never seen guys so drained emotionally. It meant so much to this team to have them there on the sideline with us.

In my mind, it is our responsibility to keep an open door for those players. This is not my program. It is theirs. It belongs to anyone who ever dropped a bead of sweat to build it, from a walk-on who never played to an All-American. Our responsibility is to make them proud of what we are trying to do. I care about the integrity and tradition of this program, and I know they care about it, too. We will play as hard as we can play, we will coach as hard as we can coach, and we will respect as hard as we can respect.

The two greatest days in our student-athletes' lives should be the day they walk across the stage to receive their diploma and the day they slip a national championship ring on their finger.

I would guess that fans don't realize the deep meaning of being part of this Ohio State family for the players, past and present. I am hoping it becomes crystal clear in this book. I believe that the strong inner feelings that the

Coach Tressel relays a play to quarterback Craig Krenzel during the 2002 win at Cincinnati.

contributors to this book lend will help everyone understand how important and how deep the connection to Ohio State is. There are some powerful messages here. It is about Ohio State. It is about football. And it is about life. It is how each person was uniquely moved and affected by the experience of playing football for the Buckeyes.

What does it mean to be a Buckeye?

It means we are extraordinarily blessed and we have an awesome responsibility to uphold the higher standards that have been set before us. It means we have a tradition that is second to none. It means we love Ohio State.

Time and change will surely show . . .
How firm thy friendship . . . O-HI-O!

—Jim Tressel

xiv

EDITOR'S ACKNOWLEDGMENTS

First of all, I would like to thank Ohio State athletic director Andy Geiger and associate athletic director Archie Griffin for allowing this book to be written with the cooperation, participation and encouragement of head coach Jim Tressel.

Thanks to sports information director Steve Snapp, who was there to answer any questions that surfaced during the process.

Jim Tressel may have graduated from Baldwin-Wallace and coached at Youngstown State, but he has already proved himself to be a true Buckeye. I want to thank him for his vision and involvement in this book and for realizing that the tradition and past of The Ohio State University is as important as its present and its future. The man is a champion on and off the playing field, and Ohio State is lucky to have him.

Coach Tressel's secretary, Deb Broeker, was vital, too, given her boss's demanding schedule. Thanks, Deb, for putting up with my seemingly endless phone calls.

Most of all, I want to especially thank each and every man who once wore an Ohio State uniform and took the time to participate in this project.

Through your words and memories I hope will come a better understanding of what it means to be a Buckeye.

INTRODUCTION

Two months and four days after the Ohio State Buckeyes won their first national championship in 34 years, I was sitting in Jim Tressel's office at the Woody Hayes Athletic Center. On the previous night, he had driven through poor weather to speak to the Urbana, Ohio, OSU Booster Club, which had presented him with a gift.

As we talked, he couldn't stop looking at this gift, and it became very clear to me that it touched him deeply. He had placed it behind his desk.

"Look at that!" he said, turning to examine it one more time. "Looks just like him, doesn't it?"

It was a bronzed bust of Wayne Woodrow Hayes.

I realized this was Ohio State's past and present greatness colliding, even if it was in a symbolic way.

One, a man so loved, feared, and respected who captured five national championships, molded hundreds of football players into men, and gave 28 years of service to the university, becoming a legend and an icon along the way.

Another, a man who resurrected the rich tradition while reaching unparalleled greatness in only his second season as head coach.

They are generations apart yet so similar in character, ethics, and ideals. They are two men who were made to lead, build, teach, help, and nurture.

Woody Hayes paid forward each and every day, especially through his charitable work and endless days and nights sitting next to hospital beds brightening the day of those less fortunate. He had a temper. He hated to lose. He lashed out. The rest of the skeptical world can remember what they choose from the man called Woody, but a Buckeye remembers the essence of the man.

When I came up with the concept for this book, I didn't intend for it to be a book about Woody Hayes—and it is not—but there will be times that you believe it is. That's because the men who played for him from 1951 through 1978 respected him, worshipped him, hated him at times, and ultimately loved him. He was the most prominent figure in most of their lives, and all these years later, they have come to understand him much, much better. What's more, they miss him and think of him almost every day.

If you don't believe he was a great man—perhaps one of the greatest figures of our time—read Rex Kern's chapter. If you don't think he had a sense of humor, read Jim Stillwagon's. If you don't think he believed in education, read Brian Baschnagel's. If you don't think he believed in love and family, read George Jacoby's.

The thing is, contrary to popular opinion, football wasn't Woody Hayes' life. It was only his conduit for making everyone else's lives better. He didn't care for money, because football was his currency for making everyone else's lives richer. He brought hundreds of young men onto campus because of this game, but once he got them there, he taught them the lessons that would make most of them wildly successful later in life.

As Rex Kern reports, about 87 percent of Woody Hayes' players graduated. They became doctors, lawyers, ministers, and presidents of their companies. And they gave back to their communities, or as Woody would put it, they "paid forward." Whether they started every game, played sparingly, or became injured, he stood by them all the way to graduation day and beyond.

In the end, I often wonder if this great university and its fans ever took that man for granted until it was too late. He did so much but was remembered by outsiders for so little.

In talking to the 2002 seniors, I realized how similar Jim Tressel is to Woody Hayes. These players never knew Woody and probably never read much about him. But coach Tressel's beliefs, for the most part, are right out of Woody's playbook for life. I know that Woody would have loved Jim's creation, "The Block 'O' of Life."

When coach Tressel visits recruits, I would doubt that he ever mentions the acronym "NFL." Neither did Woody, who rarely even mentioned football in selling Ohio State to high school seniors. In coach Tressel's Foreword, he refers to a scene when Woody spent time at the bedside of Jim's father, Lee, the legendary Baldwin-Wallace coach. Now if God ever put two greater and yet humble men in one room at the same time, I wouldn't know when that would have been.

Lee Tressel's son James Patrick is a throwback all right. He has thrown us all back to the good times. Ohio State fans already have benefited immensely and will continue to relish having him pace that sideline each autumn Saturday wearing his scarlet and gray sweater vests. But more important, Ohio State's players will benefit more. Understand that Kenny Peterson never even realized "Carmen, Ohio" existed until his junior year when Jim Tressel was hired.

Coach Tressel believes that "like coach Hayes said, you really can't pay back. So it is about paying forward in so many ways. We have a responsibility to teach that to our young men and to do it every day."

One day during the compilation of this book, he called me and said, "You want to talk about paying forward? You have to go talk to Max Fisher! Now there's a man who has paid forward." It turned out that Max M. Fisher was recovering from a broken hip at his Palm Beach, Florida, home—about five miles from where I live. I called him and scheduled a visit.

You've heard of the Fisher College of Business? It's named after Max, who donated $20 million to build it. One of the most noted philanthropists of our time, Fisher was born in Salem, Ohio, but built an empire in Detroit. He became a key advisor to Presidents Nixon, Ford, Reagan, and Bush Sr., specializing in Middle Eastern affairs and Jewish issues. He has served on more boards and task forces than he can count. And he has given away more money than Congress.

But you know what his passion is?

Ohio State football.

"I played, you know," he said of his days with the Buckeyes in the mid-twenties, "but I hurt my knee pretty bad and that was that."

In front of his large-screen TV, Max Fisher never misses a game, and he enjoyed the 2002 championship season as much as anyone. "Wasn't that great?" he said, his 95-year-old eyes twinkling at the idea of Ohio State finishing 14–0 and number one. "That season made me feel young again. I wanted to go out there to the Fiesta Bowl, but you know when you get older . . ."

As I got up to walk out of his mansion, a butler, a nurse, and a personal assistant scurried to take care of him, and he sat up in his bed. "Hey, don't forget," he said. "Tell that Tressel fella I sure would like to have dinner with him some night."

Now there's a meal where I wouldn't mind being a fly on the wall—one of Ohio State's biggest benefactors meeting its living icon. Two Buckeyes who believe in making a difference, you could say.

As I have traveled the country and lived in Florida since graduating from Ohio State in 1982, I often have been asked by non-Ohioans: "What is a Buckeye, anyway?"

The way I see it, if you have to ask, you'll never understand.

You are a Buckeye if the Oval is more than a shape to you. If you realize that taking the time to watch the leaves fall there on a sunny autumn day will reward you in ways you never thought possible. It is then that you know William Oxley Thompson may have the best view on earth.

You are a Buckeye if you return to campus, no matter how many years it's been since you took that final class, and you find yourself drawn to the falling water from the fountain at Mirror Lake. It truly is a mystical place, perhaps your favorite.

You are a Buckeye if you check your watch by the giant clock tower of Independence Hall.

You are a Buckeye if that giant horseshoe is your Saturday place of worship.

You are a Buckeye if the sounds from the TBDBITL are as sweet to you as anything the Beatles or Sinatra ever created.

And you are a Buckeye if the sweetest sounds of them all are the words and music to "Carmen, Ohio."

Our alma mater brings so much emotion from the toughest men. Vaughn Broadnax named his daughter after it. Jim Marshall, who left school early to play pro football in 1958, still cries when he hears it. Cie Grant is proud to claim that he has sung it in front of thousands of fans. And now, Jim Tressel brings every victory to an official finish by facing the band and bellowing it out with his warriors surrounding him.

In this book, you will read about the many traditions Ohio State football players have embraced and nurtured through the years.

There are many references to "gold pants," a tradition started by former coach Francis Schmidt in 1934. Someone asked Schmidt how the Buckeyes would fare against Michigan that year, and he replied, "They put their pants on one leg at a time just like everybody else." From that, each Ohio State player has been awarded a gold charm in the form of a pair of football pants for each victory over the rival Wolverines. By the way, Schmidt's Buckeyes whipped Michigan 34–0 that year.

This is why these Buckeyes' words and messages are so vital today.

From Jim Stillwagon's disdain for individualism to Randy Gradishar's intense love for tradition to Jim Otis' boyhood dreams being realized to John Hicks' love for his teammates to Brian Baschnagel's dogged determination to succeed on the field and in the classroom to Pepper Johnson's intensity—they have each contributed to the tradition that has been built day by day, season by season, decade by decade.

From Charlie Ream's first days on campus in 1934 through the senior class of 2002, which wears national championship rings as you read this, this book will give you some insight to what they did, how they felt, what they thought, and all that they believed in.

Ohio State football has been and is a way of life, and without it, there would be a large void.

The men who have played it come from places all over the country—from Ashtabula to Zelina, from California to New York. They arrived as big-eyed freshmen with large fears and bigger dreams, and they departed as men possessing a concrete understanding of teamwork, commitment, perseverance, and dedication.

They arrived part of one family but left as an integral and lasting part of another. They made friendships that will last their lifetimes. They sang "Across the Field," they earned gold pants, they won Big Ten titles and national championships, and they fell in love—not only with the football program but with the greatest university in the land and its unmatched traditions and ideals. They became Buckeyes, a concept they discovered lasts for life.

Here are some of their stories.

—Jeff Snook

The

THIRTIES

CHARLIE REAM

1934–1937

AS I LOOK BACK ALMOST 70 YEARS, I am proud to say that I played football at Ohio State during a time when two of our greatest traditions were created—the "Gold Pants Club" and "Script Ohio."

I arrived in Columbus from tiny Navarre, Ohio—a little place near Massillon—and nobody knew anything about me. I had listened to Ohio State football on the radio and had heard of all the big names, and it wasn't too long after I enrolled in college and walked on to the team that I was scrimmaging against those big names.

I remember I got into the Tower Club in the stadium and lived there, paying $12 a month for room and board. I always came in late for dinner and got to know the cook pretty well, and she let me eat at about 7:00 every night after practice. The food was pretty good, because I went from 175 pounds up to 218 pretty fast.

It was a great thrill to be at Ohio State. There were something like 60 or 70 players on the freshman team and about 50 of them were handpicked by the coaches. We would practice in that big field south of the open end of the stadium. I played tackle for my first two years and later switched to end, and of course, we had to go both ways in those days.

As a freshman, one of my jobs was to clean out the stadium after a game. I remember sweeping up after one game with a teammate, Charlie Maag, and he told me, "They promised me the stadium when I came here, but they never told me I would have to clean it!"

But we didn't have scholarships then; we had to work at different jobs to make a few dollars.

Francis Schmidt was a great offensive coach, and he would hold three-hour practices. For the first two hours and 30 minutes, we would practice offense and then save a little time for the defense. I guess he just figured defense would come naturally. He was real profane, though. He spent a lot of time screaming and cussing at the referees. But the reason he had been hired is because OSU was losing to Michigan all those years earlier. People were tired of losing to Michigan.

As the legend goes, when he was hired, he said, "Michigan puts their pants on one leg at a time same as everybody else." That is what he did say. Simon Lazarus, the president of Lazarus' store, and Herb Levy, president of the Union Company, were big, big football fans. They put their heads together and came up with the "Gold Pants Club." They created this charm made of gold that would be given to every letterman who played on a team that beat Michigan.

I am proud to say that I earned three pairs—during the first three years they were given away. Today, my wife still wears a pair on a necklace.

Not only did we never lose to Michigan, but they never scored a point on us from 1934 to '37. We beat them 34–0, 38–0, 21–0, and 21–0. In that final Michigan game, I remember tackling their punter in the end zone for two points on a cold, cold day in Ann Arbor.

It was a big thing then, but now those gold pants have become really big. I get calls every once in a while that somebody wants to buy a pair. I don't even ask how much, because why would I ever want to sell a pair of them? They mean too much to me.

The biggest game we ever played in was the 1935 Notre Dame game at Ohio Stadium. It was called "the Protestants against the Catholics," and I happened to be one of the few Catholics playing for Ohio State. I think there were ninety thousand fans there that day, and we jumped to a 13–0 lead at the half. But Francis Schmidt had taken out a few key players early in the fourth quarter, and the substitution rule then meant they couldn't come back in for the remainder of the quarter. In the end, they threw a touchdown pass on the final play to beat us 18–13.

That pass was from Shakespeare to Milner, and the saying went that a Protestant boy threw a pass to a Jewish boy to lead the Irish over the Buckeyes. That was the only loss we had, and it cost us the national championship. Let me tell you that we hated like hell to lose that game.

That also was the year we played the University of Chicago and Jay Berwanger, who was just a great, great player. We beat them 20–13, but Berwanger won the first-ever Heisman Trophy that year.

3

The next year, 1936, was when the band developed "Script Ohio," but being in the locker room, we never got to see it. I have enjoyed it ever since, however.

This was during the Depression, and nobody had any money. A ticket to the game cost $3.50, and a program was a quarter. When I was a sophomore, we had our training table at Jim Rhodes' restaurant. Jim later became governor of Ohio, but he was a big Ohio State fan before that. Before games, we would bus out to the Columbus Country Club, have a big dinner, and stay in those dorms upstairs. We would watch some film of our opponent and then go to bed.

As a sophomore, I joined the Betas and ended up living in the fraternity house on 15th Avenue the next two years. Funny thing was that Francis Schmidt's house was close by, but he had a reputation for being such a lousy driver that nobody wanted to ride home with him. We would rather walk and get there safely.

Which reminds me, Esco Sarkkinen was in my fraternity. He was my backup when I was a senior. Later on we got to be good friends, and Esco coached all those years under Woody Hayes. He must have had 20 pairs of gold pants.

The strangest thing happened to me later when I played with the Iowa Seahawks in 1942. I was in the service and Ohio State was on their schedule. Here I was playing my alma mater—now that was awful strange for me. Still, it was a thrill to go back to Columbus and play them, but I remember they wouldn't let me in the Ohio State locker room. That '42 team was a great one—they lost only one game and won the national championship. Anyway, they whipped us pretty badly that day [41–12]. I remember one of our linebackers would look at me and say, "Who ran by me that time?" That Ohio State team wasn't big, but boy were they ever fast.

I don't know if anybody else ever played for Ohio State for a career and then played against them, too. I do know one thing: I've always been proud to say that I played football with the Ohio State Buckeyes.

During Charlie Ream's four seasons, the Buckeyes had a 25-7 record and never allowed a point to Michigan.

JAMES LANGHURST

1938–1940

IN 1937, I QUALIFIED IN FOUR EVENTS (discus, shot put, low hurdles, and high hurdles) for Willard High School to go to the state track meet in Columbus. I won the low hurdles, and a big, burly guy came up and put his arm around me. It was Francis Schmidt. "Jim, congratulations on your win. I would like you to come to Ohio State University to play football for me, my staff, the university, and for the whole state of Ohio," he said.

That one line was a thrill that I never forgot.

We had some great times and great wins, and I remember one of the funniest things that ever happened at an Ohio State football game, a few years before I played. Stan Pincura was the Buckeyes' quarterback, and he was a great cutup, a big jokester. Back in those days, they would shoot off a gun at the end of each quarter. This one time, he was running in from the sideline and the official shoots off the gun. Stan grabbed his heart, twirled around a few times, and fell to the ground. The crowd was stunned. They thought he had been shot. Tucker Smith, the trainer, and his aides ran out onto the field. "Are you OK?" Tucker said, standing over him. "I am OK," Stan answered, "but how's the crowd taking it?"

When we played Southern California in Columbus in 1938, they beat us 14–7 and the winning touchdown came when we punted and Glen Lansdale returned the punt 70 yards up the right sideline. Ross Bartschy had got trapped inside and didn't stay to the outside as he was supposed to. The next week, Bartschy was dropped to second team for the game at Northwestern. When

James Langhurst was sole captain of the 1940 team.

the game started, the coach was sitting on the end of the bench as he always did. Bartschy saw to it that he would sit next to the coach. Throughout the game, he kept jabbing the coach in the ribs and asking him to put him in the game. He spent the whole game finding fault with his replacement. Finally, in the third quarter, the coach got up and went to the other end of the bench.

A few minutes later, he got up and walked back to Bartschy. "Bartschy," he said, "I am coach of this team. *You* go down to the other end of this bench!"

That 1938 team won only four games, but we won six the next year to win the Big Ten championship. After Michigan's Tom Harmon had won the Heisman Trophy in 1940, he told me, "Jim, I would be happy to give up the Heisman Trophy for what you got at OSU. You played on a Big Ten championship team [1939] and you were elected captain."

Nothing surpassed being named captain of that 1940 team. It's really the greatest honor a guy can have. As the years went by, I sort of became obsessed with the idea of being a captain. I figured that from 1890 through 2002, Ohio State has had 215 captains, and I am proud to say that I was one of them.

By the way, Francis Schmidt is the only Ohio State coach to shut out Michigan four years in a row: 1934 [the last time it wasn't played as the season's final game], '35, '36, and '37.

The greatest player I ever played with at Ohio State was Don Scott. He was from Canton McKinley and was our quarterback. He was about 6′4″ and 220 pounds. He could pass, run, and kick . . . just a great athlete and a great guy. Sadly, a pilot, Don was killed in World War II.

One of the games I remember most was in 1939 when we beat Minnesota 23–20. I broke loose for an 80-yard run for a touchdown, but the official called it back for backfield in motion. He threw the flag when I was about five yards downfield. The films later showed that no one was in motion. (Ironically, in 1949, I began my officiating career at the high school level and later moved on to the college level until retiring in 1974. I have some great stories from officiating, such as the time at the Sugar Bowl when a big tackle for Notre Dame lost his false eye. We called timeout and started searching the field and finally found it. I asked him, "What would you do if something happens to your good eye." He replied, "I would become a football official!" I have to admit, that was a good one.)

Anyway, having graduated from and played at Ohio State, and having been a captain, I've always supported OSU—win or lose—and that's what a true Buckeye is all about.

James Langhurst was named MVP of the 1938 team.

The FORTIES

WARREN AMLING

1944–1946

I WAS FROM PANA, ILLINOIS, and I wanted to be a veterinarian, but the University of Illinois did not have a College of Veterinary Medicine, and I also wanted to play college football when I arrived at Ohio State in 1942. I thought you just tried out for the football team like you did in high school. I wasn't recruited or anything like that, and nobody ever asked me to come out for football.

My roommate that first year was Lou Groza, and he encouraged me to come along with him to practice. Eventually, I worked my way onto the team, and my dad footed the bill for college all the way through. His only requirement was, "I am putting you through college, and if anything happens to me, you've got to see the younger ones get the same opportunity."

Freshmen could not play varsity when I entered college, but because of the war, they relaxed the rule and allowed them to play so teams would have enough players. When things settled down, they put the rule back.

Here are a few of my memories:

The 1944 Michigan game was quite a game. They had gone ahead 14–12, but we drove 56 yards late in the game to beat them. Les Horvath went over the goal line, and I had called the play. That win gave us an undefeated season. We were Big Ten champions and we thought we were national champions, but Army, because of the war, was voted number one. I think we were the civilian champs.

Even with the war on, we still had good crowds. It was something for the people to look on positively. Columbus was a big football town, but the crowds weren't as large because of the fuel rationing.

I saved a letter from coach Carroll Widdoes, dated May 24, 1945, that read in part:

> In four weeks, we will be started on the preparation for the 1945 season. Last year's wins were the result of our fine attitude and hard working during the summer drills. We must work conscientiously and at full speed to be ready to meet our opponents this fall.
>
> You men have a great responsibility. You must lead the way so that the new men get the right kind of start. Being on time, going all out in practice, observing training rules, are some of the best ways you have of getting us started right.
>
> Start working out if you have not already done so. You will need to be in condition to make the effort you will want to make. When you are in shape, it's fun—when you are not, it is just plain hard work. . . ."

This is a story that I have told several times over the years, and people always get a good laugh out of it:

For the Illinois game at Ohio Stadium in 1945, I was appointed as an acting captain for the coin toss. Coach Widdoes instructed me, "If we win the toss, defend the north goal, since the wind is blowing from the north. If we lose the toss and the Illini take the north goal, we will receive."

Then, as now, the wind in the stadium played tricks. Just before the toss, I looked at the flag, and it was blowing the opposite way. We won the toss and I said we would defend the south goal, so Illinois chose to receive. As I jogged off, I glanced up at the flag and the wind had changed directions again!

Coach Widdoes asked, "What did we get?"

"Neither," I replied.

Thank goodness, Coach was an understanding man. Fortunately, we beat Illinois, my home-state team, 27–2.

"Wid" just didn't care for the pressure of being a Big Ten coach. Sometimes we needed a chewing out, but he wasn't a chewer.

There was another funny story I always remembered. A teammate had been injured and a timeout was called. The team physician rushed onto the

12

Warren Amling was a two-time All-American—as a guard in 1945 and as a tackle in 1946.   *Photo courtesy of Warren Amling.*

field with several trainers. After looking over the injured player, the team doctor shouted to the trainers, "Damn it, don't just stand there, get a doctor—this man is hurt!"

I am ashamed to say that in '46 when I was the captain, we had a poor record (4–3–2). It was an up-and-down season all the way. We had a lot of returning servicemen on the team, and these guys had been through a lot of things in the service, so you could understand training rules didn't mean a lot to many of them. It would have taken a very special coach to win under those conditions, and perhaps I wasn't the leader I should have been, either.

When you get a grant-in-aid now, you sign up to work for Ohio State football for four years, so you are going to eat and sleep football. We played a game on Saturday, and didn't think about football until Monday afternoon when we practiced. The pressure wasn't there to win like it is now.

One time I remember attending a football banquet at Mount Sterling [Ohio] High, along with All-American Bill Hackett and Les Horvath, who had won the Heisman Trophy a few years earlier. Afterward, a small boy came up to me and commented on my not talking much. He looked me up and down from head to toe, and he said, "Maybe it's just as well. . . ."

I have a quote I like which I often used with my children, attributed to Abe Lincoln: "It is better to remain silent and thought a fool than to open your mouth and remove all doubt."

Being elected into the OSU Athletic Hall of Fame in 1982 means quite a bit to me because it included all OSU athletes, not just football players.

I was always very proud to be called a Buckeye.

Warren Amling, a member of the OSU Athletic Hall of Fame and the National Football Foundation College Hall of Fame, died at University Hospital on November 1, 2001. This chapter was compiled from past interviews and submitted by his family.

BOB BRUGGE

1944, 1946–1947

WHEN I ARRIVED AT OHIO STATE in 1944, I was just a kid—and I didn't have any confidence. I was going to go to Baldwin-Wallace because I didn't think I was good enough for Ohio State. I was just a Podunk player from Podunk Parma, Ohio. Nobody knew where Parma was, but my teammate and good friend Les Horvath was from there, too. We grew up about two streets apart from each other.

As every Buckeye knows, Les became Ohio State's first Heisman Trophy winner that season. Les was a great guy, but he really was just an average runner, an average passer. But there was nothing average about that man's smarts. He was the smartest guy playing football. He was a great tactician who could outthink the opponent.

It is no wonder he became such a great dentist. I remember Les was going to dental school at the time, and when I kept getting teeth knocked out playing football, Les would fix them for me. I would go see him, and he would fill my cavities with gold fillings. I would say, "Les, I can't afford these fillings. How can I pay you?" He said, "Don't worry, this one's on the school."

Our coach, Carroll Widdoes, was such a nice person. He was almost too nice, almost like a second father to everyone. Everybody loved him. He's the reason I went to Ohio State. But you know, he just couldn't take the pressure. It ate him up.

I was the right halfback, and behind Les that year we won 'em all. Didn't lose a game and won the Big Ten championship. I remember the Illinois game was moved to Cleveland, and we played in front of about seventy-five thousand at old Municipal Stadium. Being from Parma, that was tremendous. Plus, Les and I scored all the points that day and we beat the Illini 26–12. It was a great day.

Big Bill Willis was a great player on our team. He was big and fast and quick as a cat. I was pretty fast back then, ran about a 10.2 hundred-yard dash. I remember in spring practice once, I ran a sweep and cut the corner and took off. The defensive back stopped and coach Widdoes asked him what he was doing. He simply said, "Coach, have you ever seen somebody catch Brugge from behind?"

Bob Brugge (left) played for three head coaches—Carroll Widdoes, Paul Bixler, and Wes Fesler—in his three seasons.

Anyway, we went on and beat Michigan and finished the season perfect, and coach Widdoes was named Coach of the Year. I guess now we are one of the greatest teams in Ohio State history, but we didn't even realize it back then. We were just having fun and winning football games.

After that, Les and I went to the East-West Shrine Game in San Francisco. We had such a great time. We were out there for a month practicing and having fun. We could go into restaurants with our "East All-Stars" leather jackets on and eat free. The game was played January 1, 1945. I remember that Bob Waterfield was the head coach of the West team. He was married to Jane Russell at the time, and we had this dance after the game. She danced with every player but me and the Wisconsin quarterback because we were the only players who were not 18 yet.

The next year was different. With the war going on, I was about to go into the navy, but Paul Brown called me and said, "I got it arranged. You are going to come up to Great Lakes and play for my team." Then he called me back when it didn't work out. He said, "That SOB admiral is not an athletic man, so he won't let you play for me." Now coach Brown never swore much, so you knew he was mad. Anyway, I didn't get to play for Paul Brown.

In 1945, I played for Camp Perry in Williamsburg, Virginia, and following the end of the war, I had three years of eligibility left and a choice to make. I had great offers from all these schools in the South that would pay me to come play for them. North Carolina offered me $10,000, a car, and if I got married, free tuition for my wife. They said they would make the check out to my dad.

So I sent a letter to coach Widdoes and said I was going to North Carolina. He called me back and asked, "What do you want to be when you are finished with college?" I wanted to coach. He said, "Well, who will know you down there? You need to come back to Ohio State."

So coach Widdoes got me a job; I was the PR man for the old Deschler Wallick Hotel downtown. Then I worked at the University Theater off of Neil Avenue. But coach Widdoes left that year to go to Ohio University as athletic director, and Paul Bixler became the coach. We didn't respect him too much. After one game at Illinois, he came into our Chicago hotel and was just sloshed. That didn't sit too well with the guys who didn't drink or smoke.

The game I remember most in '46 was at Southern California. We had about ninety-two thousand in the stands, and I hurt my Achilles tendon. Ernie Biggs taped me up good, and I averaged about seven yards per carry. We won 21–0. Only one thing bothers me to this day. I never scored against our biggest rival. Never scored against Michigan.

One home game I remember the most was when we were playing Minnesota and we fell behind in the first quarter. I was engaged then to Lois, who became my wife for life, and she was coming to the game. In the second quarter, I threw for a touchdown, ran for another, and set up a third. The crowd was going crazy. After the game, I asked Lois what she thought and she said, "Well, I didn't get to the game until halftime, but I loved the second half."

It was the greatest thrill of my life, playing football for Ohio State. Something like that stays with you for life.

Bob Brugge was a starting back on the 1944 team, which had a 9–0 record but finished ranked number two behind Army.

WILLIAM "BILLY" NEWELL

1947–1949

I LIKE TO SAY THAT MY FAMILY HELPED build Ohio Stadium. My Ohio State tradition is a family tradition, starting with the construction of our now famous "Shoe." My father's OSU civil engineering classes on reinforced concrete included survey labs involving the construction of the foundation for Ohio Stadium from 1916 to 1918.

It would turn out to be a place over the next 80 years where I came to play, watch, and love the game of football. Buckeye football.

I have always been a Buckeye fan. Upon graduation from Columbiana High in 1946, there was no question where I was headed.

Football tryouts were much different then because the war had just ended, and many, many men who had previously served were there to play football. Not many of us had just come from high school. Cuts were based on wind sprints and who was the fastest. If you weren't in the top 20 of your group, you didn't make it to the next round. I wasn't very big, weighing only 165 pounds, but fortunately I was fast enough, so I made the team and became a starting defensive back my junior and senior years. In fact, I don't think we had anyone on the line who weighed more than 235 pounds. Just compare that to today's players.

Billy Newell gains yardage against Missouri in 1949. *Photo courtesy of William Newell.*

Coach Wes Fesler had a tradition of rewarding players with silver dollars for good plays. In my case, I earned one for each interception. Problem was, they didn't pass as much as they do today, so my chances were limited. For my career, I earned 13 silver dollars, which held the OSU career record for interceptions for some time. My final interception came in the 1950 Rose Bowl, setting up a touchdown in our win [17–14 over California]. That was a great day.

Both of my brothers, John and Richard, served in World War II and then attended OSU and graduated with me in the College of Engineering.

What I am proud of is the fact that my two sons continued our Ohio State tradition. My oldest, William F. Newell Jr., worked in the athletic training program for three years, beginning during Ernie Biggs' last year. Bill Junior taped Archie Griffin's ankles during his freshman season. My second son, Marvin, worked on the equipment staff with longtime equipment manager John Bozick. Both graduated from OSU.

Through our association with Ohio State, either as a player, training staff member, or equipment staff member, we each experienced the honor and tradition of running out of that tunnel at the "Shoe" on game day. Nothing in the world compares to that feeling.

As the years have gone by, my love for my school has never diminished. I have had some heart problems, and it took three nitro tablets to get me through the 2002 national championship game. I have been, and will always be, a Buckeye. I know one thing: with Jim Tressel at the helm of OSU football, the continuation of pride and tradition is assured. The Ohio State University is the best, and it deserves the best.

William "Billy" Newell earned three varsity letters.

DEAN SENSANBAUGHER

1943, 1947

I USED TO LISTEN TO OHIO STATE GAMES on the radio, and my dad took me to Ohio Stadium when I was a kid, so that was my first exposure to Ohio State football. I remember thinking how awful big and beautiful that stadium was. I was from Uhrichsville, and I figured I would head to Muskingum for college, until I met Paul Brown. You can say I liked him from the start.

When I arrived on campus in 1943, I worked out all summer long and I got to know all the other players, so I figured I might get to play early. As it turned out, I started the entire 1943 season as a freshman halfback. I don't know if anybody did that before me, but I know it didn't happen again until 2002 [Maurice Clarett].

In that first game, I gained 99 yards, but we lost to the Iowa Seahawks.

Paul Brown was an honorable man who demanded respect, and he knew his football. He was a fair man, and he never ran you down, but that was a way of making a point. He worked with you to make you better, and he was a very good coach. I remember one time in practice, I was really going around right end, but I tripped and fell flat on my face. I headed back to the huddle and Paul handed me a blade of grass. "Here," he said, "this one won't trip you up!"

That was pretty funny. That season against Great Lakes, I returned a kickoff 103 yards, which remains the Ohio State record. Funny thing is, I don't remember a thing about it. I really don't.

Dean Sensanbaugher picks up nine yards against Missouri in 1947. *Photo courtesy of Dean Sensanbaugher.*

The best part of that whole time was what happened following the '43 season. My hometown of Uhrichsville, Ohio, threw me a little party at the local theater. I was at this party having a good time, and I got a call from Ohio State and they asked me if I wanted to play in the East-West Shrine Game. Back then, it was always held on New Year's Day in San Francisco.

Well, I didn't have to think long to say "yes."

I went back to Columbus that night, and somebody went to pick up my shoulder pads and helmet and they took me to the airport. I flew to Chicago, and then the entire East team left from there on a train for San Francisco. We stopped twice to practice along the way. Boy, that was a good time. Ohio State's Cy Souders was with me, and we had a lot of fun.

I knew I had a pretty good game there, but I had to read the old scrapbook to jog my memory. The headline of one story after the Shrine Game read: "The Dean of Yardsticks." I ran for 129 yards, which was a Shrine Game record, and returned an interception 24 yards and was named the game's most outstanding player. It ended in a 13–13 tie.

After the game, they arranged for Cy and me to go down to L.A., and we went to a movie studio to see a picture being filmed. Humphrey Bogart was the actor, but I don't remember the picture. Now there was some history being made, but we didn't know it at the time. We were just having a good time. Cy was a lot of fun to be with. After that, we took a train to New Orleans, then to Chicago and back to Columbus.

The next year, I attended West Point and played on that great Army team with ["Doc"] Blanchard and [Glenn] Davis. Now there were some great players, and great guys, too. Blanchard was about 6'2" and 220 pounds and won the Heisman that year. Davis was very, very fast, and he won it the next year. Those two guys were already famous at the time. We ran the T formation back then, and we could score some points—we didn't lose a game and won the national championship.

I remember one time after a game, Blanchard and I went to New York to a dance hall where you buy tickets and find a gal to dance with. We danced a few dances and left, but everybody recognized him back then. It was a lot of fun.

That next year, 1945, I went into the army.

23

I was ready to serve. I did my basic training in Louisiana and then they shipped me to California. We kept thinking, "Today's the day." But they sent me back to Amherst College in Massachusetts. They wanted me to eventually go back to West Point, but I really didn't want to become an officer in the army.

I ended up back at Ohio State in '47. That's where I wanted to be and where I belonged. Against Purdue that season, I returned a kickoff 98 yards, and this one I remember. I caught it at the goal line and ran to the left sideline. I cut back to the right and then back to the left, and finally, I got caught from behind at the 2-yard line—and we never did score. I guess I can remember that one because I just didn't make it to the end zone—got caught from behind.

I remember we used to practice every day outside the open end of the stadium in that big field. There wasn't much west of the [Olentangy] river back then. Just a few farms and open field. Anyway, we didn't win many games that year, and I didn't care much for Wes Fesler. Not many of the fellas did, but Ohio State was very, very good to me. I got my degree in education in '52 and have been a Buckeye ever since.

Dean Sensanbaugher's 103-yard kickoff return in 1943 remains the longest in Ohio State history.

CECIL "CY" SOUDERS

1942–1944, 1946

I N 1938, I HAD PLANNED TO GO DOWN TO LSU and play football there, until Ohio State assistant coach Ernie Godfrey came to Bucyrus and I told him what my plans were. Well, Ernie went to my high school principal and did his research and discovered that I had a steady girlfriend, Jean Hoover, who was a cheerleader.

So what did Ernie do? He visited one of Jean's classes and told her that if I went to LSU, those Southern girls wouldn't let me come back up North. "Not my guy," she told him. But then she told me, "You had better look into Ohio State." Plus, my parents were happy about that. She and Ernie won out, and I decided to head to Columbus.

I met Francis Schmidt, the head coach, and we headed to lunch driving his Caddy on the wrong side of the street, down Neil Avenue with streetcars going full blast. Ernie told him to slow down and watch where he was driving. I thought we were going to have a bad crash before I became a Buckeye. Schmidt was a rough, old cob. He was a wild man, a wild driver, and a wild talker. Every other word out of his mouth was a cuss word.

But I had made my decision. Sorry, LSU. I began my football career at Ohio State in the fall of 1939. They told me they would get me a job there, and it was sweeping the stadium. On Saturdays after games, I had to sweep up all the peanut shells, but I always found a few coins to keep me going.

My freshman year, I was on the taxi squad coached by Ernie, and our job was to go against the varsity offense. One day, I stopped about six straight plays and Francis Schmidt stopped practice and yelled, "Who in the hell is that kid? Get him the hell out of here right now!"

Cecil "Cy" Souders warms up his kicking leg before a home game in 1942.
Photo courtesy of Cecil Souders.

Later during that fall, Jean and I decided to run off to Kentucky to get married, and we didn't return to school for three years. By that time, we had a young daughter, Sharon. I got back in 1942, and Paul Brown was the head coach. I think Paul was very similar to Jim Tressel—he was strict and a very mature man. He ran a tight ship.

That group in 1942 was a great group of boys. They were all first-class types of people, and school was the major thing for all of us. I played behind Bob Shaw that year, but I played in every game. We lost only one game, at Wisconsin, when everybody got sick. At the time, we thought we got sick from the water at the hotel, but I had read years later they discovered it was from the water on the train ride up there. They said they forgot to change the water and it became stagnant. Well, I don't know of anybody on that team that didn't get sick that day.

That was our only loss, and as everybody knows, the '42 team became Ohio State's first national champion. Paul Brown left after the '43 season.

I played the first three games of the '44 season, and I reported to the navy right after the Wisconsin game. It was then that I played for Paul Brown's Great Lakes team. Ironically, in the first game for Great Lakes, we went up against Wisconsin—a week after Ohio State had beaten them in Columbus. This tackle for Wisconsin asked me, "Do you have a twin brother who plays for OSU? You look just like this guy I played against last week in Columbus."

When I got out of the navy, I was drafted by the Washington Redskins, but I wanted to come back to Ohio State to play one more season. I had a good year in 1946, and I am sure glad I did. The down part of that was that Michigan ran right over us [58–6] that year, but I ended my career with two pairs of gold pants.

I also remember playing the Chicago Bears in the All-Star Game in front of 105,000 at Soldier Field.

Being inducted into the OSU Athletic Hall of Fame was a tremendous honor for me and for my family. To me, it was already a great honor just playing football at Ohio State. I was from the little town of Bucyrus and didn't know much about college football. You just work your way along and do the best you can do.

Well, Jean and I celebrated our 63rd anniversary when Ohio State won the national championship, and the whole family was in Phoenix to see it. We'll always be Buckeyes.

27

Cecil "Cy" Souders, the Big Ten's Most Valuable Player in 1946, was inducted into the Ohio State Athletic Hall of Fame in 2002.

HOWARD TEIFKE

1943, 1946–1948

T HE FIRST TIME I HEADED TO OHIO STATE, I took a bus from my hometown of Fremont. It was the fall of 1943, and I rode the bus all the way
to downtown Columbus, not realizing it could have dropped me off near
campus. So then I had to find my way back. . . . I was just a young kid lost
in the big city. I was kind of homesick right from the start, and my uncle was
very sick once I got there. He passed away a short time later, so I returned
home. I was only 17, and I wasn't turning 18 until that October. The team
was a bunch of kids that year; the season after that they won the national
championship, because everybody else was in the war.

Bill Willis was playing and so was Gordon Appleby, but the rest of us were
just kids. We weren't old enough to be drafted yet.

We had 33 guys on that '43 team, and I got to play a little bit, but most of
the starters played both ways in those days. I remember hitting Elroy Hirsch
once that season, and he bounced off of me and just kept going. I think he
may have been the greatest player I ever saw.

The next year, I enlisted and headed overseas.

I remember we were somewhere in the Atlantic that November of '44 and
we had the Ohio State–Michigan game on the radio. The guys loved the fact
that I had been there playing a year earlier. I remember it was a close game
at the half, and then we got out of range and lost the reception. It was
much later when I found out that Ohio State had won, 18–14, and I think
Les Horvath had a big game that day.

Howard Teifke's Ohio State career was interrupted by his two years of military service during World War II.

Photo courtesy of Howard Teifke.

I was in the air force—a gunner on a B-24—and I flew 26 missions near the end of the war. We still lost planes, but it wasn't like it was a year earlier. At that time, they had a bad ratio of being shot down, but we never were attacked by German fighter planes. I was still in Italy on VE Day, and they sent us to California to retrain us on B-29s and we were headed for Japan. Then they came over the PA system at the base: "Fellas, the war's over. Stay on the base and everything will be free tonight." That was VJ Day. It was pretty wild, and I had wanted to go into L.A. so bad that night, but we stayed on the base.

After the war, I thought about going to North Carolina, but finally I said, "I am going back to Columbus, if Ohio State will take me." We were on the GI Bill, and you could go wherever you wanted to go. That next spring, we had 220 guys go out for spring football—a dozen centers, a dozen right guards, a dozen left guards, and so on.

Paul Bixler was the head coach by that time, and Paul just couldn't handle the talent. He wouldn't let anyone play but the starters—guys like Tony Adamle, Cy Souders, Joe Whisler, and Chuck Csuri. I was playing behind Tony Adamle, and he got his teeth kicked out in the Minnesota game. Four or five plays later, he was right back in the game. We were ahead of Illinois late in the game that year, and we threw an interception that they turned into a touchdown. The next week, we were so down that Michigan beat us 58–6. It was 55–6 and they kicked the final field goal. I remember screaming at one of those Michigan players: "What the hell is wrong with you guys?"

Wes Fesler came in to coach the '47 team, and he installed that 5–4–2 defense. They couldn't run against us, but they could pass it on us. We didn't have much of a team that year [2–6–1], but we got better by the next season. I remember we were beating Pittsburgh so badly [41–0] that some of their players told us, "You guys are the best team we've ever seen."

But we never beat Michigan in my time, and I never got a pair of gold pants. I thought we were primed to beat them in '48 in Columbus when they were ranked number one, and we jumped ahead 3–0, but lost 13–3. That was my last ballgame. It was a very sad day for me. Nobody likes to lose to Michigan.

All in all, it was a great adventure to go to Ohio State. I wouldn't have gotten there, or stayed there, without football. The farthest I had ever been was Cleveland, but because of Ohio State—and the war—all of that changed.

Over the years, I haven't missed too many games. The '68 team was a great team and the '69 team was one of the best, too. I remember we were at the '69 Michigan game at Ann Arbor and my wife said before the game, "We don't look like we want to play today." Sure enough, we lost a tough one.

I still go to most every game, because I am a Buckeye to the core. Coach Tressel has brought back so much already that you can't help but love the guy. The tradition, so great for so many years, will live on.

Howard Teifke started at center and linebacker in 1948, a season in which Ohio State finished 6–3.

JOE WHISLER

1946–1948

THE GREAT PAUL BROWN RECRUITED ME to Ohio State in 1943, but I never got to play for him.

I did play freshman football at Ohio State for Ernie Godfrey, but we never saw coach Brown much. I have to tell you, that '43 freshman team was loaded with talent. The sportswriter Paul Hornung claimed that was the greatest freshman team he ever saw. We were larger and faster than the varsity squad, which had won the national championship earlier. Lou Groza was on that team, but he went into the service and never came back, and we had other great players. I think we could have beaten most varsity teams.

We played three freshman games that year and won all three of them, beating Indiana, Pittsburgh, and Michigan.

Anyway, I received my draft notice and entered the navy the following year during World War II. My experiences in the navy weren't too bad. I was on a landing ship tank, which transported troops to battle, and we saw a lot of storms. There were times cracks went through our ships.

After the war, I was 22. I was sadly out of shape, but I had three years of eligibility remaining. I was 5′11″ and weighed about 240 pounds, because there really was nothing to do on the ship but eat. So I came back to Ohio State and worked out on the track all summer and got down to about 212 pounds.

I had a great start to the '46 season, scoring both touchdowns in the first game [a 13–13 tie with Missouri] and all three touchdowns in the next game

32

Joe Whisler finds running room during a 1948 game.   *Photo courtesy of Joe Whisler.*

at Southern California [a 21–0 win]. That made it the first five touchdowns of the season. What I remember most was that trip to Los Angeles. We took three DC-3s to get there, and we stopped off in St. Louis. Then we went on to somewhere like Albuquerque, but before we got there, so many of the players got sick on the plane. Hal Dean had been a paratrooper during the war and he got sick! Oh, that poor stewardess . . . she got sick herself just because she smelled everybody else getting sick. I felt so bad for her. We then spent a night in New Mexico and practiced there before heading on to California. Out there, we just ran right by USC.

There was one game I don't remember. At Northwestern that year, I started to make a block and the linebacker's knee hit me in the head. It knocked me out cold. I woke up wearing street clothes, and I was sitting on the bench. Later, they put me back in and I scored another touchdown.

We had some fun while traveling in those days. On this one trip back from Pittsburgh in '47, we had this little prop job of an airplane and we were delayed for some reason. Well, the boys went to the gift shop and bought all these windup turtles. Here they were having turtle races right out there near the runway by the airplane.

What still doesn't sit well was I didn't have the honor of beating Michigan. We lost to them in '46, '47, and '48. My senior year, we scored first and went ahead 3–0, but we just didn't finish the game. I thought that would be the year we would beat them. They were our rival, and I sure didn't get a pair of gold pants. That was one thing I didn't understand about Wes Fesler. In his first practice of the season, the emphasis was on beating Michigan. I thought that was really premature. I think he was 0–3–1 against them, so it didn't work much.

I guess I had a pretty good year in '48 [Whisler rushed for 579 yards on 129 carries], because they voted me MVP of the team and that was quite an honor.

Playing at Ohio State was a great, great experience. I got my bachelor's degree in education in 1949, and even though I left Ohio State, I never stopped rooting for the Buckeyes.

Joe Whisler, a running back/defensive back, led the team in scoring in 1946, '47, and '48 and was named MVP of the '48 team.

The FIFTIES

HOWARD "HOPALONG" CASSADY

1952–1955

GROWING UP IN COLUMBUS, I visited Ohio Stadium often as a kid, sneaking into the giant horseshoe to watch the games with other kids. We would climb over the fence a few hours before the games and hide somewhere in the stadium until they opened the gates. Then we would keep moving throughout the game, just so we didn't get caught. Ohio State was a great team, the hometown team, so it was just natural to want to see them play. I liked all the big players, like Curly Morrison, Les Horvath, the Hague boys . . . we really didn't have heroes that were ballplayers in our day; we just loved watching games and rooting for the Buckeyes.

I never figured I would go to college, because nobody in my family ever went to college. Why would I go to college? But I played football, basketball, and baseball, and I pole-vaulted on the track team at Columbus Central, and suddenly, I realized I had a chance to go someplace. I visited Notre Dame, Bear Bryant at Kentucky, Wisconsin, Indiana, and Ohio University. I knew I wanted to play baseball in college, as well as football. There were times I didn't figure I was good enough for football, because I was never that big. I weighed about 155 pounds, and everybody in college football was so much bigger than I was.

Woody Hayes invited me and my high school coaches to meet him for lunch downtown one day. It was at the corner of Broad and High Streets, right there on the northwest corner. Esco Sarkkinen was with him, and

Woody just said, "I want you. You can do it." Heck, I figured if I didn't make it at Ohio State, at least I was still home. I always loved Ohio State as I grew up. Dave Parks and Frank Howell [Cassady's high school coaches] were there with me, and they handled everything for me. I guess in the end it was a group decision about what would be best for me—I was going to Ohio State to play football and baseball.

I graduated from high school in January of 1952 and enrolled at Ohio State in March, and one thing Woody didn't want me to do was sit on the bench for baseball as a freshman instead of playing spring football. You have to remember that Woody Hayes didn't have the power at that time that he did later. This was his second season, and what was their record in his first? [It was 4–3–2]. He was humble at that time, and it seemed he was fighting an uphill battle. The newspapers and fans were on him pretty good, and nobody knew if he would make it.

When I showed up for camp that summer, I was cannon fodder for the varsity. We were to open the season against Indiana, and I was running Indiana's offensive plays against the varsity. Funny thing is, we were beating them with it. I never even had a uniform until the Thursday before that Saturday opener. I remember that if you dressed for the game, your parents got tickets, and that was my goal for that first game. On Thursday, Woody told me, "Hop, go down and get a uniform; you are going to play on Saturday."

This was my choice—No. 13 or No. 40. I sure as hell didn't want No. 13, and I knew that Route 40 runs right through Columbus, so that was how I got my number.

In the Indiana game we were getting beat 13–0 at the half, and the crowd was unhappy, when I heard Woody yell something like, "Get the redhead up here!" He meant me, and I don't think the other coaches had any idea who the hell he meant. I went in for Fred Bruney, and remember we played both ways back then. As I was headed out for one of the substitutions, Fred grabbed me and said, "You're staying in here and playing the rest of the way—both ways."

I scored three touchdowns, including one on an interception, and we came back to win [33–13].

I played in 36 of the next 37 games over four years, missing that West Coast game [at California] my freshman year with a broken shoulder. They taped it down and I played the next week against Illinois. Even though I scored a lot of touchdowns and accumulated a lot of yards, I can say that I really loved

Howard "Hopalong" Cassady (No. 40), who became an instant two-way star after coming off the bench to score three touchdowns in his first game, finished third in the 1954 Heisman Trophy voting, then won the award in 1955.

playing defense more than I loved playing offense—after getting hit, you could hit back.

In those four years, we didn't lose many games. We went from nothing to national champions.

We won 'em all in '54, but the thing I loved about it most was beating the heck out of Michigan [21–7] in Columbus. That team up north—there's nothing like whipping them.

There wasn't that much TV then, but definitely the Heisman Trophy was the top award to get if you were a college player. But the only way I knew much about the Heisman Trophy then was because I finished behind [Wisconsin's] Alan Ameche that year. It really didn't bother me at all about not winning the Heisman—I had baseball season and started right into it. I do remember I returned an interception 88 yards and we beat Wisconsin 31–14 that year, but they voted for Ameche.

In '55, we knew we couldn't go to two Rose Bowls in a row, so spoiling Michigan's season and winning as many games as we could was the big thing for us. They were supposed to beat us pretty good that year, but I don't think they crossed the 50-yard line the whole day, if not for one penalty, and we beat them 17–0. We didn't go to the Rose Bowl, but neither did Michigan.

39

When I went to the Downtown Athletic Club for the Heisman, [assistant coaches] Esco and Gene Fekete went with me. Woody was too busy recruiting. I can only say it was a great honor for me, and it's something you appreciate as the years go on.

Our teams were a great success story in Ohio State history, and Woody said many times later that I was a large part of his success when he first got to Ohio State, and that always made me feel honored and awfully proud. I was one of his first recruits, and he often said later that was the start of Ohio State football as we know it, and I was more than happy to be a part of it.

What can I possibly say about Woody Hayes? He kept on me from day one all the way through, but I never gave him any reason to get mad at me. I never argued with anything that man said. He handled everything for me. He was a great man—the greatest I've ever known.

He was always out to help people wherever and whenever he could. He was always visiting the hospitals, and over the years, I signed a lot of footballs for him to give away. He taught all of us well. He taught us how to be a success and how to give back to other people. After I came back when my playing days were over, Woody and I would have lunch two or three times each week. I could talk to him at any time, any day, any place. I got into a little trouble a few times, and Woody was always there for me. He was up-front, honest, and straightforward.

They just don't make 'em like him anymore, do they?

He was a Buckeye's Buckeye. A real man. A great man. He lived and died the way he was, and he never changed in between.

The day he died, March 12, 1987, I was in Fort Lauderdale with the Yankees, and my family called [wife] Barb, and she then told me. I won't forget the sadness of it—it was one of the saddest days in my life.

I am just like the rest of his players—we loved Woody, and we loved Ohio State. Everything that happened to us at Ohio State helped make our lives easier. It worked out real well for me, and I have told every coach at Ohio State that I am always there for them if they need me to do anything. Being a Buckeye is something that never leaves you. It is a large part of me, and it always will be.

Howard "Hopalong" Cassady, nicknamed after the famed movie cowboy Hopalong Cassidy, finished his career with 2,466 rushing yards. He was a two-time All-American and became Ohio State's third Heisman Trophy winner, winning in 1955 by what would be the most lopsided vote in the award's first 33 years. He also was named the Associated Press Athlete of the Year in '55. Cassady is a member of the Collegiate Football Hall of Fame and the Ohio State Athletics Hall of Fame. A first-round pick in the 1956 NFL draft by the Detroit Lions, he played ten seasons in the NFL—eight with Detroit, one with Cleveland, and one with Philadelphia. A shortstop at Ohio State, he is a long-time employee of the New York Yankees.

GALEN CISCO

1955–1957

I WAS FORTUNATE THAT MY HIGH SCHOOL COACH at Saint Mary's, Ohio, was Jack Bickel, who had been a halfback at Miami, Ohio, under Woody Hayes. He coached a lot like Woody did, so I knew what to expect if I ever went to Ohio State. Well, sure enough, Woody recruited me, and I looked at plenty of other schools, but I had no intention of going anywhere else.

When I first met Woody, what impressed me was how much he knew about me. He made it seem that he couldn't do without you. And he made it known that Ohio State would be good for you. He said, "Ohio State could do more for you after you graduate, because you are from Ohio, and you probably are going to stay in Ohio after you graduate. Why go anywhere else?"

I am glad I took his advice.

I arrived in 1954, thinking that the campus looked bigger than the whole state. It really was unbelievable that all those students could go to one school. It was just mind-boggling to me.

As freshmen, we got to go against that national championship team in practice, and we got beat up, but that helped us in the long run.

As a sophomore, I had worked my way up to second team and was doing pretty well, but during this one practice, I was lined up with the first team. We didn't have pads on, just our helmets. [Jim] Roseboro was at right half-back, Hop [Cassady] was at left half, and I was the fullback. Woody called a sweep to the right side, and I thought it was a sweep to the left. Well, Cassady and I bumped heads and Hop went down. Woody was shaking

41

me and standing over me and screaming at me. I just kept thinking, "Get up, Hop! Get up!"

Finally, Hop got up and he was fine. He never said anything to me about it. I really thought I had screwed up big-time, but four plays later, Woody asked me, "Do you know these plays now? Well, get in there."

To start that season, we played Nebraska and beat them at home before we went to Stanford. Stanford had John Brodie at quarterback, and we held them to 6 points but lost 6–0. An outside linebacker, that was the first time I got to play, but from then on I played most of the games there. We lost to Duke, and those were the only losses that season, but the Big Ten had put us on probation and we couldn't go to the Rose Bowl.

I still don't know what that was all about. From what I heard, a lot of athletes had jobs and some didn't show up for work but still got paid. But we weren't on scholarships then. [The Big Ten adopted a grant-in-aid for athletic scholarships, based on need, in 1956]. We had put together a pretty good streak in the Big Ten [17 consecutive wins] until Iowa beat us 6–0 in '56. We also lost the Big Ten title that day, and we were so flat after that, we got shut out the next week by Michigan, 19–0.

We had ended the season on a real down note, and we were picked in the middle of the pack for 1957. I had been chosen a cocaptain with Leo Brown, and it was a big honor. I don't know what I did to deserve it, but I always cherished that. We opened with TCU; they had a great back in Jim Shoffner, and he tore us up. We lost 18–14.

We went to Washington the next week, and that is when Don Sutherin, our place-kicker, turned it around when he ran about 67 yards and got us going. We won 35–7 and then got on a real roll in the Big Ten. We were real fired up for that Iowa game because of what happened the year before. I remember Richard Nixon was in the stands for the game, and Iowa was ranked fifth and we were sixth. That game decided the Big Ten. We were trailing 13–10 when Bob White came in and just started running over people. Here was this big powerful fullback, and on that final drive, he must have carried seven or eight times for 70 yards, and Dick LeBeau carried only once on that drive. We won and then kicked Michigan 31–14 to put us in the Rose Bowl.

Galen Cisco cocaptained the 1957 national championship team with Leo Brown.
Photo courtesy of Galen Cisco.

We had a great defense that year. We must not have allowed 100 points the whole season. [They allowed only 92.] I know one thing: we didn't give up many points in the fourth quarter that year. Woody's theory was, "Whoever wins the second half wins the game," and that applied to that team.

We had some great players then, because I think I counted once that there were 21 guys in professional football that I had played with at Ohio State. Anyway, we won a national championship in '54 when I was a freshman and in '57 when I was a senior. That was a great way to begin it, even though freshmen couldn't play, and a great way to end it.

After my eligibility was up, I had about two quarters left to graduate and I was signed to play baseball. Woody called me in and asked, "After the baseball season, what are you going to do? How about coming back and help coach freshman football and you can pick up a few classes while you're at it."

Ernie Godfrey was the freshman head coach, and he had plenty of assistants, but that was Woody's way of making sure I graduated. After the next season, he asked, "Now what are you going to do? Come back again, because you did such a good job." I ended up coaching the freshmen from 1958 through the 1961 season. And I graduated.

Those days at OSU completely organized my future, and the whole scenario of it set me up for life. I learned that you could cope with everyday things that you run across in life. You become better prepared to deal with any setbacks. I ended up coaching in the major leagues and had a great career, and I really have Ohio State, Woody Hayes, and all of my teammates to thank.

Galen Cisco, captain of the 1957 national championship team, spent 30 years as a pitcher and manager/coach in professional baseball.

JIM HOUSTON

1957–1959

YOU WANT HUMBLE BEGINNINGS? I started my illustrious football career at Lorin Andrews Junior High in Massillon as a seventh grader at the time my older brothers were playing on the high school team and my oldest brother, Lin, was playing for the original Cleveland Browns.

I had to play football!

Guess what? I was cut from my seventh-grade team because I was too small. I didn't like to be hit, either. I remember coach Roger Price telling me that I wasn't good enough, so he cut me. I was humiliated. What would my mom, dad, brothers, and friends say?

Things changed, fortunately. After my Massillon High days, I was looking forward to college. Two of my brothers had gone to Purdue. Woody Hayes came to my house to recruit me and never said anything to me other than the normal greeting. But he convinced my mother that Columbus was much closer than Purdue. My mother simply said, "It *is* closer than Purdue." So I agreed with her and became a Buckeye.

I remember when they first called my name to come off the sideline at Ohio State. I almost peed my pants. As I ran out to the huddle to take my position at end, I couldn't remember any of the plays. Once the quarterback started his cadence, it suddenly came back to me. Ross Bowermaster was starting ahead of me, but he got hurt in the third game of the season. So I played the rest of the season both ways, averaging 44 minutes every game, and I played all 60 at the Rose Bowl [a 10–7 win over Oregon].

Jim Houston (No. 84) starred at end for the Buckeyes from 1957 to 1959 and was a two-time All-American. *Photo courtesy of Jim Houston.*

One of my teammates, Dick Schafrath, was a very good blocker. We were both about 6′3″, 220-plus pounds—which was good size back then. He had calls so that we could define our blocking scheme. "Run it" was if he was facing a six-man defensive line, man-on-man blocking. "Rack it" was a double-team block by the tackle and the end. Schafrath would make the calls.

Against second-ranked Iowa my junior season, we were facing Alex Karras, an All-American at right defensive tackle, and John Klein, a 6′5″, 255-pound left defensive tackle. I remember Woody calling a sweep once, and Dick saw the alignment and yelled "rack it." John's first move was up, and Schaf stuck him in the chest with his helmet and then I blew him away. I think we gained about 18 yards on the play.

A few plays later, Woody called the same play. It was his "three yards and a cloud of dust" scenario. John Klein was over Schafrath again. Dick called "rack it," and I saw John's eyes get real big and he said, "Son of a bitch." We did it to him again for a big gain. When Dick and I got back to the huddle, we couldn't stop laughing. And that went on for several plays. We won 38–28.

During my senior year, I was a captain but we just didn't get the job done. We had a lot of injuries and had to play young players. I still made All-American, but I would have taken another Rose Bowl trip instead.

There were many ups and downs, but all in all, Ohio State was a great experience. The coaching I received from Woody Hayes and [assistant] Ernie Godfrey was responsible for my later success with the Cleveland Browns. Not bad for someone who once wasn't good enough to make his seventh-grade team.

Jim Houston played 13 seasons with the Cleveland Browns.

GEORGE JACOBY

1951–1953

I GREW UP IN TOLEDO AND ALWAYS WANTED TO GO to Ohio State, but by the time I was a senior I had considered West Point. Problem was, you couldn't go to West Point and be married, and I was very serious about my girlfriend, Nina. My childhood dream had always been to play football for the Buckeyes, and I wanted to stay close enough so my dad would be able to see the games.

Coach Wes Fesler recruited me to Ohio State, and I arrived in 1950. Wes was a fine man and a top-notch gentleman, but he made people mad at him at that point and he wasn't going to last. Why? He had lost to Michigan again [Fesler had an 0–3–1 record against Michigan]. That was the famous Snow Bowl, and it turned out to be Wes Fesler's final game.

I'll never forget our first meeting with the incoming coach. I was sitting in the front row and Woody Hayes looked at me, and he asked, "Jacoby, is that you?"

"Yes sir, it's me," I replied.

"I told you I would get you sooner or later," he said. Woody had recruited me when he was at Miami. It was the beginning of a long relationship.

When Woody was hired, everybody said, "Oh God, he'll never fill the shoes Fesler left behind. It will be a disaster." The fans were tough as hell on him those first three years, but Woody got through it. After my freshman season, he called me for a talk one day. I had been an honor student at Toledo Libby, but he said, "Jacoby, I see your grades have fallen down here; now what's going on?"

I told him I kept going home to Toledo on the weekends to see my girl-friend. "Is it serious?" he asked.

I told him it was.

"Then why the hell don't you marry her and bring her down here?" he told me.

So we got married on August 11, 1951, and Woody was largely the reason.

Once we were married, we ended up doing our laundry at his house. Anne Hayes was just a lovely lady, probably Ohio State's best recruiter. And she was a great cook, too, even though Woody always had me dieting. I played a lot that sophomore year, going both ways as everybody did. I was an offensive tackle and a nose guard. I was 5′11″ and about 225 pounds, but I could have been a lot heavier if I didn't watch what I ate.

At the time, we were recruiting Hubie Bobo and they put him up in a hotel. Well, one of those Southern schools came up and stole him away. So they got Hubie back up for another visit. We lived in this little apartment on High Street, and Woody called me. He said, "Jacoby, I got a favor to ask of you. You and your wife need to take Hubie Bobo back to your apartment and keep him there. Don't let him out of your sight." Nina was up all night long, checking to make sure nobody got to Hubie, but we got him signed.

The thing about that High Street apartment was there was no parking. I would park on the street and get parking tickets all the time—must have had 10 or 12 of them. I called Woody about it once, and he just said, "I'll take care of it." He did, but I had to run extra laps for it.

We had one rule that seemed excessive back then, the so-called Tuesday rule. [Assistant coach] Bill Arnsparger would knock on our door and remind us, "No sex after Tuesday." My wife and I really didn't understand that rule, and we always wondered who was telling that to all the single players, but Woody really liked Nina.

She would come to practices, and if Woody was in a good mood, he would look at her, wink, and nod toward the bench. That meant it was OK for her to go sit down. We used to go downtown to check into the hotel before games, before we would go eat dinner and see a movie as a team. One night, Woody, who never had any money on him, said, "Jacoby, let me borrow 10 bucks." I said I didn't have any money but my wife did. "Where's your wife? Get her, because I need some money to get back to campus," he said. Nina gave him the money, and Woody said, "I'll send you a check this week." Sure enough, a check came in Wednesday's mail.

The most embarrassing time of my career was when I missed the Purdue game in '52 with a freak injury. Our kicker, Thurlow "Tad" Weed, was one of my fraternity brothers. I was always kidding him that kicking was easy and that anybody could kick, so one day in the front yard of the fraternity house he told me, "OK, Jacoby, you think it's so easy, let's go." So what do I do? I break my toe. There was a picture in the newspaper of me at the Purdue game, sitting on the bench in a suit with my big toe all bandaged. In the stands that day, some guy a few rows behind Nina was telling the story: "I heard Jacoby got hurt by chasing his bride around the bedroom and he tripped on the vanity stool." Just then, Nina stood up and told him, "No, he didn't break it from chasing his bride around the bedroom. How do I know? I am his bride!"

Anyway, Woody was a little ticked off at me for that injury.

I can always say that I blocked for two Heisman Trophy winners, Vic Janowicz and then Hoppy. They were great players. Man, Vic could do anything—he just ran like a deer. The game I remember most was when we beat Michigan 27–7 in my junior year. It was Woody's first win over Michigan. I was playing nose guard and dropped into coverage on this one play. The quarterback looked right at me, and I was thinking, "Damn, he's going to throw it right to me." He did and I got a big interception. The next year, I was the team's MVP and a cocaptain with Rock Joslin. Both of those honors are very special to me to this day.

After I graduated, we continued to go back to home games. One time, Nina was pregnant with our first son, and we stopped by to see Annie after the game. We were getting ready to go home and she said, "George, Nina can't ride all the way up to Toledo like this. You just take one of Woody's double beds in the front bedroom. Don't worry about it—Woody watches film all night, and he won't be home until about 6:00 in the morning."

Woody had this big bedroom in the front of the house with two double beds in it. Well, Nina and I were sleeping in one of them, and sure enough, at about 6:00 A.M., the door opens and here came Woody. He went into the bathroom and then sat down on the edge of the bed. It was still dark. My wife woke me up. She said, "George, Woody's here. He's on the end of the bed."

I said, "Coach?"

He said, "Jacoby, what the hell are you doing in here?"

This was after I was gone, but he still recognized my voice.

George Jacoby was an All–Big Ten tackle in 1952 and 1953.

Photo courtesy of George Jacoby.

When Annie would come up to Toledo, she would always tell people, "My husband got into bed with this man's pregnant wife." She always thought that was funny.

Years later, as our boys, Jeff and Douglas, started to grow up, we would take them to campus. Woody would pull them aside and tell them about how important it was to get a good education. Then we would get in the car and they would say, "Dad, Woody says we have to mind you and be good boys."

He was a great man. I see a lot of him in coach Tressel in the way he runs a program, too. Nina and I have been loyal fans of Ohio State since I graduated, and we will be until the day we die.

George Jacoby was MVP of the 1952 team and cocaptain in '53.

ROBERT "ROCK" JOSLIN

1951–1953

BEING FROM MIDDLETOWN, I was deciding where to attend college. I was signed, sealed, but not yet delivered to Purdue when Wes Fesler talked to me. "You're an Ohio boy and you need to be loyal to your state school," he said.

And after thinking about it for a while, I knew I had to attend Ohio State.

That first year, coach Fesler spent a lot of time after practice working with me to groom me to replace Vic Janowicz a few years down the road, and I have to say right here and now that I have played with many great players like Hop Cassady and others, but Vic was the best there ever was. He was just the best and he was always helpful, but I never got to replace Vic because coach Fesler left and they brought in a new coach before the 1951 season.

We had heard a lot of stories about Woody Hayes before he arrived at Ohio State, like the time he got into a fistfight during a Miami of Ohio–Cincinnati game, but we really didn't know what to think of him. As a matter of fact, most of us didn't want to play for him.

I remember one of his first temper episodes came when Bill Wilks got Woody upset during a practice. Well, Woody told him, "Take this football and stick it up your ass." Bill left the field and never came back, but he did go on to become a great basketball player.

Well, I got along with Woody pretty well because I was very self-disciplined and I was tough on myself, so I didn't need anybody else to be extra tough on me. But he was a tyrant in those days. He was tough. And you know how some guys were tough but fair? Woody really was tough and unfair at times. I remember we were going up to play Michigan, and you could dress 38 players on the road back then. Well, he was planning on not dressing Bill Mott. Now Bill Mott didn't play much, but he was one of the greatest guys on the team and he was a senior. It was his final game! I told Woody, "The guy's a senior and his parents are going to be up at the game. You just can't tell him he can't dress for his final game." I told him to not dress some sophomore, and he finally agreed.

Anyway, Woody came in that first year and changed our offense from the single wing to the T formation. He converted me from halfback to end, and I think I was the only starting sophomore on that '51 team. It's a great trivia answer, but I scored the first touchdown at Ohio State under Woody Hayes. I ran this little hook pattern, and Tony Curcillo threw it low, just off the grass. I got my hands down and picked it right from the grass and rolled over for the touchdown. We beat Southern Methodist 7–0.

When Woody changed the offense, he converted Vic from a single-wing, Heisman Trophy winner to the left halfback position in the T. Now there were jokes going around that there was only one man who could stop Vic and that was Woody Hayes. That first year under Woody we lost 7–0 at Michigan, and there were not a lot of happy people in town. I remember one game at the stadium, and I am not sure exactly when it was, but the crowd was chanting, "Good-bye Woody, Good-bye Woody."

The worst blowup I saw from Woody came after we played at Pittsburgh. He came in after the game, and the locker room door was still locked. He knocked the door off the hinges to get in. He told the starting offensive guys to go sit down, and then he started in: "You look like bunch of f——ing clowns out there." He really let them have it. And we had won that game [16–14].

That next season, we played without a captain after Bernie Skvarka was elected. He had a kidney removed and represented us in street clothes for the season. I was injured in the Purdue game, tearing a knee ligament. So we headed into the Michigan game and the doctors weren't sure if I could play. Well, Dean Dugger got coldcocked right away, and they carried him off the field. I told Woody, "I need to get in this game. I can play; send me in." So he put me in there, and Michigan had this All-American safety by the name of Perry. I went down as a decoy a few times, but I thought I could get behind him. So we called the play and John Borton hit me on a pass, and I just got my feet in before the end line. Thirty-three yards and a touchdown!

Robert "Rock" Joslin was an end for three years and cocaptained the 1953 team
with George Jacoby. *Photo courtesy of Robert Joslin.*

I caught another touchdown later and ended up with 10 catches. We won 27–7, and it was Woody Hayes' first win over Michigan.

Woody came up to me after the game, happy as can be, and all he said was, "Joslin, you were right." He later told John Borton, "Joslin personally saved my job." I guess he was real worried about getting fired in his second season if we lost that game to Michigan.

In those days, when you went to the movies, they would show newsreels before the movies. So I had a date with this nurse and we went to the movies. The newsreel they showed was a recap of the Ohio State–Michigan game and it was how "Joslin catches touchdown passes to lead Ohio State over Michigan." You could just say that it ended up as a great date. Now you can't get any better than that. But the best thing was pleasing my parents. My father was a great fan, and he went to all the games. I know I made him proud.

One time, my dad came up to town and took a few of us out to dinner. We ended up drinking beer and eating ribs somewhere downtown. He dropped us off, drove 90 miles back to Middletown that night, and then went to work the next day at the steel mill, telling his friends, "I was out having a beer with Vic Janowicz last night. . . ." He was proud of me.

My senior year in 1953, George Jacoby and I were elected captains. George basically took care of the defense and I took care of the offense. They put in a new rule that limited substitutions that year to just one player, and John Borton was the one who came out of the game. I really struggled on defense. I weighed about 190 pounds. Michigan ran the single wing, and I was not that good of a defensive player, and we lost our final game [20–0].

Woody was always good to me, though. Years later, I worked in Ashland, Kentucky, and I sat on a few boards back then, and the school football team was having a banquet. They came to me to get a guest speaker and I called Woody. He said he had just had his gallbladder taken out. I remember waiting at the airport in Ashland, and Woody's plane rolled in. He said he had to go to the men's room, so I went with him and he opened up this briefcase. He pulled out a needle and gave himself an injection. I said, "Coach, what are you doing?"

He said, "I've been a diabetic all my adult life."

I never knew that, and I thought I was pretty close to him. I just never knew. Anyway, he gave a great talk that night about education and making the kids study and taking good courses. The parents loved him.

55

Another time, we had a captains' reunion in downtown Columbus, and Woody and I happened to park next to each other. As we got out of our cars, he started in on this *Hustler* publisher Larry Flynt. He got up to speak that night, and he took off on this long tirade about Larry Flynt. As we walked back to our cars later, he asked me, "Was I out of place about that Flynt stuff?"

What could I tell him? "Of course not," I said. "Coach, that was great."

After all these years, you really don't remember the surgeries, lacerations, broken bones and all the bruises. But you don't forget that 33-yarder that helped beat Michigan. I wrote coach Tressel a letter recently about what Ohio State means to me and I even went back to "Carmen, Ohio" for the words, "While our hearts rebounding thrill . . ."

My heart still rebounds with thrill. It really does.

Robert "Rock" Joslin, who led the team in receiving in 1951, scored the first touchdown in Woody Hayes' OSU career.

JIM MARSHALL

1957–1958

DURING MY SENIOR YEAR AT COLUMBUS EAST, I had made high school All-American and I could have played at several colleges, but I knew two places I wouldn't dare visit. Woody Hayes had talked to me often, and he said, "You visit any school you want to, but don't you dare go up there." I don't think he said the word *Michigan*, but I knew where he meant. He didn't want me visiting Michigan or Michigan State. I think he did say once, "We don't give a damn for the whole state of Michigan."

I had visited the Ohio State campus so much; I was impressed with the Oval, and I loved going down to Mirror Lake. The kids were sitting around it and just being mellow. I would walk over to see the buckeye trees planted for each All-American. The tradition and history of the place impressed me from the beginning. Bill Willis had gone to my high school, and I knew he was like a legend around there, and I really wanted to follow in his footsteps.

It just seemed natural for me to become a Buckeye, because I already felt like one.

That freshman year, Jim Parker taught me how to be a man. He kicked my ass every day in practice. We would scrimmage against the varsity, and Jim beat on me every day. He wanted me to answer the call. I knew if I ever could beat him, I could beat anybody. I remember many years later, he was with the Colts and I was with the Vikings, and I had sacked Johnny Unitas. As I rolled over and looked up, there was Jim Parker just nodding, like, "You have come of age."

58

Jim Marshall was an All-American selection at tackle in 1958. *Photo courtesy of the OSU Archives.*

The next year, when I was a sophomore, we won the national championship. I can still remember how well the Rose Bowl treated us—they gave us these cashmere blazers and a pair of binoculars.

I remember the first time I got an A in English. Woody had never shown too much emotion with me, but he looked at my grades and then looked up at me. He just gave me that look that he was proud of me. I will always remember that.

After my junior year, I left school to sign with Saskatchewan of the Canadian Football League [CFL]. I got a signing bonus of $3,000, and I bought a Pontiac Bonneville convertible. Later, I might have regretted leaving school early, but now I don't because I was one of those guys who had to go through the school of hard knocks.

It's like that song Sinatra sang: "Mistakes . . . I've made a few, but too few to mention."

You can imagine, Woody didn't like me leaving early, but he stayed in contact with me throughout my career. Woody Hayes would never abandon you even if he felt you made a mistake on the field or off of it. He was always on me to come back and get back in school. Just before he died, he called me and told me, "Jim, I have been asking you this, how many times; it is time for you to come home." I really didn't know what he meant, but I think he wanted to see me before he passed on. I didn't go back. I had been in an airplane crash and had so many injuries that needed to heal.

This is what I still remember when I think of my college days: the fanatical dedication of the Ohio State fans, "Carmen, Ohio," the band in a quick march with a whispered version of "Fight the team across the field, show them Ohio's here. . . ."

Whenever I hear either one of those songs, they bring tears to my eyes.

Those are feelings that will always be there for me.

Jim Marshall, after playing one season in the CFL, went on to have a brilliant NFL career—playing one season with the Cleveland Browns and nineteen with the Minnesota Vikings.

TOM MATTE

1958–1960

Coming out of Shaw High School in East Cleveland, I had several opportunities to play college football, but Woody Hayes came to my house and sold my parents on Ohio State. He didn't worry about recruiting me—he recruited my parents. He guaranteed my mother that I would graduate from college if I came to Ohio State, and once he did that, I knew where I was headed.

Woody Hayes and I hated each other for most of my career.

I was always joking with the coaches and just having a lot of fun. I got a 1.5 GPA my first quarter in school. Woody called me in and asked, "Tom, how do you like school?"

"There is Northburg and Southburg [campus bars] and a lot to do around here," I said. "I love it."

He told me, "If you don't get a 3.0 GPA, you will lose your scholarship!"

I didn't screw around with my grades too much after that. He scared the shit out of me and that's all it took. It was the wake-up call I needed.

On the field, he switched me from halfback to quarterback, and I had never played quarterback and I didn't want to play quarterback. But he put me at second-string quarterback between my sophomore and junior years. I'll never forget what he did that spring. We had two spring games, and in the first I took the second-string offense right down the field and had a great day. I threw for five touchdowns and ran all over the place. In the second spring game, Woody would call the play and then go tell the defense what the play would be. I threw five interceptions. He just made me look like a complete ass.

So we had one more practice remaining because it had been postponed due to bad weather, and I told [assistant coach] Bo Schembechler what I was going to do. Bo said, "Tom, don't do it."

"Bo, he made a complete ass out of me," I told him. So I did it—I fumbled the ball from the snap six times in a row. I would pull my hands out early on purpose and just kept fumbling.

Well, Woody got so mad. "Bo, what the f—— are we going to do? What are we going to do?" he screamed.

Then he came up and gave me a forearm shiver and hit me so hard, I could have owned the school. Now I was laughing and he screamed again, "Bo, damn it, what are we going to do?"

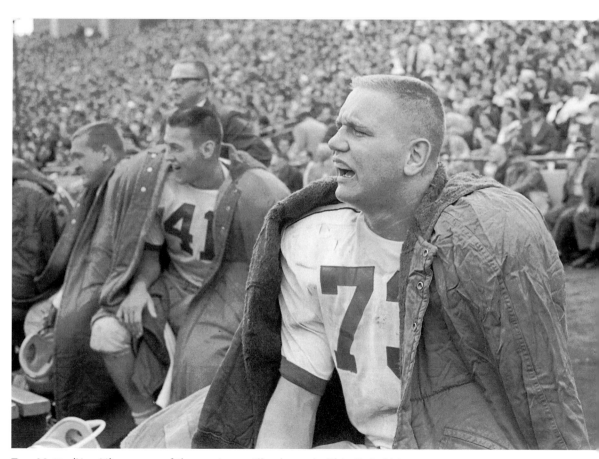

Tom Matte (No. 41) was one of the most versatile players in Ohio State history.

Then he hit himself in the temple and he went down like a sack of potatoes. Bo looked at me and said, "When he wakes up, he's going to kill you."

It turned out he had to have five stitches in his head. I went back to the dorm and went into hiding, and he came looking for me. He told me, "You will never, ever play quarterback for me." I said, "I don't want to. I want to play halfback or defensive back."

We opened up the '59 season and we fell behind Duke 7–0 at halftime. It was about 98 degrees and I was playing both ways that day. He grabbed a center and a fullback and me, and we went to our practice field right out in back of the locker room. Right out at that open end of the stadium. This is at the half! He said, "I may have to put you in at quarterback, so let's work on a few things."

We got down to two minutes to go in the game during a timeout, and he said, "Matte, go in at quarterback. Roll right and if somebody is open, throw it. If not, run it. On the next play, roll left and do the same thing."

On one play, I went the wrong way and it turned into a naked reverse of some sort and I ran for about 40 yards. We won the game 14–13, and I came in on Monday and I was thinking I was the cat's meow. He always had the roster posted with the depth chart, and I saw I was the third-string quarterback, but I was taken off my other positions. That season, we were 3–0–1 when I played quarterback and 0–5 when I didn't play. Now that is when we really started hating each other.

I had screwed off during my junior year. I was just always loose and having fun. I was living with a bunch of swimmers, and they were crazy guys—we got kicked out of four or five apartments. Before my senior year, Woody said, "You are worse than Vic Janowicz and Hubie Bobo combined."

Now I knew I was bad, because those were two guys who had a reputation for getting a little wild. Before my senior year, he told me, "You have a choice—you can either come live with Anne and me or you can move back into your fraternity house."

That year, I had lunch with him every day and dinner with him every night. He would tuck me in, because he gave me ulcers. We learned to get along, but he never gave me any credit. The other thing he did that really hurt me was when we voted for captains before my senior year, he told the team, "There is one guy you can't vote for, because he gets enough publicity." That still hurts.

In my senior year, I would play the game and have three hours to have dinner with my family or friends, and then I had to be back at his office to look at the film. He was like a watchdog over me, but I had a pretty good year [All-American, All–Big Ten] and it made it possible to get drafted high by the Baltimore Colts.

I had six credit hours left to graduate, and Woody called me three times during my rookie year, asking, "Are you coming back?" each time. I told him I would. As I walked off that podium with my degree that next winter, he grabbed me by the arm and took me to a telephone. He called my mom. "Mrs. Matte," he said. "Your son just got his degree, and my obligation to you is fulfilled."

We ended up getting along much better after that. Later, when he came to the East Coast, he always stayed at my home. In fact, we became really good friends. He became such a special person to me. One time we talked about all we had gone through.

He told me, "You know, you were such an immature kid; you just needed guidance."

I told him, "I didn't like you at all."

"Did I get the best out of you?" he asked.

"Yes."

"Well, what do you think of yourself today?" he asked.

I told him that he helped make me who I am.

Looking back on it, I guess I just needed a kick in the ass every once in a while.

I understand him a lot better now. He was a very intelligent guy, and he made you focus. His football theories were basically military theories. He always explained himself and explained why he did certain things. He was very unselfish, and he considered us part of his family. There is no way to overestimate the effect he had on my life.

Those all are similar things I love about Jim Tressel—he got us back into caring for the players and made the players interested in being a team.

The strongest friendships I have, I made at Ohio State—my fraternity brothers, teammates, Jack Nicklaus. I am very proud of Ohio State, and I have always been proud to be a Buckeye—I can tell you that.

Tom Matte was selected in the first round of the 1961 NFL draft by the Baltimore Colts, where he played for 12 seasons. He was named to the franchise's 50th anniversary team.

AUREALIUS THOMAS

1955–1957

I WAS BORN IN OKLAHOMA, but I was destined to be an Ohio State Buckeye. I played football at Manual Training High in Muskogee, Oklahoma, for a coach named Walter W. Cox, who was a graduate of Oberlin College. Coach Cox first recommended that I consider moving to live with my sisters in Ohio to try to earn a football scholarship.

This was in the early fifties, and the schools were segregated in Oklahoma at that time. He knew I would have more options if I would be living in a place like Columbus. At that point, I decided to go to spend the summers with my sisters and work, and then I would return to Oklahoma. Before my junior year, I decided to stay in Columbus, and I attended Columbus West. My coach there was Mack Pemberton, and he was convinced I should attend Ohio State.

Coach Pemberton called Woody Hayes and we scheduled an appointment. Most of Woody's linemen at that time were about 6′3″ and 240 pounds, but here I was, a 6′1″ and 195-pound tackle. When he saw me, Woody wasn't convinced Ohio State was the place for me.

So I decided I was headed to Cincinnati. I had been selected to play in this high school All-Star Game in August of '53. While preparing for that game, [I found out that] a lot of the players there had scholarships to Ohio State. I was outperforming a lot of the fellas there, and the Ohio State coaches noticed it. Once they saw that I could get the job done, they made me an offer. My brother had played at Maryland State, which is now Maryland Eastern Shore, and he was an All-American. He taught me so much about technique as a lineman, and I made up for my lack of size with good technique and plenty of hustle.

In the fall of 1954, the week before the opening game, I was supposed to be on the second team, but Jim Reichenbach was injured and couldn't play, so I was elevated to first team. We were having a scrimmage at the stadium, and it was about 105 degrees that day. I worked about 45 minutes with the first team that day during the scrimmage and then they called for the second team. Well, I was a second-teamer, too, so I stayed on the field and worked with them for another 45 minutes. Then after the scrimmage, we did our running around the field. When it was all over, I went into the locker room to get an orange juice, and the next thing I know I am waking up in University Hospital. I had heat exhaustion, and I had lost too much water.

I was there for 28 days. It was a serious situation, and it took that long for my body chemistry to adjust. I had lost about 15 pounds. About four or five other players had heat exhaustion, too, but my case was severe. I remember waking up in the hospital, and I moved my fingertips to open my eyelids; they were open but I couldn't see. They had two tubes going into my arms to get me the necessary fluids. Woody and all the other coaches would visit me, and they made it clear that I had my scholarship whether I ever played football again or not.

Things changed that day, from the standpoint of how they tried to prevent problems with the heat and how everyone looked at practicing in those conditions.

The doctors at Ohio State began researching it and doing scientific studies. They took that problem and made it a big project. They started to weigh players before and after practice. They convinced the coaches that players must have as much water as possible during practices. Before then, we couldn't have water, period. They started giving them salt. They even changed the uniforms. They used to make the jerseys that were real thick so they could be worn for five years. They recognized that once the jersey got wet with sweat, it was like having a big wet blanket over your body and your skin could not breath. So they started making the uniforms lighter.

Doctor Bob Murphy then went around to other universities and taught these new principles and told about his research.

When I look back on it, I realize I am blessed because others have passed due to heat exhaustion.

65

Aurealius Thomas was one of the anchors of the offensive line during the 1957 championship season.   *Photo courtesy of Aurealius Thomas.*

I slowly worked back the energy and stamina and began my playing days in 1955.

Woody was known for his detail and his no-nonsense planning. We made a trip to the West Coast for a game, and in the air he had us extremely busy. We didn't waste any time. We were eating, getting our ankles taped, and having various kinds of meetings with our coaches. We landed and then went directly to the locker room and practiced. When it was over, we were riding on the bus to the hotel, and I won't name the guy, but he told me he made a date with the stewardess. I said, "We were getting taped, having all those meetings with the coaches, and all that; how did you find the time?"

I averaged 52 minutes a game during my senior season, playing guard on offense and nose guard on defense. I made All-American, and we won the national championship. Because of my problem, I studied health in college and paid very close attention to my health from that day forward.

I am proud to say that I still feel very close to the university and I look upon my days at Ohio State with great fondness.

Aurealius Thomas was named an All-American guard in 1957.

The
SIXTIES

WAYNE BETZ

1960–1962

I WAS BORN AND RAISED IN OHIO and ever since I could think, I had these goals: I wanted to go to Ohio State, play football for Woody Hayes, and play in a Rose Bowl. Then in high school, I realized I wanted a career in chemical engineering, and I discovered that Ohio State University had a great program.

Later, Woody Hayes wooed my mother and convinced us that I would get a great education if I became a Buckeye.

How could I not?

When I think of Ohio Stadium, sometimes I think of our freshman coach, Ernie Godfrey. At practice every day, he would point to Ohio Stadium and tell us, "It was not built in a day." He knew that we would need many days of practice, practice, practice to gain our potential. But Ernie also said such things as, "Pair off in groups of three and scatter out in little bunches." I always wondered but never asked Ernie, what did scattering out in little bunches really mean?

In the late fifties and early sixties, football got away from the 60-minute "iron men" that played both ways. Limited substitution was allowed on a change of possession. If the defense gave up the ball, you had to get the quarterback and other key offensive people in the game first, and linemen were generally the last to be substituted. Consequently, defensive linemen and linebackers were required to play offense for a few plays, so we had to practice with the offense, too.

Wayne Betz (No. 55) rushes a North Carolina quarterback during the 1962 season opener.

At such a practice, before a game against Michigan, I was in at offensive guard. In the huddle, Woody called a guard-trap play on the end. Somehow, I got the call wrong and I crashed into the other guard behind the center, causing a fumble. At that moment, I thought that Woody would probably beat me to a pulp for my mistake. We got back into the huddle, and Woody asked, "Betz, what kind of engineer are you studying to be?"

I answered, "Chemical engineer, sir."

Immediately, he snapped, "I'll never drink another drop of water again!" Lesson learned.

He wasn't known for his humor, but Woody could be as funny as anyone.

Before the start of one game, we were in the locker room and Woody asked von Allen Hardman to go outside to see what was happening with the weather, since there had been a possibility of lightning and storms. The team was facing Woody, receiving our last-minute instructions, when von reentered the room behind Woody. He had coat hangers sticking out of the ear holes of his helmet. The team sort of snickered, and Woody whirled around and saw von. "What the hell are you doing?" Woody asked him.

"Just checking for lightning, coach," von replied.

I thought Woody would die on the spot.

That man was very serious about winning, however. Woody always stated that a football game has only two outcomes—"either you win or you lose"— and if you are going out there to lose, you might as well not even go out to play the game. But he was one of the most compassionate people that ever existed off the field. He really would give you the shirt off his back if you needed it. Woody also believed that education came first. He stated over and over that the real reason for being at Ohio State was to receive an education and that playing football was secondary.

This may sound strange to most Buckeye fans, but Bo Schembechler was one of my favorite assistants. Bo was the defensive line coach, and his heart was always behind his players. He did everything in his power (including arguing with Woody) to allow his players to be the best they could be. He valued each of us as a person and taught us how to really function as a team.

Which brings me to Michigan and the game I remember most. We were undefeated in 1961 as we went to Ann Arbor. The wonderful part about the game was after our last touchdown, which made the score 48–20, Woody, not wanting to run the score up, called for the extra point. The players in the huddle decided that 50 looked better than 49, so we went for two points and made it. All of us were lucky enough not to be kicked off the team! Woody finally took credit for the call.

Winning the Michigan game really was winning the season for us. We won against Michigan in three of my four years. Earning those "gold pants" awards was always special.

As far as teammates, I'll never forget the speed and power of our All-American fullback, Bob Ferguson. I really don't think he ever lost a yard rushing in his college career. He could carry half of any defense on his back for 10 yards. He was just an astounding athlete.

My only real regret was not going to the Rose Bowl in 1961 when the faculty council voted that we shouldn't go. [The school's faculty council, against popular opinion, voted to turn down the Rose Bowl's invitation. The controversial decision angered Woody Hayes for years to come. He often said it hampered his recruiting efforts.] Sadly, one of my chemical engineering professors was a member of the faculty council that voted "no." After hearing my story about always wanting to play football for OSU and go to the Rose Bowl, he stated that if he knew that anyone felt that strongly about going to the Rose Bowl, he would have voted for us to go. I came just short of picking him up and throwing him out of the window from the third story of the chemical engineering building that day.

To this day, it is still a disappointment to me.

Sometimes, I hear the critics say we should abolish athletic scholarships. I can say that a football scholarship allowed me to get a wonderful education with a degree in chemical engineering. That degree enabled me to have a very satisfying and successful career in my field and an opportunity to raise a family of four and retire early at the age of 58 to enjoy the great retirement life. Ohio State helped make it all possible.

Wayne Betz was a member of the 1961 national championship team.

73

ARNIE CHONKO

1962–1964

WHEN I WAS RECRUITED TO OHIO STATE, I already was a huge Buckeyes fan. My older brothers, Andy and Allan, always listened to the OSU and Notre Dame games on the radio on Saturday afternoons—either by switching channels or by using two radios. There was no TV in the early fifties. I was always thrilled to hear the exploits of Bobby Watkins, Hubert Bobo, "Hop" Cassady, and Dave Leggett, along with Jim Parker and Jim Houston, but I admit that the exploits of John Lattner and Ralph Guglielmi at Notre Dame were equally important to me.

Woody Hayes pointed out to me that Ohio State was the only place for an Ohio lad, particularly one interested in medical school. Indeed, Wayne Woodrow asked the dean of the medical school to show me around the medical school campus within a half hour of my arrival for my official recruiting visit. Dean Richard Meiling told me that I needed to maintain a 3.3 GPA to prove to the admissions committee that I was serious about medical school. I was just a quiet kid from Cleveland, and I can recall thinking that I may have bitten off more than I could chew. Of course, Woody spoke up and told Dr. Meiling that he knew that I could do that—and more—particularly with the discipline of athletics in my background.

Woody also pointed out to me that Notre Dame did not have a medical school and that he had several former players in dental school at the time. "We have the best darn medical college in the Midwest right here in good old Columbus . . . so forget about even visiting that school up North!" he told me.

However, Woody was not thrilled to learn that I wanted to play baseball in the spring rather than attend spring football practices. My brothers, who had played baseball and football at Ohio University and Notre Dame, respectively, told me to insist on a written agreement from coach Hayes prior to my signing the letter of intent. I was concerned about Woody's notorious temper, but I decided to ask for the letter. Needless to say, Woody was only mildly irked and pointed out to me that his word was his honor. I thanked him for his interest and pointed out that coach Ara Parseghian at Northwestern and coach Bump Elliott at Michigan had agreed to my baseball-in-the-spring request in writing. I also mentioned that both of those schools had excellent medical schools. Woody's reaction was swift and measured: he wrote a very nice letter to me, asking me to attend spring football practice during my freshman year but allowing me to pursue baseball in the spring of the last three of my undergraduate years. He also added a handwritten P.S. stating his concern that I would be making a great mistake if I attended the "school up North." What he did not know was that I hated Michigan all my life and I found it impossible to matriculate at Ann Arbor despite the greatness of the Michigan academic and athletic programs.

I was won over by the traditions of the horseshoe—Ohio Stadium—and the sounds of that great band that I had seen on several visits to Ohio State games with my high school football team. Moreover, I sensed that coach Parseghian would not stay at Northwestern.

Thus, a shy, pug-nosed kid from Parma followed his childhood dream and headed to Columbus to join the rigorous program of Buckeye football . . . and baseball.

I worked hard in school and on the athletic fields at Ohio State. I spent 36 hours at OSU hospitals during my freshman year after suffering a concussion when tackling teammate Bo Scott in a full-scale scrimmage in the stadium on a fall Friday afternoon in 1961. When I was led into the locker room after the concussive blow, apparently Woody asked me to identify him. When I drew a blank, he shook his head and told the trainers, "Get his butt to the hospital." I awakened in the OSU neurosurgery observation ward 30 hours later in the middle of a conversation with my brother Al. The next two weeks were without serious contact for me, and it led me to wonder if I should forget football and play only baseball.

However, I can honestly say that the lure of playing on the horseshoe grass was too great and I pressed forward through spring practice, a subsequent

75

Arnie Chonko shares the Ohio State record for interceptions in a game, thanks to picking off three Indiana passes in 1964. *Photo courtesy of Arnie Chonko.*

separated shoulder, and Woody's wrath. He would say, "You can't make the club in the tub."

I persevered and got a break when Eddy Ulmer left school due to academic difficulties. I was inserted into the defensive backfield and won a starting job and flourished as a sophomore. I continued to work hard and improve during my junior and senior years.

Words cannot express how thrilling it was for me to play football for OSU, in the Big Ten, and in the horseshoe along the banks of the Olentangy. I remember the courage and camaraderie of my teammates, the game-saving interceptions and tackles, and key goal-line stands that we accomplished as a team. I remember hating Woody for the grueling thrice-a-day preseason practices in the hot August and September sunshine. I still remember being "chewed out" and kicked in the ass by Woody for minor mistakes at practice and then being praised to high heaven by him a week later on his TV show! He was a volatile character, but he always meant well for his players.

And get this—he even came to several baseball games when we won the Big Ten title during my senior season in 1965, when we went on to finish second in the College World Series. Football players Bo Rein, Don Harkins, and Jim Reed also were on the team.

We all know that Woody hated to lose. Once, he almost attacked the USC Trojan mascot riding the white horse in the L.A. Coliseum when they scored a late touchdown in 1963. "I am going to knock that asshole off that ——damn horse if he comes around that ——ing track again," he said. Another time, I intercepted a pass in a scrimmage at the stadium, and as I was getting tackled, I lateraled to Paul Warfield, who ran it in for a touchdown. I thought we made a wonderful play, and all of a sudden, Woody came and kicked me in the butt. "What is a smart guy like you doing making a play like that?" he said. "You could have fumbled!"

In contrast, he could be enchanting and charming while discussing Ralph Waldo Emerson's essays or the history of Western Europe following World War I and World War II.

The key to his judgment of you was giving intense effort on your part. He believed that you could "outwork the other fellow." He worked hard and expected those around him to work equally as hard. His favorite saying was "nothing good in life comes easy." His football program was an example of that philosophy. He was honest and he ran a program that was academically focused and without recruiting scandal. I think the best attribute of coach Hayes was his interest in his players' academic careers and his loyalty.

He encouraged me to aim high and pursue a career in medicine, and he was very supportive of me when I was exhausted and transiently depressed during my sophomore year in medical school. "Chonko, you damn fool, you need to learn that you cannot know everything about medicine as a young doctor—that's why they call it the *practice* of medicine!" he told me. "Call Dean Meiling and he will tell you the same thing."

He bought me a new suit of clothes for graduating Phi Beta Kappa as an undergraduate and another when I graduated summa cum laude from the Ohio State College of Medicine. He even helped my wife, Barbara, find a teaching position in the Columbus area when we married after my freshman year of medical school. When you became a Buckeye, he and his wife Anne adopted you as family, and you were never forgotten, particularly if you were a good citizen during and after your playing days.

I have fabulous memories of my years at The Ohio State University, as an undergraduate and in medical college. All of these memories are intertwined with the figure of Wayne Woodrow Hayes.

As our alma mater states, "Time and change will surely show, how firm thy friendship O-HI-O."

It was a great honor for me to wear the scarlet and gray uniform on both the football and baseball fields. To leave the horseshoe with the Victory Bell ringing in my ear remains an indelible memory in my life.

78

Dr. Arnold Chonko was Academic All–Big Ten and an All-American defensive back in 1964.

DWIGHT "IKE" KELLEY

1963–1965

I DECIDED WHERE I WANTED TO GO TO COLLEGE one day in Ann Arbor, Michigan. I was visiting Michigan on a recruiting trip, and it was November 25, 1961, the day that Ohio State beat them 50–20. I knew then that I wanted to play for the Buckeyes.

I came from Bremen, Ohio, a town of 1,200 people near Lancaster, and I first remember seeing Woody Hayes when he came to the Fairfield County All-County sports banquet. He was such a dynamic individual. My dad absolutely loved him, and so did my mom for that matter.

And I came to love him, too.

What can I say, Woody was Woody.

He was kind: after I came to Ohio State, my dad was watching practice in the spring on a fairly cold day. Woody noticed him and sent one of the managers in to get him a coat. I don't think people ever realized to what extent he cared.

In my four years, I remember that Woody missed practice once. On that day, he disappeared from practice, and I found out later what had happened. He had gotten word that a young student had just broken his neck playing intramural football . . . I guess one of the managers had gotten a message to him. Woody left practice to go to University Hospital. He took an autographed football and stayed there with that boy until his parents showed up. Woody didn't want him to be alone.

He was a teacher and a historian, and he always tried to make a difference.

He made sure that you knew the difference between right and wrong. Now this sounds corny, but all those lifelong lessons that he taught us, they

80

Dwight "Ike" Kelley anchored the middle of the defense from 1963 to 1965.

are all true. He would say, "When you get knocked down, you only have to get up one more time." You later find out that life is like that. You get knocked down in life, you dust yourself off, and you jut that jaw out there like Woody did, and you get right back up.

And he was a competitor: in my junior year against Illinois, they had about 18 or 20 returning lettermen and they were ranked pretty high [number two]. Dick Butkus was quoted as saying, "Ohio State's my meat, because they run straight at me and that's what I love."

Well, Woody was made aware of this. He got up in front of us and said, "Hmm, hmm, that son of a bitch won't know where we are coming from!"

He had us so sky-high for that game, we were throwing up before it. We beat them 26–0.

We had started out 6–0 that year by holding on to beat Iowa 21–19. I remember that Iowa's quarterback, Gary Snook, ran the option for a two-point conversion to tie us, and I tackled him just short of the goal line.

The next week, we got beat pretty badly by Penn State, and then we later lost to Michigan. But we beat them up there in '63 and '65, so two out of three ain't bad.

The next year, in '65, I can remember the announcement of captains like it was yesterday. Of all the great athletes we had on our team, to be elected as one of the two leaders was one of the greatest honors I had ever received. To know my teammates thought that much of me . . . I can't put it into words. I was just one of those crazy guys, that when I crossed that sideline, I was ready for war. Being a captain was greater than All-American status. It came from my teammates, not some sportswriter who didn't know me from Adam.

One time that season, Woody grabbed me and Greg Lashutka, because we were the captains. There was some kind of demonstration on the Oval. He took us down there to speak to the group, to try to get the crowd to disperse. It's an example that he would try to do anything he could to correct the situation any way possible. He cared about people, and he loved that university like no one else.

He was very opinionated, as everyone knows, but you never had to guess where you stood with Woody Hayes.

The character and integrity of that man were above reproach, and I believe today that Jim Tressel is a chip off the old block, but he's got a few more years to put in before he reaches legendary status like coach Hayes.

81

I really think that coach Hayes had a soft spot for our class, because we were so close. There were always five or six of us hanging out together— Tom Bugel, Will Sander, Greg Lashutka, Bobby Lykes, Ted Andrick, Bob Funk, Don Unverferth, Tom Barrington, and Doug Van Horn.

I also stayed very close to Woody after my playing days were done.

One of the times I visited him was when they left the sponge in him after his gallbladder surgery. So I went to the hospital and he had a nurse that looked like Sergeant Shultz outside his door. "He's not receiving visitors," she said. "Tell him it's Ike Kelley, and if he doesn't want to see me or he is tired, that's fine," I told her.

So she came back out, and I could tell that she was disappointed, because Woody wanted to see me. "Ike," he said, "do you know why I am in here? Goddamn it, you know why they left a sponge in me? Too damn many doctors. Yep, there were too many doctors. All these doctors were around there and somebody just forgot."

With me having a position at Worthington Industries in personnel, Woody would call often and ask if I knew of anything or anyplace for certain people. He would always try to help somebody get a job. One day he called me and said, "Ike, can you bail me out of jail?"

82

I said, "What?"

"It's one of these charity things, and I need money to be bailed out," he told me.

"What do you need, a couple of hundred?"

"No, no," Woody said. "Fifty would be great."

I remember the times he spoke at the all-sports banquets, he never charged a speaking fee. They would want to give him the money, and he would donate it right back to the booster club. Woody was Woody. He was always giving back.

One time, Bruce Ruhl, Greg Lashutka, and I were involved in a children's fund-raiser and we met down at the Jai Lai. We asked coach Hayes if we could put his name on it. Woody walked in at about 10:00 A.M., and right away he said, "Well boys, is this a good charity?"

We all said, "Absolutely."

He said, "That's good enough for me. I'll do it."

We were sitting there all prepared to give a litany of reasons to do this charity, and that's all he wanted to know. He trusted us. So then we sat there for two hours and talked about history. It got to be about noon, and suddenly he said, "Hey, you boys had better get back to work." But that's the way he was, you could sit there all day and talk to the man.

After the Gator Bowl incident [coach Hayes' firing], he wasn't accepting calls or anything, but he had committed much earlier to speak to the chamber of commerce. Nobody was getting through to him on the phone. The president of the chamber kept calling and never got through, so he called me to see if coach Hayes could still speak.

I went down to his house, and the shades were drawn. I knocked and I saw this little face stick out through the blinds. I heard Annie say, "Woody, it's Ike Kelley." I walked in and a couple of other players were there. "Ike, I just kind of canceled everything," Woody told me.

I told him how they really wanted him to do this and that they would send transportation right to the house, pick him up, get him there, keep the reporters from him, then get him out the back door and right back to the house. He wouldn't have to talk to anybody else. So he called the chamber and told them that he would do it. I went that night, and I'll never forget what he said in his speech: "Expect nothing less from a man than his full potential, or that is exactly what you will get."

When Bob Funk, our place-kicker, passed away in the early eighties, I got a call out of the blue. "This is coach Hayes; are you going down to Bob's service in Marietta? Would you mind a couple of riders?"

That day, Annie and Woody rode with us, and I remember we got a history lesson all the way down.

There is no way to really explain what that man meant to me, but I know I cried like a baby on the day he died.

Playing for him at Ohio State was an experience afforded to me that I never, ever thought was possible. My goal wasn't to play major college football, because I never thought I was that good. But Woody Hayes made me believe I was. It was an experience that molded my life. It gave me a direction to follow, a direction that I have used since I graduated.

As I sit here, I can't put into words what it meant for me to attend Ohio State and play football at the greatest university in the country.

Dwight "Ike" Kelley was named an All-American in 1964 and '65, becoming Ohio State's first two-time All-American linebacker.

REX KERN

1968–1970

WHEN I WAS A BOY, MY HEROES HAD NAMES like Havlicek, Lucas, and Roberts, and as long as I can remember, I wanted to go to Ohio State to play basketball for the great Fred Taylor. Fred was bigger than life to me. As I developed as a basketball player, he started recruiting me out of Lancaster High School, and my dreams were coming true. But I was pretty good at football and baseball, too, and I had several colleges to choose from. I could have gone to UCLA to play for John Wooden or North Carolina to play for Dean Smith. Ohio University had a great baseball program, and I considered going there, because they would let me play all three sports, and I also was drafted by the old Kansas City Athletics during my senior season.

Then Wayne Woodrow Hayes walked into my life.

It seems that everybody around me met him before I did. He came to one of my basketball games in Columbus, and I was thrilled to death, but it was a game in which I had the opportunity to tie it at the end, and I missed a free throw. "I would like to talk to Rex," he told my parents, "but if he is anything like me, he won't feel like talking after getting beat."

So he left.

One day I was walking down the hallway at Lancaster High, coming out of the locker room, and there he was, walking toward me. He just said hello and kept on walking. He was headed to the principal's office to find out what kind of person I was. He had already talked to my football coach.

Then Dad, who was a barber, got home and told me, "You'll never guess who was in the chair today."

"I have no clue," I told him.

"Coach Hayes came down and got his hair cut today," he said. "He talked about getting an education at Ohio State. He talked about paying back and paying forward, but he didn't talk much about football."

I knew where I wanted to go to college, and when I finally decided it was Ohio State, Woody and Fred agreed that I could play both football and basketball. The real thing that sold me on Ohio State: coach Hayes and coach Taylor both convinced me I would get a good education and the academic support would be there if I needed it. I started thinking that I would be the first in my family to get a college degree, so I told them both I would become a Buckeye.

"OK, Rex, I need you to call these kids," Woody told me, giving me a list of recruits. "There's this kid out of Cleveland we need to get. His name is Larry Zelina. If we get him, it will complete one of the best classes Ohio State has ever had."

One of my first days on campus, I was in the physical education building and I met Rufus Mayes. I saw "Rufe" take off his shirt, and I never thought his shoulders would stop. I never saw anybody that big.

85

Well, we got Larry Zelina and the amount of talent on that freshman class was phenomenal. We knew it immediately after that first day of freshman practice. We must have had 10 or 11 high school All-Americans, and I firmly believe our class was the beginning of another era of Ohio State football. These guys were so athletic that they could play any sport. Take Jack Tatum. "Tate" would have been one of the all-time best running backs if he had stayed on offense. He was that good.

As freshmen, they called us the "Baby Bucks." We would practice against the varsity defense in 1967, and one day illustrates what kind of talent we had. We were in goal-line offense, and the defensive coordinator, Lou McCullough, and our freshman coach, Tiger Ellison, were going back and forth.

"OK, this is what Purdue is going to be running on the goal line," Lou told Tiger. "Let's see if you can score on us."

We gave it to John Brockington, and he would score without anybody touching him. "OK, let's see what the Baby Bucks can do from the 3-yard line," Lou shouted. So they moved it back to the 3-yard line, and we gave it to Larry Zelina and he scored. They moved it to the 6, and we scored again. Tate would score. Then Leo Hayden. They couldn't stop us. Now Lou's starting to get upset. "Dang it, Tiger, you're not running the play right; you are not blocking this the way you are supposed to," he yelled.

Tiger would just say, "You can't stop our Baby Bucks!"

Earle Bruce was coaching the defensive backs that season, and he had this tackling drill for them where they had a five-yard square. They would line up, three defensive backs in this square, and give the ball to the freshmen and they would have to tackle [the freshmen]. First Zelina, and he would get by all three. Brock would run right over them. [Ron] Maciejowski would get through. Tate would make it easy. I would make it. Earle would get so upset with those defensive backs, but they couldn't tackle us. Some of them couldn't touch us.

That next spring, toward the end of spring practice, I had what I thought was a nagging hamstring pull. It had bothered me toward the end of freshman basketball, and one day I couldn't get out of bed or even tie my shoes. So the doctor diagnosed it as a ruptured disk in my lower back. I had back surgery at the end of June, and back surgery was a big deal in those days—not many guys came back from it.

86

When I came out of surgery, coach Hayes was in the room. He took my parents out in the hall and told them, "Listen, if Rex never plays a down for us, he'll get his degree from Ohio State. I'll see to that!" My dad told me that conversation later.

Heading into that fall of '68, I didn't think I would be ready, and I wasn't sure how my back would hold up. But I improved and got ready to play, and I was number one on the depth chart.

Woody was such an organized disciplinarian and we had our routine the day before the game. He even taught us how to pack our bags and what to put in them for our overnight stay. We would go to the golf course, eat filet mignon and those cinnamon rolls that everybody loved, go see a movie, and go back to the hotel. We would have a brief meeting, watch a little film, drink some hot chocolate, and eat our cookies and an apple.

Before that first game, we were opening against Southern Methodist, and my roommate was Jim Otis. Woody would come by and figuratively tuck us in. Well, let's just say that my intestines were working too frequently that night. Woody came in and said, "Jim, how are you feeling?"

"I am ready to play, but if Rex goes to the bathroom one more time, you're gonna have to sleep with him tonight," he told Woody.

"Oh no, oh no," Woody replied. "I got to have my fullback rested and ready to go."

Now I was thinking that Otis would be sleeping in Woody's room and Woody would be sleeping next to me. He summoned Dr. Murphy to the room, and Dr. Bob told him, "Rex will be fine. He's just a little nervous."

I remember the exciting part about that next morning: it was the motorcycle escort to the stadium. Coach Hayes was sitting in the front, and I was across the aisle from him. My eyes were as big as saucers, as these motorcycle cops led us down through campus to the stadium. Kids were clapping and rooting for us and cheering at the bus. We got off, and there was a crowd waiting to greet Woody. It seemed that Ohio State football was larger than life.

So the game started and SMU was passing it all over the field. They set an NCAA record at that time for 76 passes in one game. Woody had told me before the season, "Rex, there will be times out there that you will notice things that me and my coaches won't notice. It will be a gut reaction, and you will have to make a decision out there to do what is best for the team."

We were facing a fourth-and-10 right before the half at about midfield, and this was one of those times. I was huddling the guys as quick as I could, but Woody was sending Mike Sensibaugh in to punt. I waved Mike and the punt team off the field and I called, "Robust, fullback delay." It was a short pass for Jim Otis, who would fake block and slip over the middle. That had to be the worst call at the worst time. SMU came on a fire game from the right corner, and Otis got held up by the defensive end. I dropped back and both linebackers were all over Otis by this time, and the corner hit me and knocked me up into the air. I did a 360 pirouette and landed on my feet. Somehow, I took off and picked up 16 yards and a first down. The crowd went wild. Then I hit Dave Brungard over the middle for a touchdown right before halftime. We won 35–14 that day, and I think it was a new era for Ohio State football. That first game had not been a sellout, and I think we started a chain of sellouts ever since.

Well, we rolled through that season, beating number one Purdue 13–0 in a great defensive game. Teddy Provost made a huge interception and ran into the end zone. We knew the Big Ten championship would go through that last game against Michigan. That fall, I was going to class from 8:00 A.M. until practice started, and I always had to take a sack lunch with me to eat on the run. One day of that Michigan week, I didn't have time to eat. We came into the meetings and George Chaump, the quarterbacks coach, said, "Rex, you don't look well. Are you OK?" I told him I missed lunch. So we went out to practice and I saw this manager carrying a McDonald's bag across the field. He walked up to George and gave it to him. George walked up to Woody and they talked before Woody called me over. He ordered, "Rex, take this bag, and go over there behind those tarps and eat this and then get back in there." So I went over and ate my hamburger, ran back in, and after practice, Rufus told me, "Woody would let you eat McDonald's, but if it were anybody else, especially a lineman, he would have us eating grass if we were hungry."

Early in that Michigan game, Tate fired in on a blitz and just decleated Denny Brown—one of those crushing tackles—and I have no idea how Denny got up. But right then and there, there was no doubt in my mind we were going to beat Michigan. At halftime, we made an adjustment and went to an unbalanced line, and Michigan had never seen it. We just did what we wanted to that day [in a 50–14 win].

Woody always said, "If you are going to fight in the North Atlantic, then train in the North Atlantic." So as we prepared for the Rose Bowl to play USC, he had the heat in the French Field House turned up to 98 degrees every day. The quarterbacks were never involved in tackling drills, but one day in there, Woody said, "George, bring those quarterbacks over here and let them hit the tackling dummy." I was the first guy up and hit the tackling dummy and fell down in pain. I had dislocated my shoulder. Woody came running up and he was screaming, "Oh shit! Oh shit!" Our trainer, Ernie Biggs, ran over and popped it back into place, but I couldn't practice and I didn't know if I would play in the Rose Bowl. But they rigged up a shoulder harness, and when we went to California, I worked my way back into shape.

I remember during practice out there, Woody had one of his megaton blowups. Paul Huff was a fullback who was injured with a bad back and watching practice from the sideline when Woody got mad about something on the field. All of a sudden, he screamed, "That's it! Everybody's running! Everybody start running!" He looked at Huffer and said, "You too! Run till I tell you to stop."

Later, I was coming out of the shower, and almost completely dressed when the equipment manager came in. "Coach Hayes, would you like me to tell Paul Huff he can stop running now?" he asked.

A born leader, Rex Kern was one of Woody Hayes' favorite players of all time.

"Yep," Woody said, "tell him to stop."

Poor Huffer had nothing to do with what went wrong on the field, and he was running all that time.

It was very hot on game day, January 1, 1969, and during pregame warm-ups, Otis said, "I am sweating so bad; these jerseys are too hot." We had always practiced in those fishnet jerseys, and we happened to have them in the locker room. Many players that day wore those fishnets in the Rose Bowl, and that was the first time Ohio State had ever used them.

When we met USC at Disneyland, I remember thinking they were the San Diego Chargers. I mean, they were huge! We were undersized on the line of scrimmage, and I was wondering what would happen during the game, but our offensive line controlled USC from the beginning. We got down 10–0 after O. J. [Simpson] busted an 80-yard run, and I got in the huddle and said, "OK, we've been screwing around long enough. Let's go!" We got back to tie it 10–10 at the half, and then our defense turned it up a notch in the second half. We could always count on our defense.

I think at that time, that game had the largest viewing audience in college football history. We were number one in one poll and they were number two, and vice versa. The Rose Bowl was the biggest game in the universe at that time, but I think the euphoria and excitement of beating the team up North was greater. There was nothing like beating Michigan that year. Still, I'll never forget the Rose Bowl. We won the national championship and I met my wife, Nancy, who was one of the princesses on the Rose Bowl court. [Kern was named the game's MVP, completing 9 of 15 passes for 101 yards and two touchdowns.]

The '69 team had one of those years where we just crushed people. We were winning by three and four touchdowns, and the starters didn't play many second halves. I think *Sports Illustrated* wrote, "Kern might win the Heisman Trophy, but not play enough to earn a letter."

In that first game against TCU, on the first play, we threw a pass to Bruce Jankowski for 69 yards. It was called back for holding. So I noticed they were in man coverage and I called an automatic: "Gold 98." Woody named it, because he always said, "This play is as good as gold." It was for Bruce to line up on the right side and run a post pattern. Bruce had tremendous speed. We hit it for a touchdown, and that was the first play of the '69 season. We won 62–0 that day.

We threw enough to keep defenses off balance, and we threw a lot on first and second down in '68 and '69.

We were 8–0, ranked number one, and had a 22-game winning streak heading to Michigan, as everyone knows. I have never really talked much about what happened that day, and I know people have always wondered, but here it is. The day before the game, it was chilly and moist and a cold front was coming in. Michigan had the artificial turf, and we were out there practicing and stretching on it, and I was lying on my back. My back had gotten wet from this turf, and I started to have a flare-up of back spasms. ABC wanted to do an interview that day, something with a Heisman Trophy angle. They had said that [Purdue's] Mike Phipps and I were splitting the Midwest vote and this game could change that. ABC was late getting there, and the longer I stood waiting on them, the colder it got.

The next day, I couldn't get out of bed. My back was killing me, but gradually it got better and I was able to move around. On that first series, I had dropped back and then shot up the middle for 50 yards, but something changed after that. [Coach] Bo Schembechler had those guys so well prepared. I always heard later that we had taken Michigan lightly. That is bullshit— Michigan played the greatest game in their school's history. I swear it was like Bo was in our huddle. They knew exactly what we were going to do. It was just an ugly day and, without question, the worst loss I ever experienced. When did I get over it?

I haven't.

That '68 team was voted team of the decade by the *The Sporting News* and one of the 10 greatest football teams of all time. I am here to tell you that the '69 team was much better. Woody always said it was the best team ever at Ohio State, but we didn't beat Michigan.

In the locker room after the game, Woody stood on a bench and told us, "All good things must come to an end. This is one of those. We will start preparing for those guys on the way back home." And we did. That will always be branded in my mind and ingrained in my heart.

He had given me a lot of freedom those first two years, but after that Michigan game, it changed. We didn't pass much at all in 1970 and I didn't know why until years later when I read it in Woody's book. He thought I was injured for most of my senior year, but I wasn't. It seemed he just didn't have the confidence to put it up, as we had the first two years. But we had so many great running backs . . . who would ever argue? We were winning and that was all that mattered.

That year, on Thursday before the Michigan game, Woody had one of his megatons again. We were running the offense, marching down the field, and two of our guys were standing on the sideline. Now as we went down the field, they were supposed to be paying attention and moving with us, but we got down to the 45, and all of a sudden Woody noticed them over there shooting the breeze, not paying attention. Well, the old man came unglued. His play cards went up in the air, he started ripping his shirt, screaming, the watch went, he was on the ground, and then he started crying. He started crying and said to Earle Bruce, "Earle, they won't play for me! They won't play for me! My God, it's Michigan week and they won't play for me!"

Now I think that was the only time I heard him say the "M" word. He always used some other term for them, but he said it that time. John Hicks was our right tackle and he had never seen Woody like this, and John was real emotional. So was Tommy DeLeone, our center. Now both of them are about to cry. "Come on, Rex, get us ready!" Tommy screamed. "We'll play for him! We'll play for him!"

It was effective.

The campus started going nuts that week. On Tuesday night, there were about five thousand students trying to find where players lived . . . holding their own pep rally. Then there was another one on Wednesday night. Woody got word of this and decided it was time to get us off campus a night early, so we spent Thursday night at the Fawcett Center. I remember that night because at about 10:00 P.M., a lot of us were hungry. The trainers told Woody that, and all of a sudden, they had to put in an order at that McDonald's down the street. Can you imagine what happened there when that order for 100 Big Macs and 100 fries came in?

We beat them 20–9 in our last game in our stadium—we never lost a game at Ohio Stadium in those three years. And it did take away a little of the hurt from the year before.

Before that Rose Bowl against Stanford, I think he made a tactical error. Woody brought the captains in to schedule the practices and [Jim] Stillwagon said, "Coach, instead of going out 14 days ahead of the game and practicing on the first day, why don't we go out 15 days ahead and just do all the media stuff, get our pictures taken, and have a relaxing day. Then the next morning, we'll go two-a-days as long as you want to."

"By God," Woody said, "you seniors are getting smarter. I love that idea."

Well, no sooner had that airplane banked out of Columbus than the trainer came on the speaker and told us who would be getting taped first in the back of the plane. That meant we would be having practice as soon as we landed. Then during the interviews that day, Woody threw the media out and we had a marathon practice. That set the tone for the Rose Bowl. It put us out of sync, broke our momentum, and really broke our trust.

Stanford was so well prepared. Stillwagon tells the story that [Stanford coach] John Ralston told him he had read Woody's book *Hotline to Victory* three times before the game. He prepared for us out of that book, and [Jim] Plunkett had one of his incredible days. We just weren't in the right mind-set for that game.

I look at my Ohio State days and put it into three categories. One, I got a great education. Two, I made lifelong friends from my teammates and classmates. Three, I got the opportunity to play the best football in the country. Our names became household names with OSU alumni, thousands of fans, and friends all over the world. It's just hard to put into words what Ohio State means to me. I am a product of Ohio State, and I am proud to say that three times I walked across that stage to get degrees [bachelor's, master's, and a doctorate in education]. I hope I became a good representative of our university.

Woody Hayes was such an incredible man to me. There is not enough space for me to say what he meant to me. He brought out the best in everybody.

All the stories don't do him justice.

One time he was in the shopping center in Upper Arlington, and this man came up to him and told him how much he and his wife loved the Buckeyes and how he just wanted to shake his hand. "Well, where is your wife?" Woody asked him. The man told him she was dying of cancer at Riverside Hospital. That evening, that man went to see his wife, and Woody was already sitting by her bedside. There are hundreds of stories like that. Woody used to just walk the halls at all of the hospitals and drop in to cheer people up—people he didn't know.

He would call me over after training table sometimes and say, "Rex, you got any tests you are studying for?" If I said no, he would say, "Let's go." You knew where you were going—you were going to the hospital with him.

We once had a teammate who had lost his best friend in Vietnam. This teammate went home one weekend, and there were some war protesters there and he got into a fight with them. Well, one of them hit him over the head with a bottle, and he never played a down at Ohio State. The injury had affected his central nervous system. Years later, Woody asked me if I remembered that teammate. I did, and he said, "Well, I got him graduated today!"

That's how much an education meant to the man, whether you played football or not. During my rookie year with the Colts, I surveyed our 17 rookies. One guy from Dartmouth had graduated, and me, and that was it. I know for the first 25 years that Woody was at Ohio State, 87 percent of his players graduated. Of that, another 36 percent went to graduate school. That tells you something about what he thought of an education.

We had one linebacker who was one of the most unlikely guys to go on to law school, but he decided kind of late that's what he wanted to do. Woody went to the dean of the OSU law school. "Sorry, Coach, no way," the guy told him. Woody then called the dean of Capital's law school. The guy looked at his records and said, "You know, son, have you ever thought about another profession?" But Woody helped get him in, and he graduated in the top three of his class. He later went to Oxford, and now he is a judge in Columbus. His name is Bill Pollitt.

94

I looked this up once recently, and there were eleven scholarships in either Annie Hayes' or Woody's names. Eleven!

Jack Nicklaus wrote me a letter once. It read: "To me, Woody was one of the greatest people in sports history. He always told me, 'I am going to get one of your kids to come to Ohio State.' He got down to my fourth one, Gary. They had made a luncheon date in Columbus on a Friday. Woody passed away the day before. Of course, Gary went to Ohio State. I will never forget Christmas Day 1969, when my dad was dying of cancer. As we finished dinner, there was a knock on our door and it was Woody Hayes. In his hand was his book, and he had written 'to the best father-son team I have ever known.' That was pretty special to me. It still is."

I had a very special relationship with Woody Hayes. We both respected each other immediately. When I got my Ph.D., he had a little party for me over at the Jai Lai. That time, he told me how proud he was of me. When they left that sponge in him during his gallbladder surgery, he had to go back into the hospital. I called up and got the receptionist at the hospital. She said, "I am sure Woody would want to talk to you. He got on the phone, and he sounded very weak. "Rex, what are you calling me for?" he asked. All of a sudden he remembered my back problems. "Rex, by God, I hear you got back problems again. You know what we need to do? We need to get you back here to University Hospital and take care of that back."

Now I was thinking, "They left a sponge in you and you want me to come back there?" But the point is, he never thought of himself. He was worried about my back.

The last time I was in Columbus prior to his death, we went to the Faculty Club for lunch. He was on his cane then, and we went to his favorite table. All of those professors would come into the club and stop by his table. That man had amazing knowledge. He could talk about sociology, business, politics, war, history, anything. We always fought over who would pay—he would never let me pay.

As we left, he said, "Rex, you haven't driven down Woody Hayes Drive yet, have you? By God, we've got to go down there!" We did, and he loved it. I took him home, and I had made up my mind I was going to tell him what he meant to me. We went to the side door, and I opened it for him. Before he walked in, I just said, "Coach, I want you to know that I love you," and I kissed him on the cheek. I think it shocked the old man. That was the last time I saw him alive.

God, I miss that man. The day he died was the saddest day of my life. Even now, it brings great sorrow to me.

After he died, I was in charge of raising money for an endowment chair in military history in his name, and it was something that Annie wanted so badly. We were $10,000 or $20,000 short, and I went to see Dick Brubaker, who was the captain of the 1954 team. Dick said, "I will take care of it." I went back to see Annie, and she was in the hospital when I told her. Tears ran down her cheek.

What a wonderful lady Anne Hayes was. She was just as good a person as he was—maybe even better, because she had to put up with him. We all did, but he made us better people for it.

Rex Kern, who led Ohio State to a 27–2 record in his three-year career, was an All-American in 1969 and team captain in '70. He played three seasons with the Baltimore Colts and one with the Buffalo Bills.

JIM OTIS

1967–1969

I CAN HONESTLY SAY THAT THIS IS NO EXAGGERATION, but from the time I learned to walk, I was a fan of the Ohio State Buckeyes and I knew that I would someday play football for them. And Woody Hayes was like part of my family from my earliest memories.

My dad and Woody were roommates at Denison, and he remained close to our family as I grew up. He would come up to Celina, Ohio, and we would go boating. I started attending OSU games at the age of five, and if you named the number, I could tell you the name of the player who wore it.

Ohio State football . . . I lived it, slept it, dreamed it. When I was 11 or 12, I would tell all my friends that I would someday play fullback at Ohio State. When we were playing in the yard, they would act like they were Jim Brown or some other great NFL player, and I always acted like an Ohio State player. Now that's tough, acting like a college player and trying to beat an NFL player!

When I got to be a high school senior, my coach told everybody I was going to Ohio State. I guess that limited the number of schools recruiting me, not that they had a chance anyway, but it limited some of the fun I could have had from those visits. Anyway, Woody came to speak at my high school banquet, and he came out to the house afterward. He pulled me aside, and he said, "I want to talk to you. I want you to know that we are recruiting other fullbacks, bigger, better fullbacks."

I said, "Coach, are you offering me a scholarship?"

He said he was, and I just told him, "Well, we'll have to find out just how good those other fullbacks are."

After that freshman season, we began to find out. After that spring season in '67, I was still third-string. Woody called me in and said, "You know, you were in there on seven of the eight drives [that the first-string defense] was scored on. Now it's OK for me to be dumb, but I don't want my assistants to be that dumb."

That day, I moved up the depth chart. I got to play a lot my sophomore year, but we were having a tough year. We had lost to Arizona and Purdue, and then I fumbled in the first half against Illinois, and Woody became pretty mad at me. I didn't play in that second half, we ended up losing, and he benched me for the next two games.

We went to Michigan with a 5–3 record, and I'll never forget that first Michigan game. Woody was so intense in that locker room. He just shouted, "If there is going to be a fight today, let's do it right here in this tunnel!"

We won 24–14.

Next season was the dream season for us. That '68 team put it all together and blended perfectly, and I want to tell the real story of what happened on the famous two-point conversion play against Michigan. We were beating them 44–14 late in the game and Ray Gillian broke a long run to get it down to the 5. We ran it three times and got nothing. We were facing a fourth-and-goal at the 5, and I just happened to be walking by Woody on the sideline. I tapped him on the shoulder and I asked, "Coach, do you want that touchdown?"

He just said, "Go in and get it! And you call the play!"

So I went in and I looked around, and the best lineman in the huddle was Dave Cheney at left tackle. I looked at Dave and said, "Now Woody wants this touchdown, and he wants it over you!"

I got the touchdown over Dave, and the old stadium was rocking like it never rocked before. Kevin Rusnak was at quarterback. We probably should have called timeout right there to get organized, but we didn't. We were trained not to waste timeouts. It really was very innocent, but we lined up to run a play just to get it run before we got a delay of game. But we didn't score [the two-point conversion]. Woody had nothing to do with it, and I take the blame for it, but Woody always shouldered the blame for one of his players.

As everybody knows, after the game when he was asked why he went for two points with a 50–14 lead, Woody replied, "Because they wouldn't let me go for three."

Preparing for that Rose Bowl, I just remember Woody turning up those heaters in the French Field House. It was so hot in there that we could hardly breathe, and it was snowing outside. Ask anybody on that team and they will remember that heat. Woody turned out to be right on that one—it was 90 degrees on game day, and we ran USC off the field in the second half. Their tongues were wagging.

There is no doubt in my mind that '69 team was the best team at Ohio State, but that Michigan game is right out of the twilight zone. Ron Maciejowski and I roomed together the night before, and we missed the bus to the stadium. It was a panicky-type of thing, with a lot of traffic ahead of us. We got the hotel guy to take us in one of those courtesy vans, and we had the guy driving on the opposite side of the highway and everything. Finally, the police nabbed us and we explained who we were. The policeman told us, "OK, we'll take you the rest of the way, but if you guys are lying to us, you're going to jail." We got there and snuck in the locker room, and I don't think Woody ever found out.

The game was a disaster, too. We had six interceptions in that game, and there were times that we never even threw the ball six times in a game.

For my career, I was a guy who took time off the clock, got the first down, and kept the yard markers moving. That was the important thing to me. Sometimes, great plays are three or four yards long. They didn't expect me to break a long run—they wanted me to get first downs and eat the clock. Well, in that game, we had a fourth-and-2 late in the first half, and I didn't pick up the first down. That play still haunts me to this day. If I had picked up the first down, we could have scored before the half, and that game might have been different.

It was the toughest loss of my career. Michigan wasn't even close to us in terms of talent, but it taught us a lesson. We were walking off the field, and Woody looked at me and said, "I am sorry. If you had carried 15 more times, we would have won this game." Then he walked away.

I played in the NFL, and I can honestly say there was never anything greater than playing at Ohio State. People at Ohio State sincerely care about you. The whole stadium is behind you. Everyone in that state is behind you. It's all first class.

Woody Hayes was the greatest man. He cared endlessly about his players. I remember one time he went around giving out neckties for Christmas. I was in the room with Teddy Provost, Alan Jack, and Chuck Hutchison. Woody opened the box and it was full of these skinny black ties. All of a sudden, somebody started laughing. Then we all started laughing. "Well," Woody asked us, "what's so funny?"

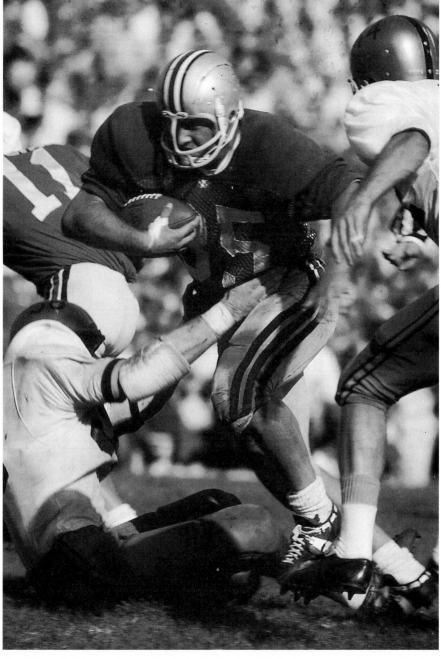

Jim Otis bulls his way through a hole during the 13–0 win over number one Purdue in 1968.

"Coach," I said, "nobody wears those skinny ties anymore. They're out of style."

He picked them up and later came back with these wider ties that were more fashionable. You can bet that somebody got chewed out on that one. He might not have been up on the current fashions, but that is how much he cared about us.

When he had his first heart attack during my NFL career, I went to Riverside Hospital to see him. The doctor told me, "Jim, just stay 45 seconds and don't let him talk."

I walked in there; the room was real cold and he was on all those monitors.

"Coach, I don't want you to say anything. I am here to tell you how much I love you," I told him. "I want you to know how much those kids need you to be ready for them, so you do what the doctors tell you to do."

As I walked out, he snapped, "Jim, when's training camp?" I told him it started in two weeks. "Damn it," he said, "are you in shape?"

We've all heard crap over the years for that Gator Bowl thing. I just tell them, "You don't know the Woody I know. Hey, Woody was a southpaw and he hit that kid right-handed." The real story is that he didn't take care of his diabetes, and the fact is that he had nodded off in the locker room before that game. His blood sugar was all screwed up, but he never told anybody that. He didn't want to make excuses.

One of the best days of my life was October 18, 1981, when my son Jimmy was born. I held him first and Woody held him second, even before his mother. Woody was in St. Louis to give a speech, and I had picked him up at the airport. Well, he had the courtesy to let me hold my son first. That great man always was and always will be a part of our family.

Jim Otis led Ohio State in rushing in 1967, '68, and '69, finishing his career with 2,542 yards and 35 touchdowns. He played with the Kansas City Chiefs, the St. Louis Cardinals, and the New Orleans Saints.

TED PROVOST

1967–1969

I WAS BETTER KNOWN FOR BASKETBALL than I was for football, coming out of tiny Fairless High, which was just south of Massillon, Ohio. I think somebody in Massillon notified Earle Bruce, who was an assistant at that time. He got the ball rolling, and then Lou McCollough, the defensive coordinator and the recruiter for our area, started recruiting me. I never met with Woody Hayes until I came to Columbus for my visit. One time, Lou was sitting at our kitchen table and my mom called him "Hank." Michigan State was recruiting me, too, and Hank Bullough was their defensive coordinator. She just got them confused, and I said, "Mom!" It was kind of funny. Ohio University had offered me a scholarship to play both sports, but I was always leaning toward Ohio State. When Woody took me over to the Jai Lai during recruiting, we talked about math and engineering because that's what I was interested in. He kept saying how good Ohio State's engineering school was. I wondered if I was good enough to play for Ohio State.

"You come from a small school," he told me. "We are recruiting you because we know you are a good athlete. We wouldn't do it if we didn't know you could play here."

In the end, it was a pretty easy decision for me.

I had heard all the stories of how tough and mean Woody was before I got there. I had heard how hard they hit and how tough practice was. We had a couple of days of practice before the varsity came in. Once they got there, the hitting was probably what they said it was like.

Ted Provost started at cornerback for three seasons.

In my freshman year, it was only Woody's second losing season [the first was 1959]. There were people trying to run him out at that point, and those airplanes were flying overhead with banners that read: "Good-bye Woody."

He told us he was trying to put together three top-notch [recruiting] classes to get it turned around. The class before us had Dave Foley and Rufus Mayes. Ours had Alan Jack, Chuck Hutchison, David Whitfield, Jim Otis, Tom Backhus, and a few other great players. And then that sophomore class that everybody knows about put us over the top.

When things weren't going well, we saw all the bad signs of Woody. My sophomore year we had started 2–3 and Jim Otis had fumbled twice before the half. We were meeting at halftime, and Woody jumped right over two rows of people to take a swing at Otis. We lost that game 17–13. Paul Huff started that next game at fullback and got Midwestern Back of the Week.

I remember that game well because Dick Himes was an offensive tackle and he was really quiet. He never said a word. Before that game at Michigan State, he got up and told how bad he wanted to beat them. They were favored to beat us badly that day, but we played one of our best games [21–7 win]. We won the next three games and beat Michigan to finish 6–3.

In that '68 season, the game I remember most is the Purdue game. They came in to Ohio Stadium the year before with [quarterback Mike] Phipps, and it was a real embarrassment [41–6 loss]. They could have beaten us 60–0 that day, and it made Woody point to that game for a whole year. They came in the next season ranked number one, and we shut them out 13–0.

The thing I remember about the Rose Bowl is that it was all business. There was no partying. We were supposed to do a press thing there when we got off the airplane, but that didn't happen. We began practicing right away and it all paid off for us.

We were so well prepared for the game, because we knew what they did with O. J. [Simpson]. We knew if we could take him away, we would win the game. I actually got my foot hurt in practice and played only for the first quarter and a half. Mark Stier covered O.J. all over the field, and I had to back him up in the secondary if he got by him. One time, I remember they threw a swing pass to him and Mark missed him and I made an open-field tackle. O.J. got up and said, "Great hit."

I get asked the question a lot, but I do think the '69 team was better. We didn't have Mayes or Foley, but Woody opened up the offense a little bit, and

103

it was easy for us. I think it was too easy. We beat everybody pretty badly—the closest game we had was 27 points [Washington and Minnesota].

We just had a letdown against Michigan and I don't know why. That junior class got to come back and beat them the next year, but that was my final game. I never had a chance to come back and redeem myself. I know if we had won that game, we would have been voted one of the top teams in the century. We still have reunions for the '68 team, but not for the '69 team.

All in all, it was a great four years at Ohio State. I can say that I am a Buckeye for life.

Ted Provost was an All–Big Ten defensive back in 1968 and '69. He is one of eight Ohio State players to record three interceptions in one game (against Northwestern in 1967).

MIKE SENSIBAUGH

1968–1970

I GREW UP IN CINCINNATI AS A PREACHER'S KID, and when it came time to choosing a college, I really didn't want to go to Ohio State. I just didn't want to stay close to home, so I visited Georgia Tech, Maryland, and Florida. But this man at my high school told me that you needed somebody to stand behind you in case you get hurt or they make a mistake with you. He said you have to make sure they won't run you off the football team or take your scholarship if you don't pan out. "Besides, 100 miles is far enough from home," he told me. He was talking about a first-class program like Ohio State.

I was planning on majoring in math, and when Woody recruited me, he told me, "Now math is a good subject. Either you have the right answer or the wrong answer."

He convinced me that Ohio State was the right school for me.

I remember getting some of the best advice of my life during my freshman orientation. [Assistant coach] Tiger Ellison was a super guy, and he told us, "As a freshman, you're a number. But go to class! No matter what the situation is, go to class. Don't sit in the back of the class. Sit right up front. Take notes on what is important. When that professor looks at you, you be looking back at him. That professor, or teacher's assistant, has gone through graduate school, and that subject is the most important thing in the world to him. So you have to make like it is, too."

That really stuck with me, and I shared this with my kids when they went to college.

The thing that I can remember from my first game, the season opener against SMU in 1968 at Ohio Stadium, was the roar of the crowd for the first time. It was something I will never forget. I got my first career interception and then got clobbered by Jack Tatum as he tried to peel off a tackler. The guy had me by the leg, and Jack hit me so hard I fumbled. But I recovered it, so I didn't make a complete fool of myself.

SMU must have attempted about 80 passes that day [actually 76, which remains an OSU opponent's record], and our secondary coach was Lou Holtz. After the game, coach Holtz told me, "I couldn't grade you, son, because I couldn't even find you on the film." I guess I was lining up pretty deep at free safety.

That was the year we became humans again. As freshmen, you couldn't play back then. We just played two freshmen games and practiced all the time. So our class was really ready during spring ball. We were getting into the mix and we would be able to play—Rex Kern, Timmy Anderson, Jim Stillwagon, John Brockington, Jack Tatum . . . what a great class.

I remember that August when we were taking our team photo. Woody looked at me in my jersey and said, "Mike, that's not your high school number. Don't you want your high school number? What was it anyway?" I just said "10" and he said, "Oh," and walked away. Rex had that number. An interesting story: Tom Bartley was the only one not in the team photo. He had a class that day and he was a senior. He probably didn't care much at the time, but then we won the national championship and that was the official team photo of Ohio State's last national champions.

That was a fantastic run that season. We were the last undefeated team at Ohio State until 2002. Let's face it, from 1968 until 2002 is way too long. We should have had a few in between.

I was punting some, and in the second game against Oregon I squibbed one off the side of my foot. I came off to the sideline and Woody started beating me on my shoulder pads, screaming, "Don't you ever do that again!" The other coaches came over to me and said, "If you ever do that again, don't run off the field toward Woody!" I said, "He's going to find me sooner or later, so I might as well get it over with."

At Illinois that season we jumped ahead 24–0 at halftime. Then in the second half, Rex got hurt. Illinois scored three touchdowns and went for two-point conversions on each and got them all to tie it. We scored again to make it 31–24 late in the game. Woody always yelled in practice, "If you miss a ball or a pass, don't beat on the ground and act like that is the first ball you ever missed. Don't do it for the fans. Just get up and make the next play."

So I had an opportunity for this interception, and I took a dive at it. It would have basically ended the game. I just missed it and I wanted to pound my hands on the ground, but I remembered what Woody had always said in practice. So I got up, and on the next play, I intercepted a pass to end the game.

I just felt that if I should get my hands on the ball, I should catch it, and I felt that way from my first game [Sensibaugh holds the OSU record with 22 interceptions].

It takes a lot to go through a championship season. But we beat Michigan and headed to the Rose Bowl to play O. J. Simpson and USC. I didn't start the game, but Ted Provost got hurt early, and I came in and played most of the game. I remember the first time they got down there, they had a first-and-goal and they run O. J. on two weak-side runs to my side. I scraped off and tackled him two times in a row. He had no place to go. We held them to a field goal and it was 3–0. Now we had watched film of O. J. and knew what he could do, but seeing it was believing it. The next time, he made this lateral move and I went for the kill. I just got a hand on him and he went 80 yards to make it 10–0.

107

We came back to win [27–16] and won the national championship. It was a great day. The great thing about that team was that there were a lot of seniors that were unselfish. Take a class guy like Bill Long. He was a two-year starter at quarterback before Rex came along. But several seniors gave up positions.

That '69 season was the most fun, because we just blew everybody away . . . until the Michigan game. I still don't know what happened. I think Rex got hurt in warm-ups and he still won't divulge what happened. We don't even like to talk about it after all these years. It was the toughest defeat ever.

We never even watched film of that loss. I remember after I got into pro ball with the Cardinals and one of my teammates was Dan Dierdorf. He said, "We beat your ass." I said it was only 24–12. "No," he said, "we really *beat* your ass physically." I guess they did. It was one of Woody's greatest teams, but that was the end of the [22-game] winning streak.

In 1978, we were playing at Canton, Ohio, in the preseason, and Jim Otis was a teammate. Woody came into the locker room to see us. Dan turned and introduced himself to Woody. Woody said, "Yep, yep, yep . . .we made a mistake [not recruiting] you." Then he just turned around and walked away. Woody disliked anything to do with Michigan. In fact, I never heard him say the word *Michigan*. He always said "those sons of bitches up North" or something like that.

We used to have to wear our names taped to our helmets during practice, and that's how I got my nickname, "Baugh." The tape with the front part of my name had peeled off, so Doug Adams and Stillwagon started calling me that. Doug Adams was the thickest-chested guy. He had upper-body strength to no end. We didn't have weights in the dorm, so he would say, "Baugh, come sit on my back," and he would do push-ups as I sat on his back. What a true friend. One of the saddest days in my life years later was the day when I heard he was killed while riding his bike.

Rex, too, was such a phenomenal person. In the locker room, they had us numerically, so with me being 3, I was next to him. During our senior year, he gave me a Bible and wrote in it: "Thanks for letting me locker next to you for the past three seasons." I still have it. What a neat man.

Another awesome player was Tatum. I really think Tatum would have been one of the best running backs Ohio State ever had. You just could not catch that man when he had the ball.

108

You know how I hated dropping interceptions. Well, I had pretty sticky fingers off the field, too. Our practice balls had "Ohio State University" ingrained in them, and I decided that they made great gifts for family members and friends. I lived right behind the football facility at Buckeye Village. So if I ever got a real good ball when I was punting in practice, I would shank one purposely over the fence and then come back and get it later. I sort of became known for that. I would stick them in bushes where we entered and exited during practices. You know those orange cones that block off parking lots? I would stuff a football right up there and come get it later.

One time, the equipment guys put me in the dirty-towel bin, covered me up with towels and jerseys, and then closed the locker room after practice. I slipped out of there later in the evening, but I had plenty of presents. It was like having a free shopping spree.

Good thing Woody never caught me. Can you imagine Woody today? I don't think Woody would have existed with the press today. You know how those coaches have to talk to the announcers coming off the field at halftime?

Mike Sensibaugh, here returning an interception against Purdue in 1969, believed if he could get a hand on the football, he could intercept it.

Gosh, Woody would have taken one of those microphones and jammed it somewhere.

Well, I earned my degree in math and I graduated in four years, and I will always be a Buckeye. I was so proud of the [2002] team. It was just time for another national championship. It brought nothing but pride. It is true that Buckeyes bleed scarlet and gray. Ohio State was the right school for me.

Mike Sensibaugh, who was All–Big Ten in 1969 and '70, holds the Ohio State career interception record with 22.

MARK STIER

1966–1968

I CAME FROM A LITTLE TOWN CALLED LOUISVILLE up in northeast Ohio, a place where few kids ever come from and go to a major college to play football. I was ready to go to the Air Force Academy, West Point, or maybe even Kent State, and then Woody Hayes came to our high school banquet that year to speak. We had another player whom everybody was recruiting and I think Woody wanted him, but he decided to go to Notre Dame.

It was a Cinderella thing for me. I questioned whether I was good enough to play at Ohio State, but coach Hayes told me that night that he had seen enough of the tapes and he told me that I was good enough. He said, "Don't doubt yourself and come on."

That night changed my life.

I loved it from my freshman days all the way through. Tiger Ellison coached the freshmen, and we had a great time. I remember Woody preaching to us from the time we set foot on campus: "You can be a superstar at Ohio State, but if you don't get your degree, you are kidding yourself!"

During my sophomore and junior years, it was very tough in terms of wins and losses. We were 4–5 and then 6–3, but that sophomore class in '68 gave us a lot of expectations. We had noticed how good they were as freshmen, but we didn't know how they would perform once the real games started.

Our defensive coordinator was Lou McCullough, and Crazy Lou would work us, work us, and work us. Lou wanted his defense lean and mean. He was great in terms of our conditioning. We would run and run before practice, and we never started practice until somebody would throw up. So we had a designated thrower-upper. Somebody had to do it, because that was the signal to stop conditioning and start practicing.

I remember that after the Iowa game [a 33–27 win], the coaches weren't happy and we had to run sprints—after the game! They wanted to make sure we were in shape, and you think we would have been by then. Our chemistry on that team was outstanding. We didn't have any racial problems. All the guys got along real well. It was a very, very close-knit team.

We always took a couple of buses wherever we went, from practice or to the airport, or wherever. The first-teamers would be in the first bus, along with Woody in the front seat. We had an assistant athletic director, and his famous line was, "All you others in the second bus." If you didn't start, you were an AYO—all you others. We had a lot of fun with that. The first bus was always pretty sedate because Woody was on it. In that second bus, we had a lot of fun.

We began 1968 and said, "Let's take them one at a time and see what happens."

112

We beat SMU 35–14 in that first game, and they set NCAA passing records that day [76 attempts] that lasted a long time. I had a couple of interceptions that day. I think that Purdue game, the third game of the season, was when we all realized we might have a pretty good team. They had beaten us the year before, and they came in ranked number one. They had Mike Phipps at quarterback, Leroy Keyes, and the whole crew. We shut them out 13–0.

Before the Michigan game, coach McCullough would put pictures of Michigan players above all the urinals and in your locker, and we had a special rug we ran over before the Michigan game.

We blew out Michigan 50–14 to go to the Rose Bowl. USC came in as a great team, but we played O.J. man-to-man in that second half and just shut them down. It was a great game, one I will always remember. That was the only time I ever remember another player coming into our locker room after the game. O.J. came in and gave a little speech about how we won the game fair and square, and he told us we were the best team. I never saw that before or since. But he went down like everybody else—he wasn't exactly hard to tackle.

I often wondered what would have happened if we had lost one game in '68, if anyone would have remembered us or if we just would have been another team forgotten over time.

Mark Stier was one of the leaders of the 1968 national championship team.

I am so glad to finally say that we are not the last Ohio State team to win a national championship. Through those 34 years, we had a lot of great teams that didn't get it done. Little did I realize how meaningful that '68 team would be over time.

Coach Hayes . . . what a guy. I never, ever to this day have seen a guy who could swear so fluently, sentence after sentence. You know, he didn't swear much off the field, though. Off the field, he was as nice a guy as you would ever want to see. But on the field . . . all the shenanigans you have heard about . . . they are all true.

What's a Buckeye? A man of discipline, a man of character, a man who plays his hardest and has some fun along the way. He wins with compassion and loses with grace.

Ohio State has always been near and dear to my heart. That phrase, "How firm thy friendship—OHIO," is pretty amazing.

And it's true.

Mark Stier, twice named Academic All–Big Ten, was MVP of the 1968 national championship team.

JIM STILLWAGON

1968–1970

IT SOUNDS FUNNY TO SAY NOW, but when I was a young kid from Mount Vernon, Ohio, I didn't like Ohio State. My dad went to Notre Dame.

I had gone to military school in Virginia, because I didn't get along with the nuns too well at my school. But I came home one time so I could see my parents and visited Ohio State. I got recruited by Michigan State, West Virginia, and all those schools in the South.

I met Woody Hayes and went into his office. They didn't have any scholarships for me, but on that day, some other high school player had told them that he wasn't coming. So they had a scholarship for me at the last moment. I remember Woody asking me what was the last novel I had read. I don't think I had read any novels, but I said *Moby Dick*. So we spent about 45 minutes talking about *Moby Dick*. Then he said, "If you are good enough, you'll make it here. And if you're not, you won't."

So I became a Buckeye.

I remember the program was in the dark ages with weight lifting at that time. I had to bring my own weights. We had a special bond on that freshman team. We scrimmaged against the varsity, and there was a lot of pride among the freshmen. From that nucleus, we had a common goal. We were all different one way or another, but we had one thing in common: to win.

As sophomores, we all took starting positions and just had a great year. We wouldn't be denied. We just overwhelmed people. We were a horse-and-plow team, and Woody was a great horse-and-plow coach. We won every game. It's hard to believe that was the last national championship team from Ohio State until 2002.

But we were so worn out after the Rose Bowl [a 27–16 win over USC] that we didn't really appreciate what had happened. Woody always believed that if too much good was written or said about you, it would make you soft. That eventually wore on us.

Our junior year, we had a great season until the Michigan game. We were number one in the country for every week from camp all the way through. Rex Kern was hurt in that Michigan game and Woody was superstitious. We had attacked people all season until that game. One of his downfalls was he would outthink himself, and I think he did it in that game [a 24–12 loss]. Woody was predictable when it was close. Bo knew Woody's mind-set, too. He knew we would run right and run left. He stacked those tackles in there on the line of scrimmage. That game set us back. It set Woody back.

As seniors, however, that game motivated us. It set us up for a revenge game against Michigan, and it was one of the greatest games I played. We beat them [20–9]. We went out to the Rose Bowl to play Stanford and went through two-a-days [practices] and we scrimmaged in a gymnasium with tennis shoes on. Woody loved to hit and hit all the time. It wore on us. We scrimmaged a lot and really had a minor uprising—a big team meeting—and it was never right after that. I think he lost sight of the big picture. Then in the game we sat back and didn't attack them. Stanford beat us [27–17]. I am not taking anything away from Stanford, but they played an eight-cylinder team playing on four cylinders.

Don't get me wrong. Woody Hayes was a great man. But was Woody Hayes a great Xs-and-Os coach? No. Was he a great leader? Yes. He could make an average player good. He could make a good player great. And he could make a great player a superstar.

I have a lot of great Woody stories, but one of my favorites is this: he always wore short sleeves no matter how cold it was. I would see him after practice in that shower for about 10 minutes, and his arms were purple like plums. Well one time he was not wearing a short-sleeve shirt, but he had on one of those mock turtlenecks. We started to call him "Woodstock" once we saw that turtleneck, and you know he sort of liked it.

My senior year was when there was the energy crisis, and Woody wouldn't drive because of the gas crunch. So I had this old Barracuda I was driving, and after practice one day Woody asked for a ride over to training table. He liked riding with me, so during my whole senior year he rode with me after practice. It was neat just listening to him. He would talk about all the younger players like Randy Gradishar who were going to be great.

Our talks were always interesting because Woody was always interesting. He used to talk about big battles in history and the wars. One time he was telling me about this famous guy from Ohio State who invented "WEFT," which was a way to identify enemy aircraft. It stood for "Wings, Engine, Fuselage, and Tail." Woody called it, "Wrong Every F——— Time." He said, "By the time you figured it out with that system, the son of a bitch had dropped a bomb on you." I thought that was real funny.

So one day after practice I was in the shower and I was telling the guys about Woodstock's theory on WEFT, and I noticed that he was in a bathroom stall listening. I could hear him chuckling about it. I could hear his cleats clattering on the floor because he was laughing so hard.

Anyway, after the Stanford game, Woody called me down to the office and started to thank me for all I had done, and he said, "Son, if you would have played middle linebacker instead of middle guard you would be drafted higher. I want you to know you made a big sacrifice for the team and I appreciate it. You are going down to the Lombardi Award thing in Houston, but don't get too excited. They won't give it to no Yankee bastard." I went down there and there's Spiro Agnew and Howard Cosell. I sat next to Red Adair listening to him talk about eating a cold turkey sandwich off the coast of some country while bullets were whizzing over his head. It was a great experience, but I was not expecting to win this thing, and then they called my name. I was surprised.

Later, they called me up and told me I also won the Outland Trophy. It wasn't a big award back then, but now it's a part of Americana. You know, I really never liked individual awards. I am against retiring numbers. I think it is the wrong thing to do. College football is about the team. It is about playing together. At Ohio State, we had a team that won. Not just one player. That was what was always great about Ohio State. We won as a team. We lost as a team. Everybody got treated the same. Everybody respected everybody. I respected and admired the walk-ons the most. We were already on scholarship, but they would come out and get their butts killed, and they were paying their way.

Individualism really is a disease. It's one thing I really like about coach Tressel. The Ohio State program is back to being a team. It's a special place

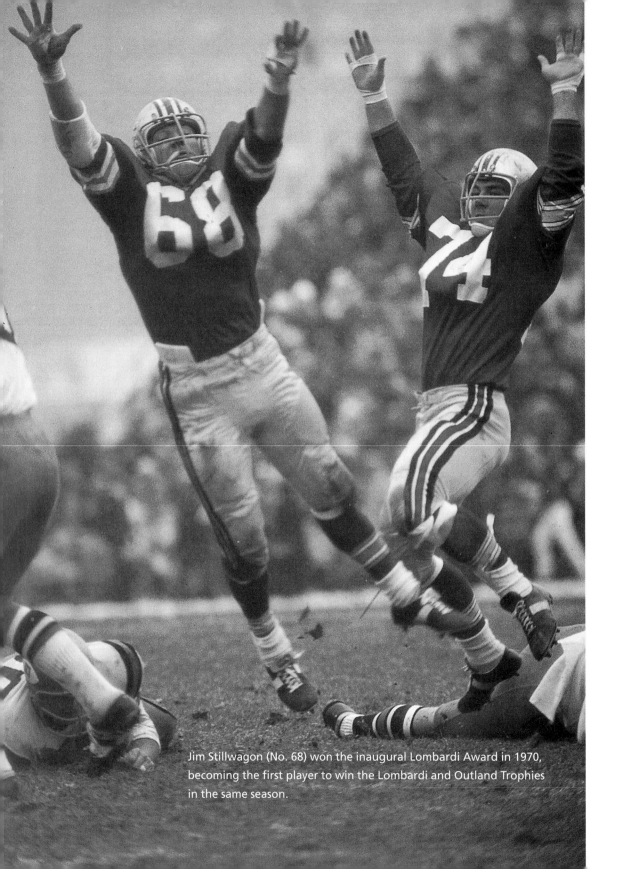

Jim Stillwagon (No. 68) won the inaugural Lombardi Award in 1970, becoming the first player to win the Lombardi and Outland Trophies in the same season.

and provides a special experience. It's really too bad that everybody can't come out of that tunnel and run onto that field just one time. You come off the ground emotionally. In this whole world and atmosphere at that particular time, you are on one of the grandest stages and part of one of the biggest shows on earth. It's very special.

Looking back, I am very thankful they had one last scholarship for me.

Jim Stillwagon, a two-time All-American and MVP of the 1970 team, became the 15th Ohio State player elected to the College Football Hall of Fame.

DICK WAKEFIELD

1969–1971

I WAS BORN IN ROYAL OAK, MICHIGAN, and grew up in Avon Lake, Ohio, loving the Buckeyes. Not that he needed to, but Woody Hayes visited me twice to recruit me, and each time he came to one of my high school basketball games. In that first game, we got beat by Bay Village 102–47 and Woody came into the locker room after the game. He said, "I'll come back the next time you play them." The day we were to play Bay Village again, it was snowing, and I got a telegram that day: "The weather's too bad. Good luck against Bay Village!" It was signed "Woody Hayes." I was disappointed I wouldn't see him that night, but right before the game, he walked in with Rex Kern. We lost that game, too, but it was much closer—77–70. During the game, he sat next to my dad and grandmother, and he buttered her up all night. She thought he was the king of the world. My dad loved him, too. He sold the parents, but he was an honest man. I remember him telling them both: "I guarantee he will get a good education."

There was no doubt where I would spend the next four years.

Once I got to Ohio State, I was awestruck. I was from a little hick town of six thousand people and I remember seeing those 11-story dorms, and all those big buildings, and I thought, "What am I going to do now?" That's where the camaraderie of Ohio State football came in. Most of the players bonded together and you quickly found out that there were many more guys with the same feelings that you had. Right away, Woody laid down the law.

His famous line was: "You don't have to like me, just respect me." I can honestly say nobody was respected more than coach Hayes. He also said something like, "If you show me a good guy that the players love all the time, I will show you a loser."

There's one thing that man never was—a loser. The thing that upset Woody the most was mental mistakes. He hated offside and holding, and when you did those things, he would jump all over you. I remember in one practice, John Brockington kept missing the hole. He was running with his head down and kept missing it. Finally, Woody started chasing him, screaming, "I am going to get you!" Can you picture this older man, running down the field, shaking his fist, and chasing John, who probably ran a 9.7 100-yard dash?

One time we were having a bad practice, fumbling and jumping offside, and not hitting the holes, and he stopped practice and told us, "I know what the problem is—you're not getting enough blood into your heads. Everybody, stand on your head!" So here we are, as a team, doing handstands. We were stopping traffic on Olentangy River Road. People were stopping their cars to watch this. And God forbid if you laughed. If you did it, you did it quietly. One time, Woody knocked the wind out of me. He hit me in the chest, and I went down. I didn't drop many passes after that. If he was alive and doing that today, everybody would be suing him.

121

Despite all that, he was a very caring man. One thing Woody had us do—when we flew to road games he would have us take out those life insurance policies for $10 each and make our parents the beneficiaries. I think the university paid that $10 for us. And then we always picked up a postcard and would write a note home to our parents. He wanted us to do that to stay in touch with the people we loved.

The guy was ahead of his time in a lot of ways, too. You know how the NFL has that instant-replay rule where teams are charged a timeout to review a play? Woody had that idea for college football when I played. He knew better than anyone that officials blew calls.

Which brings me to the 1971 game at Michigan. We were 6–3, having a down year because of injuries. We had 12 starters out for that game, and we were heavy underdogs. The night before the game, Tommy Marendt, a starting defensive end, came down with appendicitis, and now he couldn't play.

We were just riddled with injuries, but we had them down, 7–3, before they got a late touchdown to take the lead. We passed a lot that season, because we didn't have the talent or depth to line up and smash people. The tackle next to me, Merv Teague, who was a hell of a player, weighed about 220. I was a 200-pound tight end/wingback. Donny Lamka was our quarterback, and he reminded me of Bobby Douglass. He would run right over you if he had to, and he was a great field general, a natural leader.

We got to late in the game, we crossed the 50, and we had a certain play set up. We knew that if we were in a two-or-more back set, they would bring their so-called Wolfman closer to the line of scrimmage. On this play, I was at tight end on the right side, but the formation was to the left. I knew Michigan was thinking, "Why is Wakefield on the other side?" The play called for Jimmy Lee Harris to run a go pattern on the left side, and we would run play-action, and I would come down underneath, running from the right side to the left side. Thom Darden, their free safety, read it and came up on me. It was a perfect pass, and as I was about to catch it, Darden came up over my shoulder and went over the top of me. He intercepted it right in front of Michigan's bench, but there is no doubt he interfered with me. The line judge was right there looking at it. I got up, and immediately I looked around for the flags. I saw a few and thought, "Great, now we got a first down." Then somebody told me, "No, it's not interference—it's on your coach."

Woody just went ballistic. He grabbed those yard markers and busted them over his knee. He proceeded to get flagged two more times. I called that official everything that he was, but he never flagged me—because he knew he missed the call. I was a senior and it was my last game, and I hated to lose to them. That play would have been a huge, huge gain—maybe even a touchdown. We busted our butts the whole game, and then we had that happen at the end.

It was not the way I wanted to end my career, but I have always been a Buckeye fan and always will be. As I sit here at my desk, I am looking at a Woody bobblehead. You have to wonder what he would have thought about those things. After your playing days are done, you go through a secondary rush with each Ohio State game you watch. After we won the national title in the Fiesta Bowl, I was so wired that I couldn't go to bed until 5:00 in the morning. And I am here to say there are no better fans than Ohio State fans.

Dick Wakefield was an end from 1969 to 1971.

Photo courtesy of Dick Wakefield.

I live in Michigan now, and I am misplaced up here because I am a Buckeye through and through.

Dick Wakefield led Ohio State in receiving in 1971 with 31 receptions for 432 yards. His 11 receptions against Colorado are tied for seventh best on the school's single-game list.

PAUL WARFIELD

1961–1963

It was May 1957 when I met a man who changed my life forever. His name was Gene Slaughter. I was in the ninth grade at Harry B. Turner Junior High in Warren, Ohio, and I thought baseball and track and field would be the only sports I would play in high school. Then my life changed in 15 minutes when coach Slaughter talked to a group of us. He inspired me to go out for football.

After graduating from Warren Harding, I had to make a decision where to play football and where to attend college. It came down to the University of Iowa and Ohio State, and I chose Ohio State for a not-very-good reason: I wanted to stay close to my girlfriend. I guess it was a case of puppy love. To travel from Ohio to Iowa was a real journey in those days, but I-71 had been completed and I could get back and forth between Columbus and Warren.

I know this isn't original, but it was the best of times and the worst of times. I played for a very demanding head coach, and sometimes it was not a lot of fun. But you know what? Knowing what I know now, I would do the same thing all over again.

What can I say about coach Hayes? Coach Hayes truly epitomized what a head coach should be. He worked hard. He was a perfectionist. He was a true patriot. He was a true Ohioan. He was honest. Very honest. He had so much compassion, integrity, and honesty, and those are the things that outsiders know nothing about the man. He made contributions to each and every athlete he brought in. The man was incredible, because he touched so many lives. He made sure we were fundamentally sound on the field, and he wanted us to be an asset to the community off of it. He made sure we had the right values off the field. Education was very, very important to him. He was adamant that we get a degree from The Ohio State University through hard work in the classroom. He was a very learned man. His father was a superintendent of schools. He proved a coach could win Big Ten titles and produce national teams and yet make sure his players got the best of educations. That's what makes the man stand above everyone else.

I remember one casual conversation we were having one time and I used the word *onlyest*. He said, "What? That word doesn't exist. There is no such word." Remember, he had a master's degree in English. He knew the language.

What I learned most from him on the field was that the game of football should be played with a total team concept. I learned to do some things that do not gain much notice, such as blocking. I later became one of the best blockers in pro football because I learned how important it was at Ohio State. Remember, I blocked for such backs as Jim Brown, Leroy Kelly, and Larry Csonka. Sometimes, you just have to take an unselfish position, and that is becoming a lost concept in team sports today. For example, one thing I do not agree with in today's terms is when somebody calls a team "so and so's team. It's the quarterback's team." No it isn't. It's everyone's team. It's their team. That's what I was taught at Ohio State, and that's how I played.

125

Everyone knows that Woody was famous for his practice eruptions. My first year when I was a sophomore—remember that freshmen could not play back then—on a Thursday afternoon, we were practicing for The Game. Michigan. We were practicing punt returns. Back then it was standard to employ two return men, and I was one of them. The other was Matt Snell. Now, it was one whale of a windy day. Matt went to field this punt, and it was blowing so hard, there was no way he could catch it. He dropped the punt. Woody came running down the field, and he referred to us as "jackasses." This was Michigan week, so everything had to be right. So we lined up and did it again. Matt said, "You take this one." So I dropped it, too. Woody was beside himself. This was the week before my 19th birthday, and Woody came running down the field, ripped off his hat, and started jumping up and down on it. Then he ripped it apart at the seams. I was thinking, "Wow, how could he be that angry to rip that hat apart at the seams like that?"

Now fast-forward to 20 years after that day. A friend of mine who worked for an NFL team would go to Ohio State to scout players. He always spent time with Woody. One day, they were talking for about an hour and Woody got up and said he had to get ready for practice. He reached in his desk and there were about a dozen of those black hats with the Block "O." He grabbed one and grabbed a razor blade and started to slit the seams. He wanted it to be ready in case he needed it to prove a point. It took 20 years, but I found out how he ripped that hat apart so easily.

In that Michigan game [which OSU won 50–20 in 1961], it had been an average season for me to that point, but I had a 69-yard run, another 48-yarder, and a catch that set up a touchdown. We had so many team leaders on that team. Bob Ferguson was a great fullback. I learned discipline and sacrifice that year. I learned it was a team sport, and that team won the national championship even though we didn't get to go to the Rose Bowl for reasons I still do not fully understand. I guess the faculty council didn't think bowl games and academics mixed too well and they didn't let us go. I remember three thousand students protesting at the student union and then marching down High Street to the capitol building.

For all four years, I was a committed dormitory resident. I lived at Park Hall, 110 West 11th Avenue. Room 909. I can still remember that. It was great camaraderie. We had great debates there. I talked about everything with my teammates. I was a halfback and perhaps I didn't put the numbers on the board that I felt I should have, but it still was a wonderful experience. Woody helped make me a complete NFL player. When my playing days were over, I had a Big Ten championship ring, national championship ring, NFL championship ring from 1964 [from the Cleveland Browns], and two Super Bowl rings [from the Miami Dolphins].

I would do the same thing all over again and go to Ohio State. I came back and got my degree in education in 1966. And when I was inducted into the Pro Football Hall of Fame in 1983, I looked out in the audience when I was up on stage and you know who I saw? Woody Hayes. That really touched me. He never told me he was coming. What a great man.

And that girlfriend who made me want to attend Ohio State and stay close to home? I wasn't dating her after about one year down in Columbus. I guess everything worked out for the best.

Paul Warfield, named All-Big Ten in 1962 and '63, went on to become one of the NFL's greatest receivers, playing eight seasons with the Cleveland Browns and five with the Miami Dolphins. He is one of only seven Ohio State players or coaches inducted into the Pro Football Hall of Fame.

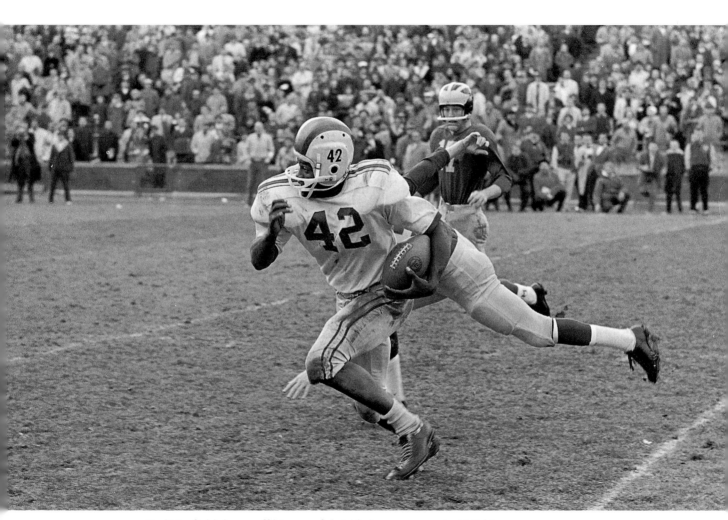

Paul Warfield shows off his graceful stride in a game against Michigan.

STAN WHITE

1969–1971

WHAT DID I GET OUT OF PLAYING FOOTBALL at Ohio State? I met my wife, played on a national championship team, got an accounting degree [and later a law degree while playing pro football], and became a young man from the boy who first stepped on campus in 1968.

Most important, I played for Woody Hayes, who molded countless boys into men. We all received demands by coach Hayes to get an education. Woody emphasized this: "The next play could be your last, but your education would never be taken away."

Those days, the athletes lived on South Campus. I lived in Stradley Hall all four years. I remember the camaraderie among all the athletes. We played basketball constantly on the 11th Avenue courts. I remember having relay sprint races down and back on the sidewalk from Stradley to Bradford Commons. Ed Smith, Jim Cleamons, Jack Tatum, and Ray Gillian were just a few that would take off their shoes at night and run . . . just for the fun of it.

And we had a lot of fun.

Naturally, most of my memories revolve around football. And, of course, the memories are always strongest from the Michigan games. The four during my stay were all memorable. Since freshmen weren't eligible, I watched from the stands as my varsity teammates closed out the unlikely unbeaten regular season in 1968 by beating Michigan 50–14.

The next day, Tony Mason, a Michigan assistant, called Woody "a big fat pig." Later, their whole staff was fired. The Wolverines hired Bo Schembechler, and we all remember that first Bo-Woody matchup in 1969.

After all these years, it still hurts. It hurts while I am writing this. It will always hurt. It will be in my gut for the rest of my life.

The 1970 Michigan game will also be in me the rest of my life, but this one I will carry in my heart. It was two unbeaten teams meeting in the biggest rivalry in sports. And we won 20–9. I intercepted a pass late in the game and returned it to the 9-yard line. A couple of plays later, Rex pitched to Leo Hayden on an option for a touchdown to cap off the game.

But what I remember most is the crowd. I played for 21 years, including 13 in pro football, and you know what? On that interception, it was the only time I ever heard the crowd during the game. As I jumped to catch the ball, I was struck by the booming explosion of the crowd. That moment is seared in my memory, and it is as real today as it was all those years ago.

The greatest player I played with was undoubtedly Jack Tatum. He was scary in person and downright feared on the field. He was the only player I ever saw who never had to break down when making a tackle. He could run full speed, adjust at full speed, and always delivered a lethal blow right between the numbers. He was as fast as he needed to be. In that 1968 Michigan game, there was one play I can still see. Jack blitzed on the outside from his monster position as Michigan All-American Ron Johnson found a big hole up the middle and was off to the goal line. Jack suddenly went into a baseball slide, got up, took off through the same hole, and ran down Johnson in what looked like a man chasing down a little boy. He saved a touchdown. What a player.

129

But my favorite player was Rex Kern. He was a brilliant ball handler, a great athlete, and the consummate winner. He later became my roommate during my rookie year with the Baltimore Colts. He introduced me to his strength, Jesus Christ. It changed my life and the purpose of my life forever.

In 1971, we had lost all of those "Super Sophomores" like Rex, Tatum, Brockington, Sensibaugh, and Stillwagon, and we had 11 knee surgeries as a team. Michigan was undefeated, we were 6–3, and the game was in Ann Arbor. But it was Ohio State–Michigan. And with three minutes left, we were still leading 7–3 on my high school teammate's [Tom Campana] punt return for a touchdown. Michigan finally scored in the last two minutes to

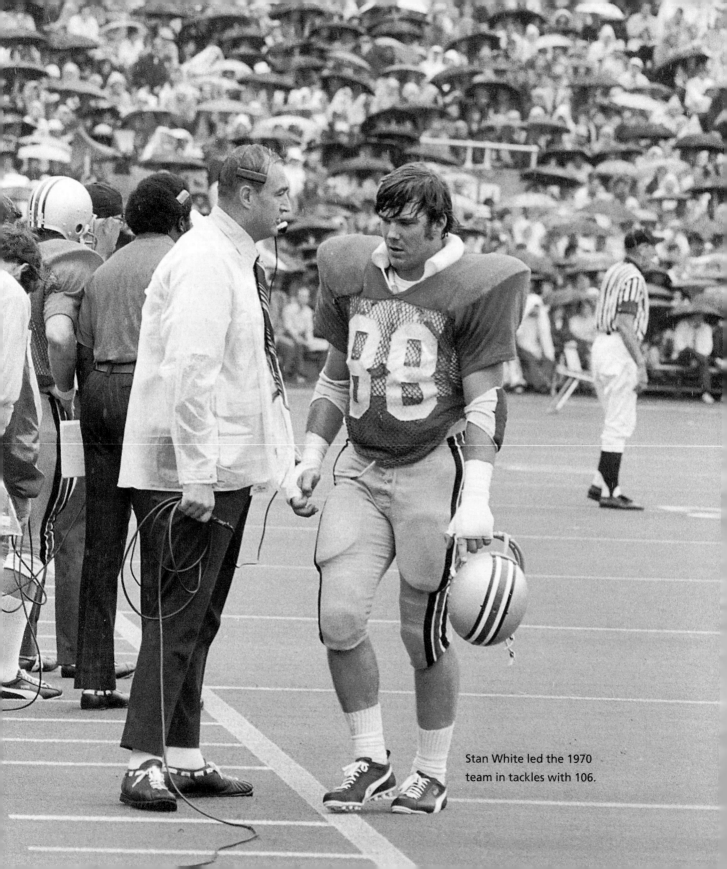

Stan White led the 1970
team in tackles with 106.

take the lead, and our final desperation drive ended when Thom Darden knocked down Dick Wakefield and intercepted that last pass.

Woody went berserk. He ran on the field. Jerry Markbreit, who later became a well-known NFL official whom I got to know well, called two or three 15-yard penalties on him. Some guys thought about restraining Woody, but most of us wanted him to go on. At least it delayed the end of our OSU lives.

When it did end, I cried. It's the only time I can remember doing that. My final game ended with Woody tearing up the sideline markers. Well, at least it was memorable.

I sent my son, Stan Jr., to Ohio State to play football. But I also sent him to grow as a man in body, mind, and spirit. I always wanted Stan Jr. to be a Buckeye, but it was beyond doubt when coach Tressel took over.

People may also think it was coincidental that the 1968 national championship came in my freshman year. The next one, 34 years later, came in my son's freshman year.

I don't.

Stan White, named All–Big Ten in 1971, played 13 seasons in the NFL, starting every game over the final 12 seasons.

DIRK WORDEN

1966–1968

HARDLY A DAY PASSES WHEN I DON'T REFLECT BACK to those experiences and memories of Ohio State. I had the honor of being named the team MVP of the 1967 season and then being named cocaptain of the national championship team in '68 [with David Foley]. To this day, I am truly proud of those honors and at the same time very humble to think that my teammates thought enough of me to bestow those titles upon me.

Ohio State football is a true lifelong fraternity, and I am proud to be part of it.

Here are some of my memories:

We struggled early in the 1967 season, starting 2–3 with losses to Arizona, Purdue, and Illinois. And the year before that we were 4–5, and everybody knows that at Ohio State, that's not good enough.

Still, it seems hard to believe now that rumors were flying throughout Columbus that a coaching change was being considered, but coach Hayes had the class to not put any more pressure on the players and coaches. He didn't want any of that "win for me" motivation. Writers and broadcasters were really on Woody then, and we had heard he had received an ultimatum to win that game or else.

About 10 minutes before the Michigan State game at East Lansing, we had all gathered in the back of the locker room after our pregame warm-up. Coach Hayes had a great memory, and he hadn't forgotten what had happened in 1965, the last time OSU had visited Spartan Stadium. Michigan State had whipped the Buckeyes 32–7. During that game, their fans constantly bombarded the field with streamers of unfolding rolls of toilet paper every time Michigan State did something good.

In his pregame speech, Woody all of a sudden jutted out his jaw and shouted, "Do you know what today is? It's Operation Constipation! They're not going to be throwing that damn toilet paper at us this time! We are going to show them where to shove it!"

We won 21–7 and it was the beginning of our own roll. We won the next three games to finish the season, and it was the start of what later became a school-record, 22-game winning streak that spanned three seasons.

It also may well have saved coach Hayes' job, but it was certain that it set the stage for great things to come for Ohio State football. I hate to think what would have happened if we had lost that game at Michigan State. Who knows? That may have changed the course of Ohio State football history.

Against Purdue in 1968, it was in the second quarter and we were in man coverage. I was covering a back out of the backfield, and he caught this pass in front of me. He stopped to cut, and I planted my foot and completely blew out the knee. My leg was never the same.

I wasn't able to contribute much, other than encouragement, for the remainder of the season, which was the remainder of my career. After the 50–14 victory over Michigan, coach Hayes and my teammates awarded me a game ball, and I can't tell you how much that touched me. I still have it prominently displayed to this day. Then I played a little in the Rose Bowl victory over USC, a game that clinched the national championship for us, before having surgery when we returned to Columbus.

In January, I had accompanied coach Hayes to New York to the Downtown Athletic Club to receive the McArthur Bowl–emblematic of the national champions. On the airplane ride, coach Hayes talked nonstop, and when he finally stopped, I had planned to thank him for all he had done for me and for all of my teammates. When he paused, I looked over, and there he was, sound asleep. I never saw him sleeping before, and it just never dawned on me that this man slept like everybody else.

I thought, "Damn, he is human!"

After we had beaten USC to win the national championship, coach Hayes had called a team meeting. He simply told us, "Remember your teammates. This is the last time we will be meeting. Remember what it took to achieve the ultimate—teamwork, preparation, hard work, dedication, and perseverance. Keep these lessons, and they will help you in whatever you do in life."

Dirk Worden surveys the line of scrimmage in the 1966 season opener, against Texas Christian.

I will always remember his words. He was right.

What can I say about Ohio State's fans? The Buckeye Nation is truly remarkable, the fans are everywhere, and it makes me proud to think that I once was part of something very special in so many people's lives.

For that great Fiesta Bowl, I was sitting there listening to all the Ohio State fans around me talking about the '68 team and the Rose Bowl and the last time we won a national championship, and I finally had to show them my ring. Next thing you know, there was a crowd around me to look at it. Then after the game, we went to this saloon near the stadium and all these guys, a little older than me, were talking about that '68 team.

"Do you remember that '68 team?" one of them asked me.

Once they saw my ring, I had 10 beers sitting in front of me.

That's just the way Ohio State is—there is so much pride from the fans on to the players.

The 1968 team had carried the torch for so long as OSU's last national champions, so it was with great pride that we could pass that title on to the 2002 national champs.

Dirk Worden was named MVP of the 1967 team.

The SEVENTIES

BRIAN BASCHNAGEL

1972–1975

I GUESS YOU COULD SAY I WAS AN OVERACHIEVER. I always worked hard at academics and athletics, because that was my way of fitting in. My family had moved 16 times because my dad worked for the Woolworth Company and he would get transferred. He would take over a store, get it back on its feet, and move on. It was our lifestyle, but I spent the final three years of high school in Pittsburgh. All that moving taught me to adapt. As far as college goes, I am Catholic and I adored Notre Dame. I was going to go there, but I also wanted to visit some other schools just to be fair to myself.

[Then–Ohio State assistant coach] Earle Bruce was recruiting me at that time, but during the recruiting process, he was named head coach at Tampa. At that time, it had boiled down to Notre Dame, Penn State, and Ohio State. Coach Bruce called me, and I was really confused, because I thought he was going to try to recruit me to Tampa. He said, "Look, I don't know where you want to go, but I am stepping out of the recruiting process for obvious reasons. I want you to know this: I can honestly tell you Ohio State is the best place for you." That really impressed me.

The first time I met Woody Hayes he came to my volleyball practice at my high school. We were practicing and I figured he would want to check out what I look like on the court, how I move, and what type of an athlete I was. But he didn't. He was over in the stands reading a book. He never once, not once, looked up from that book. It was *Animal Farm*. Then we went out to dinner and we talked for three hours at this restaurant. In those three hours, he never once mentioned football. Not once. That impressed me.

You can say he sincerely impressed me from the beginning. I could tell he was really concerned about me and my well-being. I mentioned I wanted to major in business and maybe attend law school later. So he promoted the business school at Ohio State and then he promoted the law school. He cited some examples of names who had graduated from both. Now I am comparing this to other coaches who recruited me. Notre Dame promised me I would go to four bowl games, play right away, and all that. All they seemed to talk about was football.

I was a running back, I liked Woody Hayes already, and I knew he liked to run the football, so I made my choice.

I was recruited with another running back from Columbus, and you may have heard of him. His name was Archie Griffin. In 1972, it was the first year that freshmen became eligible to play, and early on in the North Carolina game, we were stumbling around and not very effective. They called Archie's name, he rushed for 239 yards, and he became an overnight hero. I was happy we won the game, but I didn't know where that left me. I have to tell you that I came to hate Archie over the next few days, and then he didn't practice that Monday because of all the bumps and bruises. I wondered what kind of character Archie had. For those few days, I was thinking about transferring and I was thinking about quitting.

Then after that practice, Archie came up to me and he looked me right in the eye. "Look, you are from Pittsburgh; I am from Columbus," he told me. "If it were the other way around, they would have asked you to go in the game Saturday and you would have done the same thing."

I wanted to hug him right there. That taught me a lot. I decided on the spot that I would be proud to play behind Archie Griffin for four years. From that beginning, we grew really close. I wasn't going anywhere. I still get chills every time I think of Archie's words to me. Right then and there, I was proud to be a Buckeye.

On the first play I ever played, I went back to return a punt. There were eighty-eight thousand people in the stands, and my knees were just shaking. I dropped the punt but jumped on top of it and recovered it. I remember Woody saying something like that was the mature thing to do.

Brian Baschnagel, here carrying against USC in the 1975 Rose Bowl, redefined the wingback position.

The starting wingback, Rich Galbos, got hurt later in the season, and I moved to the wingback spot. I guess it was a blessing in disguise. It was very much a role-playing position. I learned to block, and they threw me passes, and once in a while they threw me a bone and I ran a counter. I think the most carries I ever had in one game was seven, and some games I didn't have any.

Woody was the greatest motivator, but he was extremely fair. It was always very positive. He motivated through intimidation and positive reinforcement, and I learned early on that you have to pay attention to where he was on the practice field. One day, Greg Hare was at quarterback and I was not in the play but I was standing next to Woody. Greg dropped back, scrambled toward Woody, who bumped into me trying to get out of the way, and then Greg threw an interception. I was still looking downfield watching the play. At the same time, Woody turned and punched me in the stomach. "Get out of the way," he told me. I never saw it coming, and I had nothing to do with the play, but I learned right then to keep an eye on Woody during practice.

He really was a perfectionist, but by the time I became a senior, I learned a lot of his tantrums were fabricated. We had lost to Michigan State twice, in 1972 and '74 when we scored but they disallowed the touchdown. (I don't think we were set on that play, after looking at the film, but Michigan State was holding us down, not letting us get another play off, and we should have been given one more play.)

So before our senior game against them, he called all the captains in and told us he wanted us to give a talk to the team about what this game means to us. He pulled me to the side and said, "Brian, when you talk to them, I want you to swear. That will emphasize what this game means to you."

"But Coach," I said, "I don't swear." I did promise him I would show plenty of emotion.

As we left the room, I heard him ask somebody to make sure there were two pitchers of water in the front of the room before the team came in for the meeting. So the team gets in there, he started in on his speech and he's getting real emotional in front of the team. He's yelling and raising his voice, and talking about how much we want to beat Michigan State, and he suddenly picks up this pitcher of water and throws it against the wall. It had to be staged, although I know his emotions were sincere.

We won the game 21–0.

141

You know, Woody never mentioned the Rose Bowl in motivating us. He always said "the Big Ten." That was our goal every year. We never even talked national championship, because there wasn't the emphasis on it then that there is now. We just said, "We have to win the Big Ten." We would prepare for Michigan for half of each week and then prepare for the team we were playing for the second half of the week.

That was our goal, to beat Michigan and win the Big Ten. My biggest regret now is that we never won a national championship, and that '73 team and '75 team were good enough to do it.

Offensively, only two things frustrated me at that time—we never changed our snap count, and when we did, we would jump offside; and in a tough game, we couldn't throw the ball effectively. We did it in practice but never had success passing in a close game.

One time we did, and I'll never forget it. We're at Michigan [1975] and trailing 14–7 and down to a fourth-down play on our final drive. Corny just looked at us in the huddle and said, "Hold hands and we're going to say a prayer." It was the first time he had done that. Now I don't think the Lord really cares who wins a football game, but it worked—he threw to me along the sideline for the first down. Then we marched down and scored a touchdown. Ray Griffin picked off a pass to set up the next touchdown and we won 21–14. That was a great team.

Off the field, Woody always encouraged us to mix in with the regular student body. He wanted us to be students before football players. One professor of mine didn't think that way. She was an economics teacher and I remember she came flying in the room on the first day, a little late and a lot flustered, and she announced, "If anybody in here is a football player, you might as well leave right now, because you will fail this course." I slouched down in my chair, but her comments motivated me. I got the highest grade on the first midterm and had a 98 on the second. The final exam was at 8:00 A.M. and I stayed up studying all night. Exhausted, I decided to close my eyes for a few minutes before I left for the test. Sure enough, I fell asleep only to wake up an hour into the test. I ran to the classroom and up to the professor. She handed me the test and said, "You were doing well, but not that well."

My roommate for four years was Garry McCutcheon. He was a quarterback and also from Pennsylvania and still is a close friend to this day. On the day of the NFL draft, in April 1976, I had a very busy day. I had a test, a paper

142

due, and an 8:00 A.M. class. I remember walking back to my apartment, just drained from all that, and I thought, "Oops, this was the day of the draft. I wonder if I got drafted."

So I got back to the apartment and Garry poured me a beer. We started to play a game of gin and he said, "By the way, the Steelers called and wanted to know if you would like to play for them. I told them I thought you would." So we played a few more hands, and a few minutes later, he said, "The Redskins also called and wanted to know if you were available in the fifth round, would you be willing to play for them? I told them that you would." By this time, we had finished our beer. Garry got up, poured me another, and said, "By the way, congratulations, you were drafted by the Chicago Bears in the third round." I could have killed him.

After the draft but before graduation in June, Woody called me into the office. "Brian, what are you going to do?" he asked me. I said, "What do you mean, Coach?" He repeated himself, but louder, "WHAT ARE YOU GOING TO DO?"

"I guess you mean after graduation. I don't know if you heard, but I got drafted by the . . ." Before I could get the words out, he picked up a book and slammed it on the floor, screaming, "There goes your law degree!" After all those years, he had remembered that conversation we had at that dinner during recruiting.

143

I told him I could do both, and besides, "I might not even make the team," I told him. We started walking down the hall, and he was yelling at me, "Brian, I know you too well. You'll make that team, play for 10 years, and never get your law degree. . . ."

I went to Chicago, made the team, and after the season, I came back to Columbus and knocked on his door to see him. His desk always faced away from the door. He never turned around. He just said, "Get out of here and don't come back until you are enrolled in law school." He was serious—he wouldn't see me. That really bothered me, so I went down and enrolled in a continuous education program to take some accounting classes. With proof in hand, I went back to see Woody one more time. I realize now that all Woody wanted was for us to prepare ourselves for the day we left the game of football.

The final time I saw him, he was in his hospital bed and was getting released that day. I visited him for about 20 minutes, and as I stood in that room, I was thinking to myself, "This man is a great man . . . he really cares about people." I guess I didn't realize what we did mean to him as players, but I really felt I touched his life as much as he touched mine. I am grateful for that. Everybody at Ohio State had such an influence on me, and yeah, you can say I made the right decision.

Brian Baschnagel, a two-time Academic All-American and team captain in 1975, played nine seasons for the Chicago Bears.

BOB BRUDZINSKI

1973–1976

I CAME FROM FREMONT, OHIO, which was a town with a lot of Michigan alumni, such as Rob Lytle, who was a high school teammate of mine before heading to Michigan. In making my final choice in picking a college, I had narrowed it down to Michigan, Michigan State, and Ohio State when I got a call from Ara Parseghian from Notre Dame. He asked me, "How about a good Catholic Polish boy like you coming to Notre Dame?"

I said, "Well Coach, I have whittled it down to these three . . ." and I heard "click"—he hung up on me.

I didn't have a real good visit to Michigan, and the guy that took me around there was a big jerk. I liked Bo [Schembechler], though, but I got bad vibes from the place. Craig Cassady was my host at Ohio State, and he was a real good guy. There were great guys there, it seemed right, and my dad wanted me to go there.

And how could you not be impressed by Woody Hayes? He really never talked about football with me when he recruited me. When he came to the home, he tried to sell the parents on Ohio State, and Dad liked him because he was in World War II and they talked about the war.

When I got to Ohio State, I roomed with this one guy whose mother had just died, and he was very depressed. It got to be really depressing for me, too. I had an eight-track tape with "Stairway to Heaven" on it, and he played it over and over and over. He just stayed in his room and played that song. He never made it—he left school after that.

It was my first time away from home, and all of the freshmen were basically scared, but everybody at Ohio State was so friendly that it didn't take too long to get adjusted and to feel at home. I remember we had to get bused over to West Campus for classes, and I hated that because I was afraid to miss even one class. If the old man found out, you would pay for it, and you didn't want to get on his bad side. He treated everybody pretty well, though. Whenever he saw me in the hallway at the North Facility, he would always say, "Bob, how are you doing today? Things OK?" I knew the best thing to do was to be quiet, keep my mouth shut, work hard, and stay out of his office. I can still see that office—he had a little bed in there.

The funny thing is that we never really had a weight room at the North Facility. They put a little Nautilus in there, because Woody went through a phase where he believed in that, but the year after I left, they built a weight room.

I played behind Van DeCree, who was a two-time All-American defensive end, for those first two years, but I got my share of practice time. Van always had some sort of injury during the week. He would point at his shoulder and say "shoulder" or at his knee and say "knee." He missed a lot of practices, but he played on Saturdays. I practiced all the time, and I really believe that had a lot to do with making me a much better player heading into my junior year, when I got to start.

One of the few times I saw Woody get real upset with one of his players during a game was in the Rose Bowl after Neal Colzie spiked the ball, which took us out of field-goal range [in an 18–17 loss to USC in the 1975 Rose Bowl]. He made a great interception and then he did that. When he came off the field, Woody got in his face and really let him have it.

The next year, there is no question in my mind that we should have been national champs. We just kicked UCLA's ass earlier in the year, and I remember what Esco [Sarkkinen] said when he scouted them before that game. He said, "They are young and good, and you have got to watch out for this team. They will be getting better and better and I hope we don't have to play them again [in the Rose Bowl]."

I admit that I don't remember much about [the Rose Bowl], or I choose to forget it, but I do remember that their linemen were huge. As my career went, it was one of the first times I could have won a championship. I never really won the big championship game. We lost that one at Ohio State, and then I played on three Super Bowl–losing teams [one with the Los Angeles Rams and two with the Miami Dolphins]. I never won the big one.

Bob Brudzinski, shown here against Purdue in 1976, was named MVP of the 1976 team.

My senior year [1976] was a very frustrating year. It was considered a down year. We lost to Missouri when they went for two points and got it, and then we tied UCLA 10–10. And we were beaten badly by Michigan, but the Orange Bowl against Colorado was one of our best games and a great way to go out.

We were getting our ass kicked early in that game, 10–0, and we came back. We were loose for that game, though, and that's why we played so well. We went to the beach and had a real good time in Miami. Plus, it was just great not being cooped up in that Sheraton in Pasadena, as we had been the three previous years. It seemed that we had a loose curfew at the Orange Bowl. I remember saying hi to "Sark," signing in at the hotel for bed check, and going right out the back door a few times. A lot of guys were doing that.

Ironically, I live in South Florida now, and one of my sports bars hosts the Broward County OSU Alumni Association when the games are on TV. We play "Across the Field" and all the other school songs, and everybody gets into it. We pack the place with Buckeye fans.

I never regretted choosing Ohio State. The fans were great, and I can say it was the best four years I could have ever asked for. I got to meet a lot of great people, people I am still friends with. I live in Florida, but I still get back to see a game once in a while. I took my two boys to Phoenix for the Fiesta Bowl, and I have never seen them get that excited about a football game. They are real Buckeye fans. It was an awesome experience. And we won the championship game, something that got away from me during my playing days.

Bob Brudzinski, a defensive end, was twice All–Big Ten and an All-American in 1976. He played four seasons with the Los Angeles Rams and nine with the Miami Dolphins.

CRAIG CASSADY

1972–1975

FOR MY STORY, YOU MUST START AT THE BEGINNING—I am proud to say that my dad is Howard "Hopalong" Cassady. He loved and adored Woody Hayes, and I think Woody felt the same way about my dad. Growing up, it was normal for me to meet Tom Matte, or Paul Warfield, or Rex Kern, or any great Ohio State player of those eras. Dad later played with the Lions, and I remember a guy like Johnny Unitas would stop by the house. I just thought that was a normal occurrence until I got older and realized that great NFL players don't stop by everybody's house.

When I became a good high school player, I wondered if I was good enough to reach the Big Ten level.

Dad always wanted me to get interested in the game of baseball, because he just loved baseball. He tried to make me a switch-hitter, and he was hoping that would be my first love. But I chose football.

When I was a senior in high school, Woody came to a couple of my games and he would ask my dad, "Is he coming to Ohio State?" Dad was good friends with Bo Schembechler, too, and one time he called Dad up and wanted to have lunch at the Jai Lai. So Dad brought me along. I think Dad wanted to time it perfectly, so we would be there when Woody was there. Sure enough, we were sitting there, and Woody walked in. He came right over to our table and said, "Goddamn it, he's going to Ohio State!"

And I did.

A second-generation Buckeye, Craig Cassady had an outstanding senior season in 1975.

I was in awe of that campus, that program, and everything about Ohio State when I got there. I always wanted to run onto that field at Ohio Stadium and be a Buckeye, and for a few years, I was an AYO—"all you others"—but I worked hard to work my way up the ladder. I didn't come in as a top prospect like an Archie Griffin or Tim Fox or Brian Baschnagel. Woody was so patient with me; he let me develop and mature. I came in at about 160 pounds, and by my sophomore year I was close to 185 and a lot faster. By then, I had worked my way onto the special teams and I did enough to earn a letter.

But coming in as Dad's son absolutely put pressure on me. It was tough, but it was also a blessing. I know Ray Griffin went through the same thing having a brother like Archie.

We had some fun in those days, because the great thing was everybody on those teams was close. I remember Ed Trepanier. When I first saw him, [Ed] would throw John Hicks off one arm and Steve Myers off another, and I would think, "What am I doing here?" He used to tape Buckeye leaves on his helmet and sit in the front row of meetings just to annoy Woody.

I was behind Neal Colzie at cornerback, and I knew I was not going to replace an All-American until he graduated.

That time came in 1975, my senior year. Before the opener at Michigan State, I was named the starter. At bed check, Woody came by to see me, and I'll never forget this: he told me, "You are going to have a big day tomorrow." I just said, "I know, Coach. I won't let you down."

Everything fell in place that day, and I had three interceptions and we won 21–0. We rolled through that season, we were number one, and how often do you get to do that? The town of Columbus was very much like it was in 2002. Then came the Rose Bowl. I am still sick about not closing it out with a win over UCLA and winning a national championship. We had beaten them so badly earlier in the season, and we would have much rather played Cal or USC in the Rose Bowl. I don't care who you are—it is tough to beat any team twice in one year.

I have always thought there was something fishy about that game, and I probably always will. We were always a zone defensive team. We had played zone all season and had practiced zone before the Rose Bowl. In the game, the only coverage we played was man coverage. So what did UCLA do? They picked us and screened the heck out of us. It was like [UCLA coach] Dick Vermeil knew we would be in man ahead of time. But how could he? We never were before and we didn't practice it before the game.

At one point, Tim Fox and I started playing zone on our own. We would fake being in man and pull out of it. Years later, I happened to be on the same flight with Vermeil in first class and I wanted to really ask him how they knew we would be in that coverage all day. We talked about the game, and he just said something like, "We couldn't beat you head-to-head, so we had to do something different." To listen to Dick talk, it sounded like he knew what we were going to do.

After the Rose Bowl, he took the job in Philadelphia [with the Eagles], and who did he hire? Charles Clausen, our defensive line coach, and later George Hill [our defensive coordinator]. I think the whole thing was too coincidental. I have always questioned how he knew what kind of defense we would be in.

I know one thing: Woody was completely upset with the defensive coaches after that game. I know that for a fact. I believe that if we had won that game, and the national championship, things would have been much different for Woody. I bet that he would have retired either after the game or within a year or two and everything would have been different for him.

All these years later, that game still hurts. But that season changed the way I felt about myself. I broke out of the shadow, so to speak, and Woody allowed me to be my own person. He stuck by me. He saw something in me that I didn't see in me. Just having an opportunity to be a part of Ohio State football, I wanted to pay forward. That feeling never leaves you.

Today, I am so proud to be a Buckeye. There is nothing better than watching that band coming out of the end zone. Just nothing like it. Now we have a coach in Jim Tressel who has brought the pride and tradition back to the program. They do everything together, as a team, the way it should be. They weren't a team under John Cooper—they were out for "me." As we all know, coach Tressel knows what the Michigan game means. It is not just another game. It is an honor to have those gold pants.

And it was an honor to play football at the greatest university in the land.

Craig Cassady holds the single-season Ohio State interception record with nine, set in 1975 (tied with Mike Sensibaugh, 1969). He is one of eight players to record three interceptions in one game (against Michigan State in 1975).

BILL CONLEY

1970–1971

M<small>Y PATH TO OHIO STATE WAS UNUSUAL.</small> I was born in Kentucky and moved to Ohio in the fifth grade, and I didn't see an Ohio State game until my senior year at Pleasant View High School. Our head coach used to get some tickets to Buckeye games, and he held a little lottery for the players. You had to pick a number, 1 to 100, and after practice one day, I hit the number. I walked into Ohio Stadium for the first time in 1967, and that was all I needed to see. It was early in the fall and the sun was shining, and I'll never forget the crowd's roar when that team came out of the tunnel. I knew that day what my goals and dreams were.

The next year, I walked on to play football at Ohio State. Back then, they would put you on a list and there were about 120 players wanting to walk on. They used the ACT score to cut that group in half, but guys were leaving on a daily basis, and after that first year, we were down to fewer than a dozen in my class.

It was tough, obviously, but the real competitiveness came as a sophomore when we got to practice against the seniors. I was at guard and I worked my way onto the scout team, but my goal was to make special teams.

It was obvious to me from the beginning that Woody Hayes was such a dynamic individual. He would walk into a team meeting and you could hear a pin drop. The things he would tell you, the lessons you learned from him— some football related, some not—turned out to be so important in everybody's lives.

All of the coaches were great coaches and great people. One time, during my sophomore year, we were going up against the first-team defense and Lou McCullough was the defensive coordinator at the time. We happened to break a big play on them, and coach McCullough was so mad, he ordered the defense to run down to that McDonald's down Olentangy River Road and touch the golden arches and come back. There were two or three fences in between, and you should have seen all these players in full gear running down there, jumping over the fences to get to the McDonald's.

In the spring after my sophomore year, I was walking down the hall of the old Biggs Facility, which is now the Woody Hayes Athletic Center, and Woody called me into his office. He said he was putting me on scholarship. I can't put into words what that meant to me. I was on student loans at the time, and I came from a single-parent home and didn't have any money. Woody made that decision on his own to give me that scholarship, and I will always be appreciative that he did that for me. And I made my goal of playing special teams and a backup role during my junior and senior seasons.

I remember after we beat Michigan 20–9 during my junior year, we were in the locker room and John Bozick, our equipment manager, interrupted Woody and said, "Woody, the president is on the phone for you."

"Which president?" Woody asked him.

When he was told it was President Nixon, he said, "Tell him he's going to have to wait—I am talking to my team right now."

Later, we found out just how close he was with President Nixon, who offered so many touching stories about Woody when he spoke at Woody's funeral.

The next year, after we flew into Detroit and started to bus to Ann Arbor to play at Michigan, Woody noticed one of our players reading the *Lantern*. The sports editor had made the prediction that Michigan would beat us pretty badly. Woody saw this and said, "Stop the bus!" He then gave us a 10-minute lecture on the fall of the Roman Empire and how it was destroyed from within. He then opened the door and threw that newspaper out, and we started up again. I think he never missed an opportunity to teach.

After I got my degree and decided to go into coaching, I became much closer to Woody. He helped me get coaching jobs, and I would stop by to watch Ohio State practices from time to time. Once he told me, "Now that you are in coaching, here's a lesson to go by: wherever you coach, coach like you will be there for the rest of your life and it will pay off."

I will never forget that.

You lived with it every day. Every day you came to that realization that once you were a Buckeye, you were part of something real special. You were part of a championship program and part of a great tradition, and you were playing under one of the greatest coaches of all time. For us, it was like fighting under Patton.

We have played football here for more than 100 years; the tradition is the greatest thing we have at Ohio State, and it is like no other school in the country. Some schools have one tradition. We have the Buckeye Grove for All-Americans, gold pants, Ohio Stadium, the Victory Bell, our marching band, and I could go on and on. Nobody has the vast tradition that we have.

In my job on the coaching staff, when it comes to recruiting, recruiting is nothing more than selling—and there is no better product to sell than Ohio State.

Bill Conley has a connection to every Ohio State coach over the past half century. He played under Woody Hayes and has been an assistant coach under Earle Bruce, John Cooper, and Jim Tressel. He serves as the recruiting coordinator and also coaches the tight ends.

TOM COUSINEAU

1975–1978

BACK WHEN I WAS RECRUITED, I had a big advantage because my dad was a high school coach and he had sent several players on to college football. Two of them were Pete Cusick and Tommy Marendt, who each went to Ohio State. At that time, you could take as many recruiting visits as you wanted. But my dad was familiar with the recruiting process and he told me right off the bat, "Don't waste anybody's time. You can't be serious about more than four schools anyway. If you visit a place and you have no notion of going there, you are taking a spot that somebody else may need."

My four schools were Ohio State, Michigan, Notre Dame, and Penn State. It became pretty simple for me the day Ara [Parseghian] left Notre Dame. I had visited the campus up there and was very impressed, and being from Saint Edward's High, there was some awful strong pressure for me to go to Notre Dame. But if Ara wasn't going to be there, I didn't want to go there. I liked Joe Paterno, but I didn't want to play in a 4–4 defensive scheme, which is what Penn State used.

The first time I met coach Hayes, he came to our school and I was running a little late. As I walked into the foyer of the building, the place was packed with people. There was this huge crowd around him, and there he was, holding court. He was holding court as only he could do. Nobody was in school—everybody was listening to him. I remember the sea of kids parted as we met.

I was excused from my class and we went down to the athletic offices and talked about everything—everything but football. That was his way.

Sometimes, he gave you the impression he wasn't interested in you for football, because he never talked about it. He left that more to the assistants. For a young guy like me, it was hard to relax around him and he knew that. He worked really hard to make you feel comfortable, but the man was a legend. He asked a lot of questions, and I think I gave a lot of one-word answers. His way was to recruit parents. When he talked to my parents later at the house, I was like a passenger in the car of my own life.

On the evening before signing day, Woody was at the house in our basement with Joe Paterno and Gary Moeller [then the defensive coordinator at Michigan]. Now there were some high-profile coaches in the same place at the same time. We all sat there and talked, but it was very uncomfortable. Thank God my mom and dad were down there with me. Coach Hayes was the first to leave. He went to the door and I followed him. He turned around and told me, "I'll be back at 7:00. You tell Mom that I like bacon and eggs, and pancakes would be nice."

Then he stuck out his hand out and asked, "Are you ready to be a Buckeye?"

"Yes sir," I said.

I want it to be clear—I didn't settle on Ohio State. That was the first real big decision of my life.

On the first day of practice, I remember Teddy Smith came off the line and hit me so hard. My face mask was crushed and I just went "Wow." I called Dad and said something like I might be over my head here, and he said, "Don't worry, everything will come to you. Give it a little time." By the end of the first week, the offense was running the isolation in 7-on-7 drills. Pete Johnson was the type of runner that you knew where he was headed once he got the handoff and started. He would get that can up in the air and head for the hole. On this day, I just headed to the spot with a full head of steam and blew it up. Coach Hayes was all upset and screaming, and he was the type of coach who would come right back with the same play. So they gave it to Pete again, and I did it again . . . I just hit Pete as hard as I could for a loss in the backfield. Now coach Hayes was really upset. He came running over and grabbed my face mask and started screaming at me. George Hill, our defensive coordinator, came over and smiled. "Great job," he told me. "Great job."

Woody was a big believer in hitting during practice. We just banged the crap out of each other. Anyway, the upperclassmen seemed to accept me from that point. I remember one night I was dead in bed, sleeping, and six of them

157

came in and gathered around me. Somebody said, "You ready? You with us? We're going out and you're coming with us. Ready to hit High Street? Let's rock and roll." That was their way of accepting me, I guess.

But that's the way it was at Ohio State. The seniors helped the freshmen and that was the great thing about it. That freshman year on the road, I roomed with Timmy Fox, because I think coach Hayes wanted me to be around a leader. Woody really believed in having older players mentor younger ones.

One of the first plays I remember in an Ohio State uniform—we were at UCLA early in the '75 season, and I was the wedge buster on kickoffs and punts. I was headed down there on one, and Wendell Tyler was just getting ready to catch the ball. I was timing it just right to be there at the same time, and all of a sudden, I got crushed high and low from each side. It turned me over and I ended up face down on the ground. I hit so hard that my face mask dug out this big chunk of grass, and it became stuck in my face mask. I was semi out of it; I couldn't see anything and I couldn't feel anything. I thought I was blinded. What a humbling experience, but we just crushed them that day.

158

Kenny Kuhn had meningitis, and I got thrown in there awful early and started most games my freshman year. Being around the guys I was playing with, I just didn't want to let anybody down. It was a great group of guys and great players. Eddie Beamon was always talking. Aaron Brown had a great year. Tim Fox was a leader on that defense. Nick Buonamici was quiet and he would lead by example. Bob Brudzinski was a great player.

To end that season, we played UCLA again in the Rose Bowl for the national championship. What an awful memory. That one still hurts.

A few years ago, my wife and I were test-driving a car in Los Angeles, and we got off the freeway. This guy was in the car with us and he said, "I know a great road we can drive on," but I didn't know where we were. It turned out that this road goes around the Rose Bowl. So we're driving around it, and I got such a bad feeling in my stomach. I told this guy, "I can't be here. I am sorry, but this brings back really bad memories. Let's get out of here."

We had such a great team in '75, but we lost all those seniors before that next season, and we had to forge a new identity, I guess. We worked really hard at trying to do that. I remember that Missouri game; we were beating them so badly that I came out of the game and I had taken my tape off. We dominated them, but the next thing you know, they came roaring back. They scored and went for two on play-action to go ahead, and I was covering the guy out of the backfield. I saw a flag and thought it was on me, but it was on the other side of the field. They got another chance and they got the two-point conversion to beat us by one point. That was a hard one to take. My family had some friends who were huge Missouri fans down for the game, and they got a little obnoxious after the game.

The one thing that stands out through those years is how much we all got along. We would go out and have a lot of fun, and there was just tremendous camaraderie. We were in New Orleans at the Sugar Bowl my junior year, and a bunch of us went to Pat O'Brien's. We were sitting around this big, round table and we were pretty smacked because we all had hurricanes in front of us. Woody had walked in there, but I never noticed him until he sat down at our table. He was talking to us like there was no big deal, because he figured those hurricanes were just fruit punch. Then he reached over and took a sip of one, and he finally figured out that the juice was just for coloring. He got up, he threw this hurricane against the wall, and the race was on. I fell out of my chair and was crawling around on the ground, going from table to table to get out of there without him seeing me. I got away. I knew that whoever he got his hands on, he would put his eyes right on them. He wanted to remember who was there. So he grabbed somebody and he ended up remembering about four faces. They had to run some extra laps or something like that.

159

He wouldn't openly condone drinking, but I think he liked the camaraderie we had socially.

Before my senior year, 1978, I was a captain, and I have to admit that I was really disappointed with what happened. I thought [quarterback] Rod Gerald had earned the opportunity to keep playing. My belief to this day is that Woody gave Art Schlichter his word that he would start from the beginning, and Woody was a man of his word. But I was surprised he would make that promise. We were an option team, and we couldn't become a drop-back team in a couple of weeks of summer camp. I had no problem with freshmen playing, but it was a mistake for Art right out of the shoot.

We opened with Penn State, and how many interceptions did we throw that day? [Five.] I remember after the third, Art was running off the field and I was running on, and I grabbed his face mask and I just got all over him. A lot of guys did that day. I know Art wanted to play better, but he wasn't ready and we were frustrated. He needed to be phased in slowly and our year would

Tom Cousineau, shown here in his final game (the 1978 Gator Bowl) holds five Ohio State tackling records.

have been different. It wasn't all Art's fault. We dropped the ball on both sides.

It was a real tough year. We wanted to finish strong and go out doing some big things, but it just didn't work out that way. We underachieved that year

[7–4–1 record]. I had played pretty well, but I would have traded it for winning.

My class had played in the Rose, Orange, and Sugar Bowls, and now we were at the Gator Bowl. At that time, Jacksonville was a crappy town. It was a terrible stadium. It was hard to live with that trip. We tried to look at it as an opportunity to play a good team in Clemson, but I don't know if we did that—from the administration to the coaching staff to the players.

We paid for it in the end.

We didn't know much about them and we got into a bigger fight than we had anticipated. They came to play that night, because it was a chance for them to make a statement. The reputation of Ohio State—regardless of what our record was—was something other teams shoot for.

People always ask me where I was when it happened. We had called a time-out, and as a captain, I was very interested in what the play was going to be, so I was right there when they called it. We were in field position where we could kick a field goal to win the game. The instructions were very clear to Art: "If the play is not there, throw it away or sit down in the middle of the field, and we can still kick it." I can still remember that conversation like it was yesterday. Well, not only was it not there, but it was pretty much double-covered. But that's why Art became a tremendous quarterback later on. He had a confidence in himself that he could make the play, and as he matured, he made plays like that.

After the interception, I was thinking, "I can't believe we blew this chance." Then all hell broke loose. I didn't think much about what Woody did at the time. It looked like a small forearm and a push to me. He didn't hurt him. We had seen him do a lot worse a hundred times in practice. I was just thinking about how we could get the ball back one more time. When [the game] was over, I ran over to shake their hands and then sprinted into the locker room. I changed and was out of there in about five minutes. All I was thinking about was that we lost my final game. Woody came in and was out of control, and I wanted no part of it. I couldn't get out of there fast enough.

I was disconnected from the aftermath. I was done. I got on a plane the next day and headed to Hawaii for the Hula Bowl. When we landed, I had heard the news [of coach Hayes' firing], and suddenly everybody wanted to talk to me about it.

As I think back, he hit me only one time in four years. It was in the spring game after my junior year. As we always did, we were playing for steaks and beans, and Rod [Gerald] had the yellow jersey on—meaning we weren't allowed to hit him. The referees were always scared to death of Woody anyway, and they were spotting the ball to benefit the offense. Finally, I got in the huddle and said, "No more of this. Let's hit him. I'll take the heat." Finally, I had a shot at him and I just decleated him. I really let him have it. I remember the crowd went "Oooh . . ." All of a sudden, I hear, "YOU GODDAMN DUMB SON OF A BITCH!" and he was coming at me with that half run, half waddle. When he got to me, he hit me right in the solar plexus. I saw it coming and tightened up. I looked around and everybody was laughing. George Hill was just howling. George came over and said, "Don't worry about it."

In the end, I loved the guy and I loved Ohio State and I always wanted to tell him that.

Years later, I had been carrying this large picture of him around in my trunk and wanted to get him to sign it. His secretary called me when he was in town, and I stopped in to his office over there at the ROTC building. He was going somewhere on campus to make a speech, and he asked me to go with him. We came back, and he signed this photo, and I finally got to express my feelings to him. I told him how much I cared about him, respected him, and how much he and Ohio State meant to me.

The next day, my wife called me and asked, "What did you say to Woody Hayes yesterday?" I said, "Why?"

"Well, he died today," she told me. I couldn't believe it. I was crushed. I believe I was the last player ever to see Woody Hayes alive.

Ohio State has been a big part of my life. The traditions, the people, the coaches, and my teammates were the best I could ever ask for. I will always be proud to say that I am a Buckeye.

Tom Cousineau, who finished his career with 569 tackles, became the first player from Ohio State to be taken with the first pick of the NFL draft (Buffalo Bills in 1979). After playing in the Canadian Football League, he played four seasons with the Cleveland Browns and two with the San Francisco 49ers.

TOM DeLEONE

1969–1971

INEVER THOUGHT I WOULD EVER BE GOOD ENOUGH to play football in college, let alone make a living at it. Heck, I went out for my eighth-grade team and quit right away because it was a lot harder than I thought it would be. I remember I had a paper route and my friends sort of ignored me because I didn't play football. Then in ninth grade, we had a 90-man travel squad and I wasn't one of them, but I grew between my ninth and tenth grades, and midway through my sophomore year at Roosevelt High in Kent, Ohio, the senior center got kicked off the team. I became the starter at center and played that position for the next 21 years.

My high school teammates were Stan White and Tom Campana, and everybody was recruiting them. When their films got sent around the country, some coaches started to ask, "Who's that center?"

My father had died when I was 12, and my mom worked at Kent State as a receptionist. Mom and I just figured that I would go to Kent State and keep living at home. But then I got my first scholarship offer—it was from the University of Pittsburgh. Mom sat there crying in our little apartment . . . I can still see her. Early on, I wasn't being recruited by Ohio State, but Woody Hayes came to our little apartment later and sat down at the kitchen table with Mom and me. He talked about history for three hours. As he got up, he said, "Mrs. DeLeone, I can promise you two things—if your son comes to Ohio State, he will graduate and he will be the starting center by his sophomore year."

I don't know what he saw in me for him to say that, but I sure didn't think that way.

When I got to Ohio State in 1968, I remember the day my mom and brother dropped me off at Park Hall. I went to the cafeteria and thought, "Look at all these students. . . ." I couldn't believe how many people were in there, but I was looking at just the football team. That was my first big shock. Right there, I wanted to go home and pump gas, but Jim Jones wouldn't let me. Jim was the study hall coach back then and later became the athletic director, but he saved me from leaving Ohio State. "Tom, if you leave," he asked me, "what are you going to do when you get back there?"

I really didn't have an answer for him.

My first practice was a real nightmare—I had to go against Jim Stillwagon. I was a freshman and he was a sophomore, and I never thought I would make it to the second day. That '68 team went to the Rose Bowl and won the national championship, but the freshmen got to go home before Christmas.

Woody was right—by the fifth game of my sophomore season, I started at center. I don't know who we were playing, but I was sitting in front of Woody during the pregame meeting in the locker room and I was hyperventilating. He looked at me and said, "You know, you wouldn't be starting if I didn't think you could do the job." That's all I needed to hear—I was fine after that.

164

That '69 team rolled through the season until the terrible loss at Michigan. I know it was the worst game I had ever played, before or since. I went against Henry Hill, Michigan's nose guard. He was a year ahead of me, and he was very, very good. Here's what I did for the next year: I cut out Henry Hill's picture and I pasted it on my dorm room mirror at eye level. Every time I combed my hair or looked in that mirror, I saw Henry Hill for a year. I studied his film intently, and the next year [a 20–9 OSU win], I got a piece of him back. Let me put it this way: Henry Hill left the game in the third quarter.

That week before the game was classic Woody. We were in the offensive huddle in Thursday's practice. He fell to his hands and knees in the middle of the huddle and he started crawling around. Both of his hands were touching our feet, and he would go from one player to another. "I want to feel your feet to see if you're ready," he said. He went all the way around the circle doing this to everybody. He came to me, felt my feet, and pronounced, "You're ready to play."

Tom DeLeone blocks against Minnesota in 1970 as Rex Kern takes the snap.

I don't know how he knew it, but I guess I was. Henry Hill would agree with him.

You know, I think it was the same week, but after practice, two girls came over and we were studying in the dorm. They brought a few beers over with them, so I was sitting there drinking this beer with them in my room when I heard somebody shout, "Woody's on the floor!"

Now Woody would come down to South Campus quite a bit, and he would always bring a pizza with him. It was almost like his disguise. Everybody would always love to see Woody down there, and they would come out to greet him. So I heard this commotion and I stuck these beers under the bed and threw a blanket down there to make sure he couldn't see them. Sure enough, he opened my door and he had a big box of pizza. He just said, "Ladies, we have a big game this week and you should probably leave now."

In my life, I never saw two girls move faster than that. He didn't offer me any pizza, either. He just turned the lights out and said something like, "Get to bed." Then he closed the door. It was about 8:30! But I went to bed. That was Woody—he wanted to see how you were living. Thank God somebody yelled that he was coming, or I would have been caught with that beer.

I have to say that I fell in love with everything about Ohio State—the traditions, running out of that tunnel . . . what an awesome feeling. It is what is right about athletics. Somebody once asked me if I had any second thoughts about going to Ohio State. I said, "Are you kidding me? None." It was the greatest decision I ever made. I will always be a Buckeye.

Tom DeLeone, twice named All–Big Ten, played two seasons with the Cincinnati Bengals and eleven with the Cleveland Browns.

DOUG DONLEY

1977–1980

I HAVE TO TELL YOU ABOUT THE DINNER that made me a Buckeye. It was the time Woody Hayes came to my house to have dinner and to recruit me. He came with assistant coach Alex Gibbs. All coach Hayes talked about was what a great school OSU was and what a great education I would get. He told many war stories, too, but he never talked about football. I could tell my parents were loving everything they were hearing, while I wanted to hear about football, playing time, the national championships, etc.

All of a sudden the phone rang; my mom answered it, and told me that I may want to take the call in the back room. I picked up the phone, and it was Bo Schembechler from Michigan calling, reiterating their interest in me coming to Michigan. I went back out to the dinner table and coach Hayes immediately asked me who was on the phone. Very nervously, I answered, "coach Schembechler." Coach Hayes immediately stood up, came down to my end of the table, stood over me, stuck out his hand, and said, "I want a handshake and verbal commitment that you are coming to Ohio State."

At that time, I was still considering Notre Dame and Michigan, but I was scared to death so I shook his hand and that was the end of that.

It was the best decision I was ever forced to make.

Woody always said, "You win with people, good people." And we were surrounded by class people. The coaches were the best in the business. The training staff and doctors were the best. They took care of our every need; they all cared about the players and were proud to be Buckeyes. The equipment guys were incredible—[John] Bozick and his staff bled scarlet and gray.

Doug Donley led the Buckeyes in receiving for three consecutive seasons.

I remember that the coaches' secretaries were people you wanted to go visit with. They were all first class.

Then you had your teammates. Woody always told us, "The relationships you develop here the next four years will last forever." He was right! The leader sets the tone. Look at what coach Tressel has done now. He instilled discipline, a sense of purpose, a pride for the program, and team unity. That's the same thing coach Hayes did.

When I think of Ohio State, I think of all the first-class, quality people, and I am proud to be a part of that. It is hard to appreciate all of these things while you are there, but when you step away and look back at the memories, the relationships, the entire experience, it truly is a great feeling.

You learned very quickly playing under Woody Hayes that beating Michigan was top priority. We started from day one with Michigan on the mind. Every practice during the season was intense, but practices during Michigan week were incredibly gut-wrenching. Any fumble, interception, or missed assignment caused an eruption of large magnitude. Players and coaches were on pins and needles all week. You didn't talk or laugh during the week. It was war.

I remember coach Hayes giving his pregame talk in the Michigan locker room, and the last thing he said was, "We are going to come out fighting." Well, he led us down the tunnel at Ann Arbor, and you are supposed to take a hard left and go to your sideline, but coach Hayes made a detour with us following him and ran into the "Go Blue" section of their student body waiting on the field. A small fight erupted, but like he said, we came out fighting. Michigan games were like no other—the crowd, the intensity on each side, the national exposure, and the feeling afterward. It was the ultimate joy if you won and the ultimate agony of defeat, that lasts forever, if you lost. Getting those gold pants was quite an honor!

My freshman year . . . it is a very intimidating time for any freshman coming into Ohio State. I played behind Jimmy Harrell, who was a great guy. He took me under his wing and taught me the ropes. He was the consummate professional. My first roommate, Calvin Murray, had a tremendous faith in God and was instrumental in helping me grow as a Christian. He was an inspiration to me. That first year is hard, and we endured it together. I could name more than 100 guys that I share a special bond with. The most unfortunate thing is that we all went different ways after it was over, and you do not get to see them very often.

169

If I could give any advice to recruits today, I would tell them to look at the head coach. He is the leader of the football program, and its success will mirror the head coach. His values, character, and leadership abilities will be a determining factor in your success as an individual and as a team. Look at the players—these are the guys you are going to battle with. Surround yourself with quality people. And this is very important: look at the school, because your education is a must. Football does not last forever. For most, it ends after your college career, and if you are lucky enough to play pro ball, your careers are short.

An education lasts a lifetime. Do not take it lightly!

I would tell the current players to enjoy this time and make the most of it. Give it your best both on and off the field. Don't look back with regrets and say, "I wish I had" but say, "I'm glad I did." You are a part of one of the best traditions in the world. Do not take it for granted. Appreciate it, respect it, and enjoy it! Keep the tradition alive by holding your teammates accountable to the standards set before you. Set a good example for the young guys coming in; they are watching you. Play the game and win or lose with class.

Ohio State football is all about commitment, excellence, character, pride, and teamwork.

When I got drafted to play in the NFL, I was two classes short of graduating. After some pressing from coach Hayes and a call from coach Tressel, who was an assistant some time after I left, I came back and finished to get my bachelor of arts.

I am very proud of that. And I am very proud that I played for Ohio State.

Doug Donley, Ohio State's first wide receiver to be named All–Big Ten (1979 and '80), played four seasons with the Dallas Cowboys.

BRUCE ELIA

1972–1974

I WAS A SMALL-TOWN JERSEY KID who was used to hanging out with his friends on the street corner until 1:00 in the morning. We never got into trouble, but that was the thing to do. We just hung out . . . about 20 guys together, all summer long. I had a good high school career as a running back/linebacker and I was about 6′1″ and 195 pounds, which wasn't huge, but it was good size for the early seventies. At that time, I really didn't know where I wanted to play college football, but I had plenty of offers.

I went to Notre Dame to take a visit on a Saturday, and my host turned in that night at 10:00 to go study. So I canned Notre Dame.

Then I went to Penn State and I loved Joe Paterno. The problem there was that I felt like I was in the middle of the woods. We went out that night and went to a Pizza Hut or something like it. That was it for Penn State.

I went to Nebraska and had a really good time, but it was too far.

Lo and behold, I got to Columbus and I knew nothing about Ohio State football, except for what I saw on television, and my host was Glen Mason. Glen had arranged for us to double-date that night.

Glen had it down real simple. We stood outside Papa Joe's on High Street and looked north and there were kids everywhere. He told me, "On the left side, we go to school and we study and we live. On the right side are the sororities and fraternities and more housing. Down the middle, we party! Welcome to High Street."

I thought, "This is simple—I am going to Ohio State."

But the truth is that I still hadn't decided after that. My dad was a construction guy, and he didn't say much during the whole process. One night he asked me which way I was leaning. I said, "I am leaning toward Penn State, but I really didn't like it there."

He then said something I'll never forget: "Why don't you go play with the best?"

We never said another word. The next day, I called up Ohio State and said I was coming. I knew then that my dad had challenged me. I was a little scared about it, and I knew Ohio State was loaded with talent. It seemed like a football factory, and I was from a small school in Cliffside Park, New Jersey.

Once I got to Ohio State, I ripped up my ankle right away and was out for a month on crutches. I would put my arm around Steve Myers and Jim Cope, and they would carry me to Papa Joe's. My ankle was the size of my head.

My sophomore year, I was about the fifth-string fullback and I could hardly get any time in practice, and now I was starting to get frustrated. They sent me to some JV [junior varsity] games and I had a couple of 100-yard games, and just when I thought I was doing well at fullback, George Hill, the defensive coordinator said he wanted me on defense. This was the third game of my sophomore year and now I was real mad. I was hurting on the inside, because people had told me Ohio State would make me a linebacker, and sure as shit, that's what they did.

On that first day at linebacker, I intercepted a pass and coach Hill got so excited. That really inspired me, so I began practicing real hard. I would come out early and stay late to learn more about the position. Little by little, I was getting better. I had [Randy] Gradishar and Rick Middleton—two future first-round picks—in front of me. The one thing I did—I went after all the running backs with a passion and I smashed them. I thought, "If they wouldn't let me be a running back, then I am going to punish the guys who are." That was my simple Jersey logic.

In the '73 opener against Minnesota, they had just come up with "Buck of the Week" and "Hit of the Week" awards that year, and I was running down on the opening kickoff and I smashed this guy who was blocking for Rick Upchurch. The guy flew into Upchurch, who fumbled, and when I opened my eyes, there was the ball right in front of me. I jumped on it, and when I came to practice that Monday, there was my picture for "Hit of the Week" and "Buck of the Week." I still have those plaques.

One day, after Champ Henson got hurt, I was sitting in the whirlpool and Woody came right up to me and pointed his finger in my face. "You are going to play fullback!"

"I will only play fullback if next year you let me go back to linebacker," I told him.

I ended up starting at fullback and had a pretty good year over those final nine games. In the third game, I went over 100 yards in one game and had four touchdowns in another, but by this time, Pete Johnson, who was behind me, had been getting better and better. By the time we got to the Rose Bowl, Pete and I were switching on and off each series.

The following year, I went back to linebacker and Pete became the full-time fullback.

That summer, before my senior season, Woody had suffered a heart attack and there were all kinds of rumors about whether he would return. Many of us were outside the building before our first meeting of the season, and we were discussing whether Woody would last the season.

"Woody will never make it."

"He'll probably have another heart attack."

"He probably wants to be buried at the 50-yard line in Ohio Stadium."

"We had better go easy on him, because he's getting too old to coach."

Those were the comments going back and forth.

Well, Woody called us all inside for this first meeting. There were about 120 players in there, including freshmen who never knew Woody aside from being recruited by him. The meeting started in typical fashion. He was talking about past accomplishments, and he was complaining that *Sports Illustrated* ranked us number one, and then he started talking about Michigan. "They'll be ready for us at the end of the year," he told us.

At this point, we were a little bored because we had all heard this talk before.

All of a sudden, Woody raised his voice. He said something like he knew he was going to have a heart attack. "I was gonna have it on Tuesday, but I postponed it until Thursday so I could hire a new backfield coach on Wednesday," he said. "I know a bunch of you think that I won't make the season. You think I'll probably have another heart attack and die. Well, f—— my heart, f—— my heart."

Then he beat on his chest in front of everyone to get the point across. Then he spoke the words I'll never forget:

174

At fullback or linebacker, Bruce Elia could star on either side of the football.

"I'd rather die a winner than live being a loser, because when you are a loser, you die a little bit each day. . . . Now let's get dressed and start practicing to win a national championship!"

I was ready to run through the wall.

The other classic Woody was after that Michigan State game that year.

We were waiting in the locker room for 45 minutes to find out who won the game, and we still had our uniforms on. I remember at the end, Archie got into the end zone and we thought we had won, but nobody was sure. Woody ranted and raved and walked around the locker room asking everybody, "Did we score? Did we score?" He came up to me and asked me. I said, "I saw the official put his hands up."

Suddenly, Wayne Duke, the Big Ten commissioner, walked in. Now Wayne was a big guy, about 6′4″, and everybody gathered around him. He told Woody, "I have to speak to your team." Woody could sense what was coming, and at this point, he started to scream, "Wayne, don't you f—— me! Don't you f—— me!"

Now George Hill had to hold Woody back so he wouldn't punch him. Woody had his arm cocked and his fist clenched and he was trying to throw a punch, but he couldn't with George hanging on his arm. He just would not accept that we lost that game. We all wouldn't accept it. I can still see Woody trying to get at the Big Ten commissioner and land a punch. He just hated losing so much.

At the time President Nixon was going through his impeachment troubles, we were at the Rose Bowl and Woody came into practice one day. He told us, "Now I want to tell you that people need friends. I visited an old friend today, Dick Nixon. Right now, he has no friends. Nobody wants to be friends with him, but I am still Dick's friend. Dick can count on Woody. Woody will be there for Dick Nixon."

Here we were thinking about the Rose Bowl practice, and Woody was telling us about his visit with the president of the United States. He was the type of guy that would help out anyone who needed it, from the president on down.

I believe it was the four best years of my life. I learned the most as a person that I could have anywhere. I had the most fun, and I acquired some of the best friends of my life. I learned what it was like to be down and what it was like to be successful. I certainly learned how to win, and I learned a lot from Woody from his speeches about being a good, moral person, to be respectful and decent and honest. I had learned most of that from my parents, but he reinforced it.

For me, Ohio State was the best place I could have ever chosen.

My family and my son are all big Ohio State fans. When I took him to the Ohio State–Michigan game a few years ago, we went over to the Schottenstein Center, and they have these little TVs where you can select Ohio State highlights from the past. Here I was with my son and they were announcing my name and some of the big games I had. That was very special for me.

Recently, I was put into my high school hall of fame, and I had to give a little speech. There were a few hundred people there, and I looked out and said, "I want to thank my father for challenging me to go play with the best. I want to thank him for challenging me to go to Ohio State. Thanks, Dad."

Bruce Elia became one of the few Ohio State players in the modern era to ever start on offense and on defense. In 1973 he led OSU in scoring with 14 touchdowns, and in '74 he led the team with 144 tackles.

TIM FOX

1972–1975

I WASN'T VERY HIGHLY RECRUITED coming out of Canton Glenwood High. I think Kent State recruited me and so did Indiana and Lou Holtz at North Carolina State. I had ruptured a kidney during my senior year in high school and missed the final three games. The Ohio State coaches never saw me play football, but they did come to one of my basketball games, and from that I was surprised when they offered me a scholarship. I was one of the last guys offered, and we had only about 12 freshmen in 1972, which was the first year that freshmen were eligible since the fifties.

My dad was dead set against my going to Ohio State. I guess he thought I would be over my head. On a recruiting trip, we were having a brunch at the golf course, and my mother was going through the buffet line and trying to balance her purse on one arm and hold the plate with the other. That is when Woody Hayes came to her assistance and carried her purse down the buffet line for her. He won her over, and from that day on, my mom loved Woody Hayes, so I had one fan of my going to Ohio State.

My first impression came on the first day—picture day. It was the first time I was in Ohio Stadium. That was great in itself, and then they gave me No. 47 and I was thinking how great this was. Then I looked around and I saw two more 47s, and that dampened my enthusiasm [Tim ended up wearing No. 12 throughout his career].

They called for all the freshmen offensive backs to go over there to get their picture taken. They called all the freshmen defensive backs to go over to another spot. I had played both ways in high school, and nobody had told me what position I would be playing. So I went up to [assistant coach] John Mummey and asked him where he wanted me. "Where do you want to go?" he asked me. He just said, "Go where you want to go." I looked over at the offensive picture and they had Archie Griffin, Brian Baschnagel, Woody Roach, and all these big fullbacks. I weighed about 165 pounds at the time. I looked over at the defensive guys and I saw only one, Craig Cassady, and thought my odds were much better over there. So I went to the defensive side and that's how I ended up as a defensive back at Ohio State. That was how it happened.

I played in every game in 1972 as a freshman and started several at free safety. I remember when we were playing Minnesota; Rick Upchurch was their tailback at the time. I think Tony Dungy was the quarterback. My main job was that I had the pitchman on the option. That was my job for the day. I played pretty well and kept tackling Upchurch, but thank God they didn't pass, because I had no idea what our coverages were at that point.

That freshman class was a tight-knit group. We all got along pretty well, but I was always afraid of the upperclassmen. I remember this big, old defensive tackle, Ed Trepanier, who never played much because he was always yelling at Woody during drills. One day at Steeb Hall, he grabbed Archie and held him out of a window by his ankle. He just had him by one ankle and it was high off the ground! I know Archie will never forget it. God, if he would have dropped him . . .

The freshmen had their own locker room in those days, and one time an upperclassman, Chuck Bonica, had been late for practice a few times. Woody said, "That's it. He's off the team." So the seniors got together and decided there would be a work stoppage until he reinstated Chuck. So they came into our locker room and told us, "Look guys, nobody is going to practice today. You just stay in here until we tell you otherwise."

So we did. Next thing we knew, Woody came busting into the room, screaming at the top of his lungs. He had let Chuck back on the team, but we were late for practice.

In my four years, we accomplished so much. We never lost a home game and never lost to Michigan, but we were 1–3 in Rose Bowls and should have been 3–1.

That 1972 USC team with Sam Cunningham that beat us was simply great. We couldn't have beaten them, but the next year, we really beat them badly in the Rose Bowl. The following year we lost to USC by one point, and that

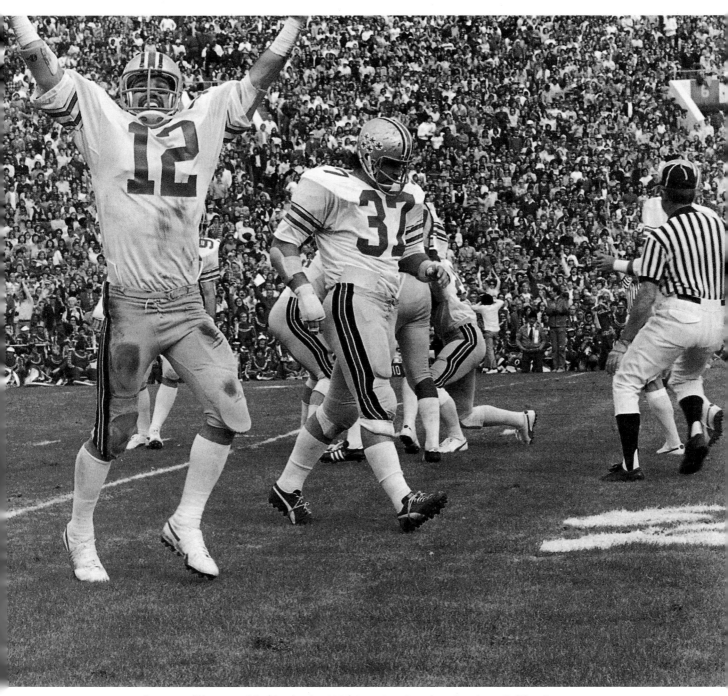

Tim Fox celebrates a big play in the 1975 Rose Bowl against Southern California.

team wasn't that good. J. K. McKay caught that pass near the sideline that still haunts me.

But none of those losses compare to the Rose Bowl at the end of my career. We were undefeated and had really smoked UCLA [41–20] earlier in the season in Los Angeles. I think the coaching staff got a little overconfident because we had beaten them so badly. Woody really liked our senior class, and I really believe he got a little soft on us while preparing for the Rose Bowl that year. He softened on bed check, saying, "Look guys, I keep waking you up during bed check, so I won't be coming by. Just sign in when you come in." Well, that was an open invitation for some guys to stay out way past curfew.

Then we stayed in our regular hotel the night before the game, and we never did that before at the Rose Bowl. We didn't really have a good game plan, either. I think we forgot to work on the things that got us there. It was definitely the toughest loss of my career. It was extremely disappointing. It still hurts. Those are the ones you remember all these years later.

We had great teammates at Ohio State. Archie was the consummate team player. He absorbed whatever Woody said. He never felt like going out and having a beer with the guys, because he felt that responsibility that Woody had put on him.

180

I really wish I would have taken the time to enjoy those years more. Coach Hayes made you focus so much. You really didn't take time to enjoy what you accomplished. The NFL was so much easier than what I went through at Ohio State. I was a young kid. Coach Hayes was a perfectionist, and he would just drive you and drive you. Nobody in pro football motivated like Woody Hayes did. He was the best at it. That work ethic stayed with me in the pros, and it does today in sales. I can thank him for that.

It really was tougher for the offensive players. Woody was in their faces constantly. I wasn't sure he remembered my name since I was on defense, but he would call me "Canton" after my hometown. I can still see him after that loss to Michigan State [in 1974] when we thought we had scored to win the game, but the refs didn't allow it. [Big Ten commissioner] Wayne Duke came into the locker room to tell Woody that the game would not be reversed, and Woody grabbed him by the lapel and lifted him right off the ground. He stood there holding him up—his feet were in the air! Then he wanted to get a bunch of us and go to the Michigan State locker room and finish the thing—men to men. But a few assistants talked him out of it.

Another time Woody let this guy from *Sports Illustrated* come in, and he spent all this time with him and he thought there would be a positive story about him and Ohio State. Well, the guy just ripped him in the article. We were at dinner, and there was this big dishwashing container up there. Woody would take a glass out of it, read a quote from the story, and smash the glass on the wall. He would read another quote and smash another glass. He must have smashed 12 glasses.

I definitely love Ohio State, and I have to tell you I was real disappointed when my nephew decided to play at Penn State. My daughter Haley was a captain of her field hockey team at Ohio State, and my other nephew Dustin is doing well there. I will always be a Buckeye. Coach Tressel has brought much of the pride back for us. I know one thing—Woody would be proud of him.

Tim Fox, a team captain in 1975, was selected in the first round of the 1976 NFL draft by the New England Patriots, for whom he played six seasons. He also played for the San Diego Chargers and the Los Angeles Rams.

KEN FRITZ

1976–1979

I AM AN OLD-SCHOOL TYPE OF GUY, and I wanted to play for Woody Hayes. If I would have been a basketball player, I would have wanted to play for Bobby Knight because he believed in the same things Woody did. I have always been a big believer in discipline, and there was nobody better at it than Woody Hayes.

I remember they shut down my high school when he came to visit me. Fran Curci was speaking that night, but kids trampled over him to get to Woody. Fran understood because he said he was always used to following Woody, but that shows what magnetism the man had.

A lot of the lessons I learned in life, I learned from Woody. That's why I went there in the first place. I knew that you learned more on the football field about life's lessons than you do in the classroom. And you could say Woody Hayes was our professor. You know what he said about getting knocked down and getting back up? That is so true. Woody taught us all to be honest and straightforward with people. He demanded respect, and we gave it to him, because he earned it.

I remember how Woody used to nickname us when he got mad at us. He would call us by our hometowns if he didn't remember our names. He would call Tom Waugh "Norwalk," and he called me "Ironton." Yeah, he would punch us in the stomach, but it didn't hurt us. We would just laugh about it. You know that coaches couldn't do that today, because all the players' parents would be suing them. Hey, if he didn't punch you, he didn't want to make you better and he didn't care about you.

I skipped class one day, and one of the professors called him. The next day, Woody woke me up and went to class with me—all day. Can you imagine the kids' reactions to see Woody Hayes walking in and sitting down in their classroom? I told him that I would never miss another class. Coaches today wouldn't do that for you.

It really saddens me to think how it ended for him. I wouldn't ever say anything negative about the man, and if you are in war, those things happen. That Gator Bowl was the most ridiculous bowl game we ever played in, and we probably shouldn't have been there in the first place. It was a fifty-five-thousand-seat stadium, and I think Clemson got fifty thousand seats. It turned into a fiasco. Those fans were very rough on us. We were spit on because it seemed that everybody there hated us. As the week went on, the resentment just built up and built up.

Then the kid made the interception and got in Woody's face. He was a fierce competitor and it happened. Everybody asks me if I was the one in the picture with him, and yes, that was me. I was trying to hold him. I'll never forget that plane ride home. It was very quiet, and Woody wasn't going to apologize. But at the end, he told us he wouldn't be the coach of Ohio State anymore.

Earle came in the next season and wanted to run everybody out of town. I think the reason we had a good football team is the fact that most of us got pissed off at him. We had a lot of unity because we all stuck together. Don't get me wrong, I like Earle and he reminded me a lot of Woody. I would play for him again. He didn't have all the pizzazz Woody had, but who did?

That Michigan game [in 1979] is the memory for me. We went up there and won 18–15 and I finally got a pair of gold pants. I really think that team should have been national champs, but we had so many injuries in the late part of that Rose Bowl against USC, we sort of ran out of gas. But I will always believe we were the better team. The greatest talent I ever saw was Art Schlichter. He could do about anything on the football field, but that day we could have used another touchdown. That Rose Bowl still is one of the greatest moments of my life. It was huge, and because of it I could understand what the 2002 team went through at the Fiesta Bowl. We all had to be tickled to death that they brought home the championship.

I really have no regrets, and I would I do it again if I could, but my body wouldn't be able to take it. My hips and lower back are a big problem these days, because we played on turf in those days and we took a lot of pounding.

184

Ken Fritz prepares to make a block against USC in the 1980 Rosebowl.

The first time I went back to Ohio Stadium later, I stood in the stands and just soaked everything in. You know, when you are playing, you really don't hear anything. But I stood there and listened as the band came out of the tunnel and realized what a magnificent thing that is. It gets you so fired up.

The memories I have of Ohio State and Woody Hayes will never leave me. It was a great time in my life, and I am very proud to have played football for the Buckeyes.

Ken Fritz, who started three seasons at guard, was All–Big Ten in 1978 and 1979 and an All-American in 1979.

RANDY GRADISHAR

1971–1973

I REMEMBER MEETING WOODY HAYES like it was yesterday. I was working in my father's grocery store one afternoon in Champion, Ohio, when my high school principal called me. He said, "Randy, you need to come back to school *now* because Woody Hayes is here in my office and he would like to see you." Woody Hayes? To see me? I thought my buddies were playing a prank on me.

Here I was . . . I had never considered going to college until my senior year at Champion High School. I didn't have any clue, really, as to what my future might hold. I didn't start playing football until the ninth grade, and I wasn't highly recruited. I thought I might be better at basketball. But here was Woody Hayes, wanting to talk to me.

I went back to school and there he was in the principal's office, waiting on me. We talked about family, education, careers, and, finally, football. Then Woody said, "Let's go see your father at the grocery store."

So we drove back to my father's store, and my dad was behind the meat counter, slicing meat. Woody joined him and they stood there for 45 minutes behind the meat slicer, talking about World War II. My dad had been in the army and had fought in the South Pacific on the infamous Luzon Island in the Philippines. Well, you know Woody was a historian and a war buff and knew everything about World War II. They hit it off right away. You could say the recruitment of Randy Gradishar was under way.

Being recruited by Woody Hayes was overwhelming to me. Remember, I grew up in a quiet little community, and when we went to Browns and

Indians games, I thought that was such a big deal. Being in a big city like Cleveland and eating in a restaurant was thrilling to me. So when Woody took me to the old Jai Lai restaurant, I was very impressed.

I could tell right away that Woody Hayes was a man of integrity.

What Woody stood for, believing in God and yourself, I also believed. He was always focused on education. He said, "Son, you are here for one reason, and that's to get an education. It will always benefit you." One of my goals was to graduate in four years. I remember Woody saying, "I'll give you an opportunity to play and that's all." He never promised starting positions. He made it clear that there was a price to pay and that price was hard work through discipline and that was the theme. My dad had taught me a good work ethic. Heck, I had worked in his grocery store since I was 11.

The other thing I learned about him right away was that he was very observant. One time, he said, "Son, you have some big feet there." I wore a size 14½ shoe and I said, "Yeah, I have a good foundation with these feet." He noticed everything about you. He didn't miss a thing.

Naturally, I chose Ohio State, committing in February 1970. It was a natural fit.

Once there, I really felt like I matured.

My military draft number was 186, and I was drafted during that summer. I moved into the dorm in August, and I enrolled in ROTC at Ohio State for the first two years. I remember all those student protests about Vietnam.

In addition to all of those changes in my life, I had to face the challenge of my own adequacy in football. While checking into my dorm as a freshman, I saw all these all-staters and All-Americans. I was all-nothing. I thought, "What in the world am I doing here?" Rex Kern and Jack Tatum were seniors and part of a national championship team, and here I was a freshman going up against them in practice. I questioned myself. One time in practice, we called a blitz and I broke free and was just about to tackle Rex Kern when all of a sudden John Brockington came out of nowhere and hit me so I hard . . . I thought he broke my sternum. But I healed, and I figured out I could play with these guys. It was somewhat of a turning point for me.

Woody always pushed us to be better. He really had a student mind set, and I did too. I wanted to get better. I wanted to learn. Woody knew how to motivate you. He encouraged you. "Goddamn it, you can do it," he would say. "You can do it!" After a while, you believed you could.

188

Randy Gradishar became one of Ohio State's most decorated defensive players.

The entire playing experience at Ohio State is entrenched in my memory, but the Michigan games really stand out. In 1971, my sophomore year, we were playing in Ann Arbor, and that's when Thom Darden interfered with Dick Wakefield and the officials didn't make the call. Woody went crazy! The next year, we made a great goal-line stand that enabled us to beat Michigan and go to the Rose Bowl as Big Ten champions.

How did Woody feel about Michigan? Let me illustrate with one story. One time we were at the Quarterback Club and the team was being introduced and a freshman had on a blue tie. Woody took one look at that blue tie, and he walked over and whipped it off that freshman. The audience went wild. We learned quickly that tradition dictated we wear ties of scarlet and gray, but we didn't know much about fashion. At the Rose Bowl one year, we went to Disneyland in those plaid coats we had to wear.

Anywhere we went, even in plaid coats, I really felt it was an honor just to represent Ohio State. I finally realized I was a part of it. I remember that John Hicks and I were chosen to be on the Playboy All-American team, and the honor meant a visit to the Playboy Mansion, but that magazine was not on Woody's reading list. He didn't believe it would be the right kind of exposure and it wouldn't do Ohio State, John, or me any good, so he wouldn't let us go. With no pictures of us, *Playboy* cut and pasted our heads onto pictures for that article.

In addition to graduating in four years, one of my other goals was to be on the weekly Woody Hayes TV show. We didn't do a whole lot of media interviews back then, and it was controlled, so we were real stilted on that show. But I got on it. And I graduated with a B.S. in education—in four years. I met my goals.

The last time I saw coach Hayes was in 1983. When I realized business would take me back to Columbus, I called coach Hayes and invited him and Anne to dinner at the Jai Lai. She did not join us, but it was typical of Woody—we didn't talk much about football or sports. He just wanted to get caught up on my life and career. Such a great man! I'll tell you one thing: he was committed to this university and to the people of Ohio. He was a real patriot who believed in the United States. He always said there was a difference between right and wrong. That man had a lot of wisdom, but what people don't understand is that he had a great sense of humility. He never thought it was all about him. Woody was like a second father to me and to most of his players.

Woody is part of the history, part of the great tradition at Ohio State. I really believe that with the long-standing tradition at Ohio State, that history will always be a part of us and we a part of it. When you go to Ohio State, you are a part of a rich history. The Ohio State University will provide the leadership and vision and will challenge you. It's about all the people, administrators, coaches, alumni, and players who care about you. It's not all about winning. It's about the values you stand for.

Living in Colorado, I find that wherever I go, whenever I mention that I am a Buckeye, eyes light up and the Ohio State tradition comes alive. It's the people and their passion for Ohio State that makes it such a great place. I am a Buckeye forever.

Randy Gradishar, a two-time All-American linebacker, became the 17th Ohio State player to be inducted into the College Football Hall of Fame. He also is a member of the CoSIDA Academic Hall of Fame and was an Academic All-American in 1973. He played 10 seasons with the Denver Broncos.

CORNELIUS GREENE

1972–1975

I HAD GROWN UP IN WASHINGTON, D.C., and played at Dunbar High, having had a pretty good senior season as a quarterback. Michigan State was the first big school to recruit me along with all the ACC schools. When Ohio State became interested and coach Hayes looked at me, he told me that he thought my neck was too small and I might get hurt playing in the Big Ten. While all the other schools were telling me I would start right away, coach Hayes told me, "If you are good enough to play here, you will. If you are not, you won't."

That put the challenge in front of me, and there was no doubt in my mind. Mom thought he was the most honest coach there was, and I really liked Rudy Hubbard, who was the running backs coach. At the time, some of the people who mentored me in D.C., from coaches to friends and neighbors, didn't think Ohio State would ever play an African American at quarterback. Some people at Michigan State had told me the same thing.

So I had a lot of naysayers who didn't think I should go to Ohio State for one reason or another, and I wanted to prove them wrong.

Woody Roach was a running back from my area, and his father drove us to Columbus that fall. We got there at about midnight. The students weren't there yet and High Street was empty. Here's this big, old university and nobody was on campus. I thought to myself, "What have I done?" You can say I was pretty homesick right away.

On the second day of practice, we had a 9:00 P.M. meeting and I was walking down the aisle when the clock struck nine. I caught a mouthful from coach Hayes that night. I knew from that moment not to be a minute late, and that was the last time I was ever late.

That freshman season was a time of doubting myself. I had to learn the whole game all over again. We ran an old-style offense in high school, and I had never run the option before. I had to learn all the plays and the footwork for a quarterback that went with them. George Chaump, the quarterbacks coach, developed me from the beginning.

We were coming right out of the civil rights era at that time, and I was a minority for the first time in my life. Growing up in D.C., I was used to being around African Americans but not many whites. At Ohio State at that time, I think we had 50,000 students and about 500 blacks, but I never once felt any racial tension. It was a learning curve for me, because I was quick to stereotype people, too. That was the best teaching experience I could have had. For the first seven weeks, I roomed with Brian Baschnagel, but Brian was from the opposite—he came from an all-white community. We became best friends.

192

Then once the season started, I roomed with Archie [Griffin], and that led to some lonely times, because he made the travel squad and I didn't. I started to get some serious stomach problems, and didn't know what was wrong until Doctor Bob Murphy diagnosed it as an ulcer. He said, "Don't worry, you're only the fifth quarterback that Woody has given an ulcer to." I guess he had given one to Rex [Kern] and to Tom Matte. From that time on, the lady at the cafeteria would never give me fried food—I had to have everything broiled. Well, I would come in and there were two or three buildings of students eating in our cafeteria, but I would have to go up and get my specially prepared meal, and everybody started thinking I was a prima donna. They didn't know the real story of my health problems.

All of my life I had kept things in when something bothered me. I never talked about my problems, and I was under a lot of pressure at that time and I was away from home for the first time. I learned how to open up, and I never had another ulcer again.

Going into spring ball of '73, I was still tied for third-string, but I had a very good spring and my confidence went up from that point. Heading into that fall camp, Greg Hare, the returning starter, was chosen as a captain. He would be the starter in the morning practice, and then I would be the starter in the afternoon practice. But Greg pulled a hamstring, and I was in there for that first possession in the first game against Minnesota. We drove right down

Cornelius Greene was so respected by his teammates that they named him MVP in 1975.

the field and I scored. We won that day, 56–7, and I had a pretty good game, and I was the starter ever since.

Coach Hayes still didn't have much confidence in me as a passer. On some third downs, he would bring Greg in, and I thought, "Who are we fooling now?"

I was really coach Hayes' whipping boy, and I would get it from him at least three times a day, because if you are a quarterback, you will screw up at least three times a day during practice now matter how good you are. He would leave me in tears, but I knew Coach loved me, because his confidence in me grew as I got older. We knew Archie was his favorite, and Archie wouldn't practice until Thursday of each week, because he was so banged up. But it didn't matter how beat up I was; I had to practice. I guess coach Hayes just figured the more work I got, the better I got.

During the Iowa game I had jammed my right thumb, and it was hurting during that 10–10 tie with Michigan. I threw one pass that day and we ran it all day. In the Rose Bowl, I threw an interception on the first play of the game, and I was scared to go by coach Hayes, but the coaches said, "That one was our fault—we called the wrong formation." We went right back out and threw that pass again and we started clicking. That turned into a great day for us. [Greene was named the game's MVP in a 42–21 win over USC.]

I went back home for a few weeks after that season, and they retired my high school jersey. They gave me the key to the city and called it "Cornelius Greene Day." On that day, the naysayers couldn't recall telling me not to go to Ohio State.

We had a lot of expectations for that '74 team, but the Michigan State loss was just devastating. We had the game in control and then gave up two big touchdowns. We drove down to the half-yard line and had 26 seconds left, but Champ [Henson] misread the hole and ran up the lineman's back. We had time to get off one more play, but they wouldn't let our guys up. After the game, when the Big Ten commissioner came in there and told us the loss was final, Woody ripped him up one side and down the other. Then he said, "Let's go to their locker room and kick their ass." I remember seeing Ray Griffin grab his helmet and head out the door—he was ready to go. It was the only regular-season game we ever lost in my four years.

That next year at Michigan, we were undefeated and everything was on the line. We were behind 14–7 and faced a third-and-11 or -12. What I remember is on the play before, I had scrambled around our own end zone and threw one up deep, and the ball was batted up into the air and finally fell down to the turf. If that pass would have been intercepted, we would have lost.

Before this third-down play, I got the group together and said, "This prayer is for the believers." We got our hands together and prayed. I didn't do it for us to win the ballgame; I did it to bring us back together as a unit. Then I called "84 barb," a play that called for a receiver wide right to run a streak pattern and for Brian to run an out pattern underneath. We got it for the first down, and Brian got the wind knocked out of him. Then we went right down the field and scored. Ray Griffin got the big interception and took it down to the 3, and we scored again to win the game.

I was being interviewed on TV after the game, and I gave all the credit to the Lord, and I couldn't believe the fan mail I got after that. People were telling me that it had changed their lives. That just blew me away.

After that season, we went to vote on the MVP for the team, and Woody started the meeting off by saying, "We will elect Archie again as the MVP, and it will be the first time that anybody has won it three straight years." Then Lenny Willis raised his hand and said he thought Cornelius Greene deserved it, and then somebody else suggested another player, so that forced the vote. It turned out that I had won the team vote by only one vote, and Archie had voted for me because that's the kind of guy he is.

The Big Ten team submitted all of their team MVPs, and the conference MVP was selected from that pool. Anytime you can be the MVP of a team, that is special, but to be the MVP of a team that includes the greatest player in the history of college football is something unbelievable. One thing I always did . . . I knew what it was like to be a freshman and not play. So when the freshmen came in, I made them feel welcome and helped them out, so I probably got a lot of sympathy votes from the freshmen.

I have no regrets at all. I couldn't have had a better college career or made a better group of friends. I am a die-hard Buckeye fan, and today when my son mentions Ohio State, he says "we." Ohio State and the state of Ohio mean so much to me because of the love and support they gave me. When I go back for reunions, I am always the next-to-last to be introduced ahead of Archie, and I always receive good applause, and that feels very good. Archie's name and number are up there on that stadium now, and that means a lot to all of his teammates.

I feel our class at Ohio State left a solid legacy there, and I am proud to be part of it.

195

Cornelius Greene, a three-year starter at quarterback during which Ohio State had a 31–3–1 record, was selected as the Big Ten's Most Valuable Player in 1975.

ARCHIE GRIFFIN

1972–1975

I GREW UP IN COLUMBUS, and I had always liked the Buckeyes, but heading into my senior year of high school at Columbus Eastmoor, I really thought I would attend college at the U.S. Naval Academy or Northwestern. When Ohio State started to recruit me, I admit I was very excited. One day after wrestling practice, my wrestling coach handed me the phone. Woody Hayes was on the other end of the line. He wanted to have dinner and talk, so we went to the Jai Lai restaurant and talked for a long time. I remember being very excited about the opportunity and the possibility of going to The Ohio State University, but after the dinner was over, I wasn't so sure they wanted me. Coach Hayes hadn't said a thing to me about football—he talked only about getting a college education.

I also visited Michigan, and it was right after Bo had his heart attack. He was at home in bed, and I liked him because he was so much like Woody. But once I realized Ohio State was still interested in me, I knew it was the right place for me. Another factor was that I had a brother at Kent State and a brother at Louisville, and I thought I would make it easier on my folks if I stayed closer to home.

It didn't dawn on me until the end of my senior year in high school that, for the first time in a long time, freshmen would become eligible that next season, but my only goal at that time was to make the varsity.

Once I was on campus, I realized how much bigger and faster the guys were than in high school. What I really remember was training that summer for the mile run. The running backs had to do it in five minutes and 45

196

seconds, and I could never make it. I tried all summer, but shoot, I couldn't get down there. It really troubled me. So we got out there that first day of practice, and I ran a five 30-something. I thought I had really done something, and then the varsity came in and I saw this big linebacker named Randy Gradishar run it in 5:15. Man alive, I couldn't believe a big guy could run that fast.

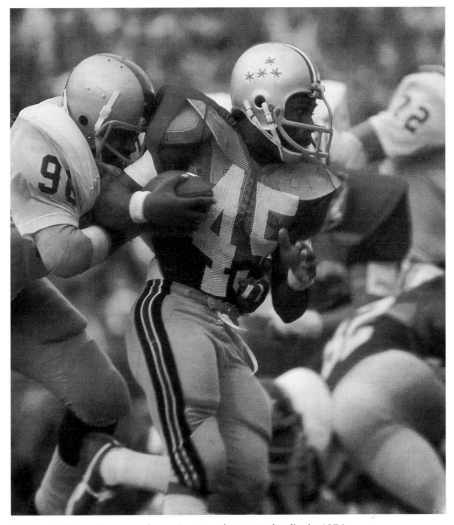

Archie Griffin rolls up yards against Southern Methodist in 1974.

I didn't know at all if I was going to play that season. I was on the scout squad, and I did pretty well during that first scrimmage, but I had no idea of where I stood. When the varsity went to the hotel before that first game against Iowa, we stayed in the dorm. So in that first game, we got to beating Iowa pretty good, and some of the freshmen got to play late in the game. I was really excited, knowing this was my shot to show them what I could do. I was thinking about breaking a long run and scoring a touchdown. They called "18 sweep" . . . to the right side. I had wondered if the holes would be there for me the way they had been all day. As the play developed, I was shocked, because there was this gaping hole in front of me. On that play, I did something fundamentally wrong—I kept my eyes on that hole and never looked back at the football, which hit me right in the hands and bounced off. I had fumbled on my first play.

That was it for me for that day—I got taken out and didn't get another carry. I really felt like I had blown my chance, and I had prayed hard just to get another opportunity. I still practiced very hard and did everything I was supposed to do that next week, but I wondered.

In the second game, North Carolina blocked a punt to go ahead of us 7–0 midway through the first quarter. At that point, somebody called my name on the bench, and I knew I was the only "Griffin" on the team, so I figured that they must have meant me. But I was so shocked that I almost went in the game without my helmet.

Thank goodness, I was in a daze that day. I really was. The guys later told me that my eyes were as big as saucers in the huddle. Next thing I knew, they were announcing over the PA system that I had rushed for a record [239 yards on 27 carries, which set an OSU and Ohio Stadium record at the time]. I really had no idea.

Things did change for me somewhat after that game. I heard what they were saying on TV that night, and I heard it on the radio when I went out on a date. I just tried not to let it affect me. I knew I was still a freshman. I was still a student-athlete, and I had my responsibilities to practice hard, go to class, and do the things I was supposed to do.

Off the field, the guys were just great. I lived in Smith Hall at the time, and we had a lot of fun. Everybody has heard that story about Big Ed Trepanier holding me out of the window there. It was really only the 3rd or 4th floor, not the 10th or 11th as the story goes, and he had me by the ankles when I told him, "Big Ed, whatever you do, don't drop me!"

The following season, I really felt like I was in a flow. I remember walking down the hallway one day after playing Wisconsin, and I had a pretty good game, and Woody was walking the other way toward me. I just said, "Hi, Coach," and he looked at me and said, "Damn it, you are the best damn back in the country. Damn it, yes you are."

And he continued on walking. That really made me feel good. I thought, "Wow, I know this guy really cares about me, and I am going to play my heart out for him."

It was a great season for us, and we won them all until we got to Michigan. That 10–10 tie really felt like a loss, at least for 24 hours, until they announced they had picked us to go back to the Rose Bowl. The year before, USC had just killed us, and we all wanted another chance at them.

That's why to this day that 1974 Rose Bowl remains one of *the* most satisfying, if not the most satisfying, games of my career. We redeemed ourselves and put it to them pretty good [42–21].

That season, we had put three players in the top six of the Heisman balloting. John Hicks had finished second, I was fifth, and Randy Gradishar was sixth. So the following year, people continued to remind me that I was a Heisman candidate. I tired to put all that talk aside and tried to do the best I could for our team, because I wanted to contribute and win a national championship. They held the Heisman ceremony so much different from what they do now. After that season, the Downtown Athletic Club called the sports information office on a Monday, and they told me I needed to catch a plane for a Tuesday press conference. I figured all the candidates would be there, but when I got to New York, I found out that I was the only guy there and they announced me as the Heisman winner. I was very happy and delighted about the whole thing, but I guess it didn't really sink in. I came back home and then had to return that Friday with my family. There was a Sunday night dance and then the presentation on that Monday.

When we got there that weekend, Malcolm McCloud of the Downtown Athletic Club had told me how emotional the presentation can be. John Cappelletti had won the year before, and as everybody knows, he dedicated it to his dying brother, Joey. Everybody was crying. Anyway, Malcolm told me, "Don't worry if you get up there and cry. It will be all right."

Well, I wasn't that type. I didn't know what he was talking about. I just couldn't see myself crying up there. So I got up to give my speech, and what did I do? I couldn't get out 10 words before I started crying. I looked out at

199

Griffin poses with the famed trophy that he won twice.

200

the audience and everybody out there was crying. I was sort of embarrassed, but I got through it.

My roommates were Steve Luke and Cornelius Greene, and when I got back home, they really let me have it. One of them said, "Great speech . . . but did you have to cry?"

The next year, I have to say that I was more prepared and I didn't break down.

That '75 team . . . now we had a team there. I think we were picked to finish about third in the Big Ten heading into that season, and I remember that
was the first spring we didn't prepare for Michigan—we prepared for Michigan State. They had beaten us up there the year before on that controversial
finish when we found out the outcome 45 minutes after the game had ended.
I still believe we scored on that final play, and I know that they were lying on
our center and wouldn't let him up so we could get the snap off.

But we opened against them in '75 and played very well [a 21–0 win at
Michigan State]. We rolled through that season, until we came to the Michigan game and fell behind 14–7 late in the game.

I really remember Cornelius calling us together in the huddle before that
final series, and he just said, "Let us pray—God, give us the strength to be
our best." We knew this was a big series and it was our last shot. He hit that
pass to Brian [Baschnagel], then I had a decent run, and we got it down there
and scored to tie it up. And Ray [Griffin] picked off that pass to put us in
position to go ahead. That was a great, great win for us. In those four years,
I am proud to say that we never lost to Michigan.

We had beaten UCLA so badly earlier in the season, so for that '76 Rose
Bowl, we were trying to guard against overconfidence. It was the fourth year
in a row that we had been out there. We all knew the ropes of the game and
what led up to it. That day, we moved the ball up and down the field, but we
just didn't score. We let them hang around, and when you do that, they are
going to think they can beat you. That's what happened.

That was my final game and the most disappointing loss I ever experienced. Period. We all thought we were good enough to be national champions that year, but we never got one. That game really hurt.

I got my degree in March of '76, a quarter early, and Woody Hayes was
there. He really liked it when one of us got our degree, and he always made
it known when one of us graduated. I felt I could go in and talk to him about
anything, and I stayed close to him over the years. The final time I saw coach
Hayes we made plans to have lunch, because I wanted him to meet my wife,
Bonita. But we never got to do that. I was driving to work on March 12,
1987, when I heard that he had died. I just turned around, went back to my
house, and sat down for a while. Then I went into the bathroom and cried.

There isn't a day that goes by—and I mean not ONE day—that I don't
think of Woody Hayes or my father. Not one day. He was very, very good to
me. He was a very special person.

Being at Ohio State, playing in the state of Ohio for my entire career, and now working here, the tradition we have gets in your blood and remains there. When you see "Script Ohio," or when that band comes down the ramp to enter the stadium, it makes the hair on your back stand up. I was born at University Hospital, I grew up here, and I played my football here. It's unlike any other place in the world—it's such a special place.

I know I was meant to be a Buckeye.

Archie Griffin, the only two-time winner of the Heisman Trophy, played seven seasons with the Cincinnati Bengals. He finished his Ohio State career with 5,589 rushing yards and an NCAA-record 34 100-yard rushing games. He also was one of six three-time All-Americans to play at Ohio State. A member of the College Football Hall of Fame, he was named president of the Ohio State Alumni Association in June 2003.

JOHN HICKS

1970, 1972–1973

NINETEEN HUNDRED AND SEVENTY-FOUR was my rookie year with the New York Giants, and we were playing the Kansas City Chiefs. After the game, a tackle for the Chiefs, Jim Tyrer, who had been in the league for years, came running over and hugged me. "You played a great game," he said.

That year, Doug Van Horn was one of our captains, and I took his place as the starting right guard. He wasn't mad. Generally, veterans don't have a lot to do with rookies, but Doug made it a point to look after me and help me through my rookie season. He took me under his wing and we became lifelong friends.

You know what Jim and Doug had in common? They, like me, were Buckeyes.

If you walk into the Woody Hayes Athletic Center today, you realize the depth of Ohio State's tradition. There have been 18 College Hall of Famers, more than 110 All-Americans, and several Heisman Trophy winners. There are too many great players to mention, but when I meet any one of them, it is like meeting one of your teammates. It's hard to explain, but that's the way it feels.

I won't forget my official recruiting trip to Ohio State. It was the Michigan game in 1968, and the Buckeyes won 50–14 and won the national championship that year. Seeing the band, the crowd, and the team in those scarlet and gray uniforms running onto the field . . . it was the greatest experience of my life.

Coach Hayes later met me and asked, "How would you like to be a Buck-eye?" I thought I was living a dream.

From that day I first accepted the offer, my life changed. I was a Buckeye, sure, but I really didn't know what that meant at that time.

When you play for Ohio State, you know you are special. I realized that as time went on. I remember after our freshmen orientation when coach Hayes met with us, he seemed to be like a stately grandfather and not the crazy general that everyone made him out to be.

The team was the defending national champions, and I was scared when I walked into the Biggs Facility that first day. I started out as the third-team tackle and the third-team guard, and the freshmen coaches really went after us that first day. After the first workout, I remember sitting at my locker next to Merv Teague. I turned and said, "I can't leave because I don't want to go back to the steel mill where I worked during the summer." Merv was from Youngstown and he also had worked at the steel mill and we bonded from that day forward. That was the last workout I had at Ohio State where I was third-team.

204

We played two freshman games that year. Remember, freshmen weren't eligible to play varsity back then. In our first game at Indiana, we were so excited we couldn't wait. The field was a mess that day, but what an experi-ence. We beat Indiana 19–7 and we were feeling pretty good about ourselves. When we came home, nobody would speak to us. Coach Hayes said we were the worst freshman team he had ever had. [Defensive coordinator] Lou McCullough had threatened to take our scholarships from us. And the var-sity? Those guys just ignored us.

The varsity was beating people by 30 points or more, and they finally told us that our win was not good enough to be a Buckeye. We got the message.

We worked harder after that first game, and we had another game against Ohio University coming up. Coach Hayes and coach Bill Hess at Ohio U. had been friends. Coach Hess used to coach at Ohio State with coach Hayes, and he always had wanted coach Hayes to schedule a game at Ohio State, but coach Hayes refused because of the risk of losing to a state school. So coach Hayes agreed that if Ohio University's freshmen played well against Ohio State, then he would reconsider scheduling a varsity game.

The week before the Ohio U. game was like Michigan week. Our fresh-man coach, John Mummey, had the varsity players come in and talk to us. Jack Tatum came in. Now Jack didn't say much to anybody, so we thought,

Tackle John Hicks had the size, strength, and mobility to become a two-time All-American.

"Wow, this must be a big game." We played the game on a Friday before a home game, and coach Hayes came out to give us our pregame speech, and the varsity showed up to watch the game. We won 56–7.

About halfway through the game, I saw coach Hayes walking back to his office, and I later found out he had placed a call to his friend to tell him that we were beating his team so bad, and not to ever call him about scheduling a game again.

At the start of my sophomore year, I had earned the starting right tackle position. I thought I was going to be nervous about my first start, in our first game against Texas A&M at Ohio Stadium. But as the week progressed, I felt like a veteran. Coach Hayes asked me how I felt, and I said I was ready to play. We beat Texas A&M 56–13. We kept winning every week. Finally, Michigan week was here. The town exploded. Michigan was undefeated. We were undefeated. Playing for the title. We had the revenge factor, and the Rose Bowl was the prize. Everyone was so uptight, but I felt relaxed. We won 20–9 and coach Hayes later told me that I had played a great game. That was the first time I had played on a championship team.

The next season was a nightmare. I got hurt in summer practice and had to have a knee operation, which knocked me out for the season. We went 6–4. I went crazy that year. I was hurt and we were losing. The next year, 1972, was the first year that the freshmen could play varsity, and we had some pretty good freshmen like Archie Griffin, Corny Greene, Brian Baschnagel, and Tim Fox.

In our second game, we were playing a pretty good North Carolina team that had gone undefeated the year before. We were losing, and the North Carolina players were saying we couldn't block too well. They were feeling they were going to beat us. A new chapter in Ohio State history was written that day. Archie Griffin ran for a stadium and Ohio State record of 239 yards, and we came back to win big. About halfway through the third quarter, I told the North Carolina players that they couldn't tackle too well. We finished that year by beating Michigan but losing to USC 42–17 in the Rose Bowl.

I would have been drafted by the pros, but I felt I wanted to play one more year and settle the Southern California score. So I decided to accept a redshirt season and play in 1973. We were loaded, and we knew we were a great team. It was one of the greatest teams I had ever played on. We steamrolled our way through the season. Michigan was undefeated, too. We tied 10–10 and it was one of the toughest games I had ever played in. I figured our season was over. Well, as everyone knows, the Big Ten picked us to represent the conference in the Rose Bowl. The Big Ten had a four-game losing streak in the Rose Bowl, and they wanted a win. We had promised coach Hayes that when we got back to the Rose Bowl, we would win the game for him. We did, 42–21, beating Southern California, and coach Hayes told us it was one of his greatest wins ever.

I finished my playing career 28–3–1, with three Big Ten championships and one Rose Bowl win, and I was the first player in the history of the Big Ten to have played in three Rose Bowls.

There are other things I remember most about playing at Ohio State:

After each game, coach Hayes would meet and speak to our families. Anne Hayes would go to the French Field House before the games and speak to them. She knew everything about every family—whether a family member had died or if there was a graduation or a birth.

It was a family.

In the locker room, coach Hayes always told us that the finest people we would ever meet would be in this room. You know what? He was right. Those teammates I had on those teams are the greatest people I have ever met. We were not a team just on the football field. We became a team for life.

Although we don't always see each other a lot anymore as we grow older, you know that we are there for each other and we will always love each other. We were and still are all Buckeyes.

John Hicks, who became the 18th Buckeye inducted into the College Football Hall of Fame, played four seasons with the New York Giants.

VIC KOEGEL

1971–1973

WHEN I THINK OF WOODY HAYES and how he became so successful, I think it started with his recruiting. He was a tireless worker, and he didn't ever want to be outrecruited or outworked by anybody. My road to Ohio State is a perfect illustration. When I was a senior at Cincinnati Moeller, I had narrowed my choices to Ohio State and Notre Dame. Woody came down to recruit me and made three visits to my house. He went out to dinner with my parents, and I remember him ordering that bananas dish for dessert—the one with the fire flaming from the bananas. It was the first time I ever saw that. I had never been out to dinner at a restaurant like this, either. But Woody was the kind of guy who wanted to get to know your family first.

So I went on my trip to Notre Dame, and I had not yet met with Ara Parseghian. I arrived on a Friday, and the first I saw him was on Sunday. I went into his office, and as I sat there he never looked up. He was reading this big pile of paper—my press clippings. He didn't say anything for about three minutes. Then he asked me, "Are you coming to Notre Dame?"

I told him, "I don't know right now. I want to take another look at Ohio State."

He said, "Well, let me know when you are ready to sign with Notre Dame."

And that was it. I thought, "You have to be kidding me." I spent no more than 10 minutes in that office and that was what he said to me. I made the decision to go to Ohio State pretty quickly. Woody Hayes had visited my family three times, and Parseghian never did.

Years later when I was with the Bengals, one of my teammates was Doug Adams, who was three years older than me. We were talking about Woody and recruiting, and I asked him if he had ever considered Notre Dame. "That damn Parseghian," he said. "He met with me for only 10 minutes."

That's what made Woody Hayes even greater in our eyes.

I remember when I went to campus for the first time as an incoming freshman. Ohio State had signed Randy Keith, too, and my parents took me and Randy up there from Cincinnati. We got out of the car in front of the dorm, and Woody came up to us and there were several seniors there, too. Somebody said, "There's Rex over there." My mom turned around and said, "I don't see any dog over there." We had to explain to her: "Mom, that's Rex Kern—the great quarterback."

The big thing on your first night at Ohio State was that Woody would come around and we would go over our vocabulary book. He had sent it to us in the summer, and we were supposed to go through it and know all these words. He would walk in our rooms and ask, "Now, do you all have your books?" Then he would quiz us on the meaning of certain words. It was Woody's Word Power class.

My first impression of Woody on the field was him going berserk . . . just beating people up. I played for coach [Gerry] Faust at Moeller, and he would scream at you, but he wouldn't punch you. You hear the stories about Woody before you get there, but until you see it person, it is unbelievable.

In that first year, you would fear him, in the second year you would accept him, and in the third you would laugh at him—but maybe not out loud in front of him.

In one game at Minnesota, during my sophomore year, we were behind at halftime. Woody gave his speech in the locker room and ended with him saying: "Let's go out there and win this game!" He started to go out, but the door was locked. So Woody broke this glass box with a fire axe in it. He got that axe and started beating this door down with it before they stopped him. We came back to win 14–12.

That was the last game we won that year. We ended by losing three in a row—to Michigan State, Northwestern, and then the Michigan game when he tore up the sideline markers.

Woody would always do something crazy on that Thursday before the Michigan game, something to get you psyched up.

Before that Michigan game, the *Lantern* had written some article with the prediction that Michigan would beat us 60 to 0. On the back of the bus that day, I remember Kenny Luttner was reading this article. Well, Woody went berserk, and he started ripping the newspaper out of Kenny's hands. He was screaming, "They're traitors! They're traitors!" Then before the game, his pregame speech was about Benedict Arnold.

That year was a bad year for us [6–4] because we had so many injuries. It was the first year of the AstroTurf at Ohio Stadium, and we had so many serious knee injuries. Your foot would get caught when you would cut, or you would get hit while your foot was planted. After that, they watered it down so it wasn't so sticky. But it got me in the '72 opener against Iowa. It was a bad injury, but I played through the first six games before it popped out for good and I had surgery.

The second game, against North Carolina, was the game Archie broke out [239 yards], but what is forgotten is that my roommate, Elmer Lippert, ran for more than 100 yards that day.

I ended up starting for all of my three seasons, except for those final five games in my junior year because of my knee injury. That is the one thing about Woody—when he gave you a shot, you had better be ready. If you made mistakes, you might never get in again. But he always gave everyone at least one chance. I got my first chance as a sophomore when Randy Gradishar injured his thumb.

The highlight had to be the Rose Bowl win over USC at the end of my senior season. They had beaten us 42–17 the year before, and we wanted to redeem ourselves. It was tied 21–21, and the defense wasn't playing well at all. I remember Woody went berserk on the sideline and punched Arnie Jones and Arnie punched him back. But [defensive coordinator] George Hill had a good game plan. He would drop our ends—Van DeCree and Jim Cope—into coverage, and it confused Pat Haden. Haden would drop back and see four linebackers there. We shut them down after that and beat them 42–21.

After the game, I told Woody, "Thanks for a great four years." He said it was the best win he had ever had. That team was good enough to win the national title, but we had that 10–10 tie at Michigan.

Vic Koegel (No. 62) chases the quarterback during the 60–0 win over Northwestern in 1973.

I really believe that when they won the Fiesta Bowl, and the 2002 national title, it was a victory for anybody who ever wore the scarlet and gray. We all took it personally—all the great players who have come through Ohio State. Just take a look at Woody's teams after 1968—almost any one of them could have won the national championship but didn't. So it was long overdue that we got one in 2002.

It was a proud moment for that team, but it was a proud moment for any of us who ever played football at Ohio State.

Vic Koegel, who as a sophomore led the 1971 team in tackles with 126, was an All–Big Ten linebacker in '73.

KEN KUHN

1972–1975

When it came time for me to decide on where to attend college and play football, it wasn't difficult. My older brother Dick was part of the great sophomore class of 1968 that went on to be national champions at Ohio State. My oldest sister, Pat, had married her high school sweetheart, Mark Stier, who was a linebacker and voted the Most Valuable Player of the '68 team.

In 1971, Dick had become a graduate assistant coach for the Buckeyes when I made a visit to Michigan. Bo Schembechler was very convincing that I should not follow in the footsteps of my brother and brother-in-law. I came home and told my family I was thinking of becoming a Wolverine. My dad said, "It's up to you." Well, word got to Woody Hayes. He called my brother into his office and threatened to fire him and not pay for his tuition for his final year if his brother did not become a Buckeye. All these years later, my brother maintains Woody was joking when he mentioned firing him.

Well, it had no effect on me anyway, but I became a Buckeye. I am glad I did.

The friendships I made with some of the greatest guys in the world have lasted now for more than 30 years. We were Big Ten champions four years in a row. My teammates, such as John Hicks, George Hasenohrl, Rich Galbos, Randy Gradishar, Rick Middleton, Neal Colzie, Van DeCree, Champ Henson, Pete Cusick, Doug Plank, Archie Griffin, Cornelius Greene, Brian Baschnagel, Pete Johnson, Tim Fox, Ray Griffin, Craig Cassady, Nick Buonamici, Aaron Brown, Steve Myers, Ted Smith, Tom

Ken Kuhn pressures the quarterback against Michigan State in 1975.

Skladany, Chris Ward, Tom Cousineau, Bill Lukens, Ed Thompson, Pat Curto, Bob Brudzinksi, and one of my best friends, Louis Paul Pietrini— "Big Lou"—are people I will never forget.

We had a guy on defense named Big Ed Trepanier. He benched 550 pounds and had a massive upper body, and he was wild looking with his helmet on. He played defensive tackle and he really helped make John Hicks the offensive legend he is today. Anyway, we were practicing one day before the season and it was second-team defense against the first-team offense. We always tried to stop Woody's offense, because we knew he would lose it if we did.

So he kept trying to run a play at Big Ed and me, and we kept stopping it. He'd run it and we'd stuff it. He'd run it and we'd stuff it. Well, here came Woody and he pushed the offensive linemen out of the way to get to Ed. He started beating Ed on the helmet with his clipboard and screaming at him. Ed just looked at him and started giggling as only Ed could. That made Woody hotter, and he punched Ed in the chest. Problem was, he hit his hand on the chest plate of the pads, and I thought Woody broke his hand. I saw tears coming out of his eyes as he threw his hat on the ground and kicked it. Then he yelled, "All right, damn it, 'Robust,'" which was our power offense.

As everyone knows, our freshman class—Archie, Brian Baschnagel, Tim Fox, Corny—was special and it was the first year of freshmen eligibility since the 1950s. The biggest play I made my freshman season, we were being beaten by Minnesota right before halftime and they were driving. They ran a play-action pass, hoping to hit the tight end across the middle. I read it perfectly and snatched my first career interception. I almost went all the way but was tripped up by their quarterback, preventing me from making what would have been my only touchdown at OSU. We went on to win, and I had 18 solo tackles. At the awards team meeting, Woody asked, "Ken Kuhn, how old are you?" I answered, "18." Then he asked, "How many solo tackles did you make Saturday?" I replied, "18, Coach." It was a memorable day.

It wasn't always memorable. As the old saying goes, I wish I knew then what I know now. I wish then I had not tried to be a character that deep down inside I am not. I came from a good home with good moral beliefs, and it was easy to give in to peer pressure. At that time, there was a lot of drinking and partying and ways to get into trouble, and I followed that path at times. It is the one regret I have.

215

Without a doubt the greatest player I ever played with was Archie. He was a champion on the field, but he will always be a true friend to me and someone whom all of his teammates and associates can look to for leadership as a great ambassador for The Ohio State University. He is truly one of a kind.

At the end of the Michigan rivalry, my class had three pairs of gold pants and also had that 10–10 tie [in 1973].

I think that after Woody and Earle Bruce, the program lost touch with the importance of beating Michigan. I am not saying coach Cooper was not a great coach or person. He was both, but I think coming from outside of Ohio and not being born and raised a Buckeye were disadvantages for him. I have the highest respect for him, but something was missing. Now with Jim Tressel, it is apparent that the Buckeye tradition is alive and well and in all of its glory. I tell everyone he is like Woody—a hard worker who cares about family and tradition. I believe that Jim will be the coach that future coaches will be judged by.

You can say I always have been and always will be a Buckeye. We are a family, a brotherhood, and a fraternity unlike any I've ever experienced. We have the best coaches, administrators, fans, the best damn band in the land, and the largest worldwide alumni association. In closing, I am sure glad I did not become a Wolverine!

Ken Kuhn, a linebacker, was named a team captain in 1975.

JEFF LOGAN

1974–1977

I BELIEVE THAT THE EXPERIENCE OF PLAYING FOOTBALL at Ohio State, while easily documented by wins and losses, statistics, bowl games, and rings, is an ever-growing one. Life experiences today continue to magnify the lessons we learned while playing football at the highest level in college, so this is not something that has yet been achieved but something that continues to grow in each of us.

My experience is unique in that my father played for Woody Hayes in his first year of coaching at Ohio State in 1951. From the very first moment of being considered by Ohio State, I wanted to become a Buckeye.

I was concerned whether I was good enough to be part of the very best, and that led me to look at football programs all over the country. I wanted to play the game I loved, and if at all possible I wanted to do it with the very best. And that was Ohio State.

During recruiting, it became obvious to me that I probably belonged in Division I football due to the interest I was receiving. I eventually convinced myself that all of these coaches could not be wrong, even though most people in my community were concerned that I would get lost at a big school.

Immediate playing opportunities at other Division I schools were tempting, and the emergence of Archie Griffin as the best to ever play the college game was daunting for a guy who played the same position. Was I willing to sit back and learn for two years until Archie graduated? I was not even giving consideration to the other excellent running backs already at Ohio State.

In the end, it was the desire to play in the Rose Bowl that was my determining factor in choosing Ohio State. I would have loved to play for Joe Paterno at Penn State, or Lee Corso at Indiana, or even Pepper Rodgers at Georgia Tech, but I could not suppress my intense desire to do it with the very best.

Fortunately, I made the right decision, not because I later became a starter and cocaptain, but because I was given the gift of the great tradition at Ohio State.

One of our greatest traditions unique to Ohio State is the awarding of the gold pants to players on a team that beats Michigan. In my time, we were 2–2 against Michigan, and therefore I own two pairs of gold pants that I consider irreplaceable.

One year I was asked to speak to the team during the week before the Michigan game, and I recall having my son Critter join me at the podium. When I completed my speech, I hoisted Critter to the top of the podium and asked him to show them what they were playing for. He reached into his shirt and showed off a pair of gold pants that were hanging from a necklace. Since that day, Critter has worn that necklace each year during Michigan week.

I maintain that we have something very special here, something only those who have been on the inside can know and understand. My guess is that most players who played for Michigan, Nebraska, USC, and the like have had similar experiences, but I will never know for sure.

What I do know is that they do not have what I have, and that is the gift of the great tradition that is Ohio State football.

You see, we at Ohio State realize we live under the shade of trees that we did not plant and we drink from the wells that we did not dig. Our opportunity, however, is our responsibility. We must recognize the gift and carry it on for the future generations of recruits who come to Ohio State.

My experience as the president of the Varsity "O" Alumni Association gave me another great chance to "pay forward," as coach Hayes used to say. It was through this position and the circumstances at hand that I was asked by [OSU athletic director] Andy Geiger to serve as a member of the head football coach search committee in January of 2001.

The selection of Jim Tressel to take over the gift was an easy one in the end, because we all knew that he knew what it meant to be a member of this particular family we have at Ohio State. He learned it from those who came

Jeff Logan, here before the Michigan State game in 1976, succeeded Archie Griffin at tailback.

before him—his father and coach Hayes. Our gift and the future of this gift is certainly in good hands, and there are always hundreds of us out there to ensure it is taken care of in exactly the right way.

Many people confuse tradition with the bricks and mortar that make up the buildings at this great institution we call Ohio State. While there are landmarks such as Ohio Stadium on the banks of the Olentangy River and the Oval, those serve only as points of reference to me when I look back on the experience of attending Ohio State and being a member of four Big Ten championship teams.

The memories of running out onto the field at Ohio Stadium for the first and last times are memories that no one else can own, unless they were one of the lucky few to wear that scarlet and gray uniform. The fans will always be remembered for their immense loyalty, and they are a big part of our tradition.

Woody Hayes always told us that the best friends and friendships that we would make would be our teammates, and he could not have been more accurate. While each of us has moved on to new lives after Ohio State football, the camaraderie of seeing a teammate at homecoming, at a reunion, or in the Varsity "O" Club room before a game is priceless. This is bigger than the concrete of Ohio Stadium and 100,000-plus screaming fans. I think we who were there to play the game and those lucky enough to get there in the future understand that this tradition of being a Buckeye is not something that you can kick or carry. This is what makes it so priceless.

Jeff Logan rushed for 1,248 yards in 1976 and was named a captain in '77.

CALVIN MURRAY

1977–1980

I BELIEVE THAT EVERY DIVISION I SCHOOL IN THE NATION recruited me, but I chose Ohio State because coach Hayes recruited my whole family. Ohio State was the only school to put me in the dorms and not a five-star hotel during recruiting, and that impressed me. Plus, the seniors had four Big Ten championship rings on their fingers, and I wanted one of those. They told me, "If you want one of these rings, you come to OSU."

So I chose the Buckeyes over Tennessee and Notre Dame.

Playing football at Ohio State changed my life in so many ways.

For example, I will never forget when it was a very hot day and we were complaining about our legs hurting. After practice, coach Hayes told us to get on the bus, and he took us to Children's Hospital. There, we saw many children with serious burns and incurable diseases, and yet many of them had smiles on their faces. It taught us that we needed to be thankful that God has given us the opportunity to play sports and to appreciate the things we did have.

Another example of how Ohio State changed my life is that I realized when you go to college, you get two educations—one with books and one with people. If you fail with people, you will fail in getting your education. Coach Hayes was the best at teaching that.

I remember in one team meeting, all the black athletes sat on one side and all the whites sat on the other side. Coach Hayes did not say a word, but for the next meeting, we all had assigned seats—black, white, black, white. Then

Calvin Murray slashes through a hole during the 1979 season opener, against Syracuse—Earle Bruce's first game as head coach.

he told us that we were divided and that no team could go to war if they were not united as one.

Coach Hayes did not believe in racism, and he knew that we had to be a family to succeed.

My favorite teammates were a lot of players, but the ones who were above the rest were Leon Ellison and Vince Skillings. I could tell so many stories about all the good times we had together. Because of Leon and Vince, my years at Ohio were some of the best times in my life. We all had one thing in common: Yeshua [Hebrew for Jesus] as Lord of our lives.

We went to the movies, played basketball, watched TV, made fun of each other, studied the word of God together, did Word Power together [this was coach Hayes' so-called freshman English class, which started at 6:00 A.M.], did study table, and cried and laughed together. We were the three musketeers, and no one could break our friendship. We still get together and keep in touch today.

Coach Hayes believed in team unity and that all of us [players and coaches] had to take showers together. It was a game to see who was going to wash coach Hayes' back. If we knew when he was coming, we wouldn't tell the last few guys in the shower, so that one of them would end up washing his back.

223

The game that I remember the most was the Rose Bowl against USC—January 1, 1980. If we had won this game, we would have been national champs. Everyone figured USC would whip us because of all the All-Americans they had—guys like Marcus Allen, Charles White, Anthony Munoz, Joey Browner, Chip Banks, and Ronnie Lott. As everyone knows, it ended with a 17–16 loss.

Another game I will never forget was when we beat the team up North in '79. I beat them only one time, and it was one the best times of my life. I remember sitting in the locker room at Michigan Stadium and coach Bruce was getting us ready. I could hear the best band in the land marching down through the tunnel onto the field. They got my spirits so high I couldn't wait to get at the Wolverines. It was the first game in which we scored a touchdown in their stadium in four years. What a great feeling!

The play I remember the most was my 86-yard reception from Art Schlichter against Washington State in '79. It remains the longest pass play in OSU history.

Watching the 2002 team win the national title brought back some bittersweet feelings, only because of our lost chance to be national champs. It still hurts today.

Coach Jim Tressel has done a great job, and he has brought back the feeling of family within the Ohio State program. We have the greatest fan support, band, and city—Columbus bleeds scarlet and gray. I am proud of where the football program has been and where it is headed, and I hope that the young men who wear the scarlet and gray will keep our family name clean.

I realize that when you travel to other states, there are true Buckeye fans everywhere, and I am proud to this day that I was the captain of the 1980 team and to realize that Ohioans always love you no matter how long ago you played at Ohio State.

I made the right decision to be a Buckeye!

Calvin Murray rushed for 2,576 yards in his career, ninth on Ohio State's all-time list.

LOU PIETRINI

1974–1976

Looking back after 30 years, I see that attending The Ohio State University as a student-athlete was one the best decisions I've made in my life. Having the opportunity to attend and graduate from one of the finest universities in the country and play football under one of the greatest coaches of all time gave me the foundation I needed for the rest of my life.

When I reported to camp my freshman year, one of the measurements we faced was a test to see if we could run a six-minute mile. I had trained most of the summer for it, and yet when it came time to do it I couldn't quite make it. I was about 200 yards from finishing when I collapsed. One of my teammates came running over to me and helped me up to finish. It turned out to be Ken Kuhn, another freshman.

Ever since that day we have become the best of friends.

I came to Ohio State from Milford, Connecticut, because I wanted to play the best level of football as close to home as possible and still get a good education. Of course, having the opportunity to play for one of the greatest coaches in the history of the game didn't hurt either.

Coach Hayes would never accept anything less than your best performance. If he didn't feel you were performing to the best of your ability, he had his own special way of letting you know—like a good roundhouse to the midsection. You knew as an offensive lineman that if you missed a block it was coming. Needless to say, it was deserved. People always ask me, "What was it like to play for Woody?" or "How about when he hit that guy from Clemson?" I always tell them that those kinds of things were not the real Woody.

Yes, he would rant and rave on the sideline and rip his shirt or break his glasses at practice, yet I always thought that all of that stuff was for show. Woody cared about his coaches and players and felt they were his family. People who did not know him would not see the time he spent visiting children's hospitals or other patients.

One of the best Woody stories that I heard was a few years ago at our 25th reunion of our 1975 team. Former assistant George Hill told us that after beating Michigan that year, Woody was given an armful of roses as he entered the arrival gate, signifying our upcoming trip to the Rose Bowl. When he left the airport, the first place he went was to Riverside Hospital. He took all those roses and passed them out to patients who did not have any visitors that day. I guess it was his way of paying forward. He always said you could never pay back, yet you could always pay forward by helping someone in need. I'm sure those roses uplifted the dampened spirits of the people who received them.

For me, many of life's lessons were learned on the football field at Ohio State, such as learning how to get back up after being knocked down and working together as a team toward a common goal. We had our offensive and defensive goals set for us during the preseason, and they were posted in our main meeting room and reviewed every week. Our number one goal, obviously, was to win the Big Ten and go to the Rose Bowl.

There were so many great players during the years I was at OSU that it would almost seem unfair to choose one as the greatest. Yet I don't think anyone would disagree that Archie Griffin would be a good choice. His work ethic and physical durability enabled him to achieve something that no one else has ever done. Everybody knows he won two Heisman Trophies, but what impressed me was the fact that he carried the football 35 to 40 times every week in the Big Ten and stayed in one piece. He was always a target, and the opposition was always trying to get that extra hit on him. He would take hits from all directions and bounce right back. The most impressive thing about Archie was that he was a real team player and leader who was always the first to credit his teammates. He never had the attitude that sometimes comes with being in the spotlight.

I have to say that I was truly inspired by the 2002 national championship team. They were in so many close games, and yet they always managed to find a way to win. They made the university proud, and they made the Ohio State football alumni very proud. They were just another reason we are all proud to be Buckeyes.

Lou Pietrini started at right tackle in 1976.

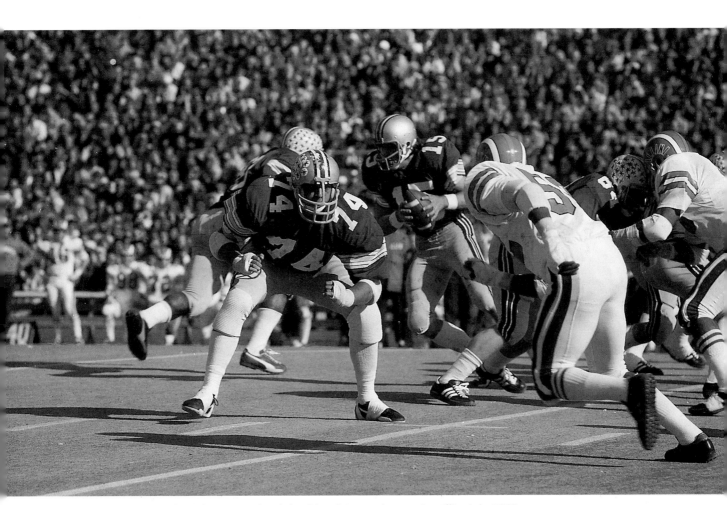

Lou Pietrini protects the right side of the pocket against Illinois in 1976.

DOUG PLANK

1972–1974

MY EXPERIENCE AT OHIO STATE was dramatic and instantaneous. Let me start by stating that my first day of summer camp was a disaster. After running a two-mile conditioning test in the morning, I coughed up my breakfast for the next 30 minutes. In the afternoon, we practiced at the stadium on AstroTurf, and I had never played on turf and was impressed by the traction. At the time, I was projected as wingback and was running the football that afternoon. On an end run, I was preparing to make a cut when I was hit from the blind side. I immediately went down on the turf and felt a sharp pain in my right knee. I did not realize it at the time, but I had torn meniscus cartilage that would float around in my knee for the next three months. I was constantly injuring the knee due to the damaged cartilage.

Finally, in November, the knee locked in place and it required surgery. During this time, I believed that several coaches and players doubted the commitment and effort I was giving. This obstacle became an opportunity for me. After the surgery, I was determined to rehab my knee and strengthen my body. The surgery convinced me to concentrate on defense because of the reduced stress on the knee. For the next few months, I listened intently to coach Woody Hayes about his philosophy of life and football. I will never forget two phrases that he constantly mentioned: "You practice the way you will play" and "The will to win is not as important as the will to prepare to win."

These two ideas became my doctrine for the remainder of my football career. I became a self-motivated player who practiced and played at game tempo every time I stepped on the football field. I was passionate to prove myself and vengeful toward anyone who was not wearing an Ohio State uniform. I treated every game and practice as if it was my last. In my desire for contact, I would hit anyone in my path.

In my career at Ohio State, I played on great teams and played behind great players. I started six games in three years because of other players' injuries. One of those starts was in Evanston, Illinois, against Northwestern during my senior season. Two Chicago Bears scouts attended that game, and I believe now that I must have played pretty well that day. The lessons I learned and the philosophy I adopted from Ohio State enabled me to take advantage when opportunity knocked. In Chicago, I became the first rookie to lead the Bears in tackles in franchise history. Every team needs players that are stars and others that fill specific roles on the team. I feel very lucky to have attended Ohio State. Whatever I gave in effort, I received much more in return with incredible memories and a fantastic wife.

One of those memories happened much later than during my playing career at Ohio State. In my last three seasons as a Buckeye, I played in three Rose Bowls. To play in the Rose Bowl was a tremendous reward for a successful season, as we all know. Many families of the players also attended the Rose Bowl game and other related activities leading up to the game. Due to the financial situation in my family, my parents could not afford the opportunity to see me play in the Rose Bowl in person. My mother was the driving force in my athletic career through high school, and I always realized that I owed her a great deal due to her love and attention to my career.

I had started in the Rose Bowl during my sophomore season against USC, and I played in each of the other two games. If I ever had a chance, I told myself that I was going to take her to a Rose Bowl game. In 1996, Ohio State won the Big Ten title and was to play Arizona State in the Rose Bowl. Because I lived in Phoenix, this was a perfect matchup for a great game as far as I was concerned.

My mom had polio when she was a child, and we struggled getting through the traffic and the crowds. We missed the warm-ups and arrived in time to see the teams take the field. My mother had a wonderful time at several Ohio State events and during the Rose Bowl parade. When she entered the stadium before the game, she was amazed at the immense crowd and anticipation for the game, but when the Ohio State team came out of the tunnel with the band playing, my mom began to cry. I looked at her and asked her if she was OK.

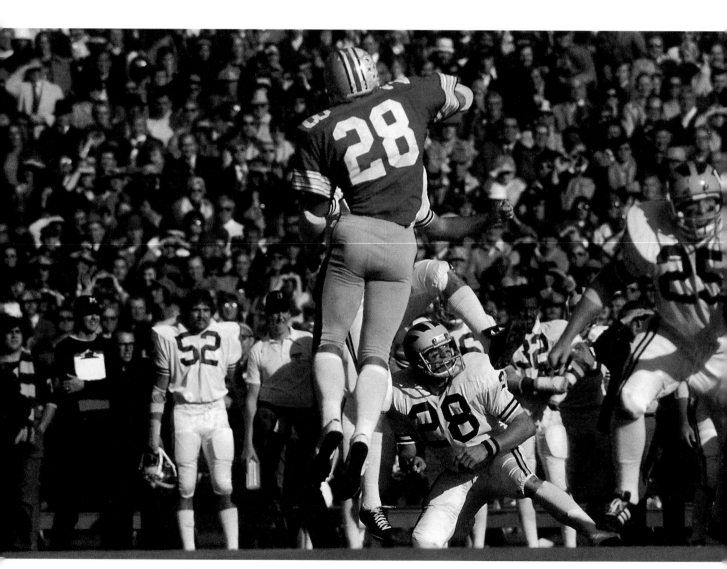

Doug Plank leaps to try to block a field goal during the 12–10 win over Michigan in 1974.

With tears in her eyes, she looked at me and said, "Doug, I wish I would have been here for you 22 years ago when you ran onto this field."

"Mom," I said, "You were here—you were in my heart!"

That day and that game—an Ohio State victory—was one of the best memories in my life.

Doug Plank was drafted in the 12th round of the 1975 draft by the Chicago Bears, for whom he played eight seasons.

231

BRUCE RUHL

1973–1976

As I was sitting in the stands in Tempe, Arizona, for the Fiesta Bowl, all those memories of why I became a Buckeye came flooding back to me. They seemed to instantly bridge the gap of those 30 years. I was from Michigan, and people always asked me, "Why did you choose Ohio State?" There were no Michigan players on the Buckeye roster at that time, and I was the first player Woody Hayes successfully recruited out of Michigan—and it was in the middle of the well-known "10-Year War" between the two schools. I became a Buckeye and a traitor.

I had established three priorities when deciding where to attend college. First, I was determined to be the first in my family to receive a college diploma. I knew that the Ohio State coaches fully supported classroom achievements, since Woody consistently graduated more than 80 percent of his players.

Second, I wanted an opportunity to play. Woody played freshmen during this era; Bo Schembechler did not. As it turned out, I was fortunate to start in a few games during my freshman year, and I played in the 1974 Rose Bowl, enjoying the big win over USC.

My third concern was to experience a quality social life. Columbus, Ohio, was all of that. Over the years, it has proved to be a great place to live and raise a family. The standard and quality of living in Columbus exceeded my expectations as I learned how the community embraces the program. I met good people and developed relationships that eventually helped me establish a career after football.

Only OSU football alumni or current players can describe the experience of running through that tunnel and onto that field for the first time. To me, it was as if I was floating on a magic carpet out to the field, while the band and the roar of the fans were our fuel. I don't recall feeling my feet hit the turf.

I have so many great memories on the field, but I will share just a few. I had three interceptions in the 1974 Wisconsin game that still stands as a school record shared with many other players. I guess it was my 15 minutes of fame. On the other side, I was the safety on the play when Michigan State's Levi Jackson ran 80 yards for the game-winning touchdown in 1974. That following season, Michigan State's plastic stadium cups featured a photo of Levi running down the sideline and OSU's No. 43 chasing. That was me.

One of my favorite assistants was Esco Sarkkinen. He had played at Ohio State in the thirties and was part of the coaching staff for decades. Esco would hold daily trivia contests on the team bus when we bused down to the stadium for practices. He would say, "Anyone with the right answers wins my orange drink." Esco also was a traditionalist. He once interrupted our ring committee meeting comprised of juniors and seniors who were engaged in designing the ring to commemorate the 1975 season. We were breaking tradition by having a gold rose on the top of the stone, instead of the "O" or "Ohio" that was usually inscribed. Esco yelled at us for messing with tradition.

Years later at Anne Hayes' funeral, I looked down at Esco's hand. He was wearing two rings—the 1968 national championship ring and the '76 Rose Bowl ring which we had designed and had broken tradition. "It was one of my favorites," he said. During his funeral, he was received while wearing those two rings and a pair of gold pants on his lapel.

Those gold pants were and still are a favorite tradition of mine. As most Buckeyes know, a player receives a gold charm when the team defeats Michigan. This tradition originated in the thirties, and being from Michigan, beating Michigan was always special for me. But defeating Michigan in 1975 at Ann Arbor for the Big Ten championship—earning another Rose Bowl berth and finishing 11–0—made that win particularly satisfying.

Everyone knows it was to Woody, too. He was somewhere between a father and grandfather figure to me. He consistently endorsed his beliefs and values to his team with passion, and although I did not always agree with him, I always respected him. I grew closer to him after he was finished

233

coaching. I think I became more than a former player; I became a friend. We met regularly and I enjoyed going over to his home to visit.

As everyone knows, Woody loved military history, and the personalities of war and the battles were often subjects of speeches on practice and game days. He took advantage of impromptu situations to embellish evil in opponents to help get us psyched up for a game. One time during a trip for an Indiana game, the Bloomington Chamber of Commerce welcomed us with a token desktop paperweight as we exited the bus. Woody encouraged us to throw the gift away. He told us to beware of smiling faces and those bearing gifts. "They are only trying to take your minds off the game and soften us up," he said.

Another time I saw him get riled up at Joe Paterno. The 1975 Penn State game was a big game, because we were undefeated and the schools had not faced each other in more than a decade. I believe Woody respected Joe Paterno because he ran a clean and honorable program. But before the game, he stormed into the locker room and repeated a conversation that he just had with Paterno. "Do you know what Joe Paterno just said to me?" he yelled. "He said, 'Woody, you're coming off that heart attack and you're working too hard; you had better take it easy.' "

"I had a notion to slap him," Woody told us. "How dare he try to soften me up!" He then went into a 15-minute unplanned speech that was one of his best. We beat Penn State 17–9.

Woody truly wanted us to be educated, and he also exposed us to great thinkers. My introduction to the writings of Rudyard Kipling came at the expense of a teammate who had snapped a wet towel at an opposing fan during a game. The fan probably deserved it, but our teammate was quarantined for the weekend to learn and consequently recite the poem "If" ["If you can keep your head when all about you are losing theirs and blaming it on you . . ."].

The player had to recite all four verses, without notes, to the team before practice on that Monday after the game. Woody was right there to help him as he stumbled to remember the next line, and Woody didn't need any notes. I framed a copy of the poem and hung it on my oldest son's wall as he grew from an infant into a teenager.

Woody often talked about paying forward. You know, don't pay back, pay forward. I experienced his conviction over and over again with his endless

A native of Michigan, Bruce Ruhl loved being part of the "10-Year War."

charitable and humanitarian actions, and many were done quietly without public notice. He often visited Children's Hospital in Columbus. We knew this, because he would apologize for leaving study table early to go downtown to visit a sick child. After our 1974 Rose Bowl victory, we returned to Columbus during the night and there were thousands of fans at the airport to greet us. Someone gave him a huge bouquet of roses. Woody decided to make a special trip to Riverside Hospital, and he asked the registration desk for names of patients who did not have any visitors that day. He passed out those roses to all those patients in the various wards. That was his way of paying forward. He was such a great man.

It went so fast. I remember my final game at the 1977 Orange Bowl. When your senior season starts to wind down, there is a realization that the clock is ticking. I was on the field during the last play as an incomplete pass fell toward my direction. We celebrated the win, but I walked off the field very slowly, taking in the smell, sounds, and sights of the moment. I knew I would not play in another game as a Buckeye. I just wanted to remember that instant forever.

From that moment forward, I knew I would become a fan of Buckeye teams to come. In the locker room after the game, the coaches went around to the seniors and thanked us for our careers and wished us good luck. I knew their sentiments were sincere. I waited until the very end to take my uniform off, because I knew I would never wear those pads and colors again. As it turned out, it was the last time I wore a football uniform.

I have no regrets. It's always been great to be a Buckeye.

Bruce Ruhl was Academic All–Big Ten in 1974 and '75.

VINCE SKILLINGS

1977–1980

O N THE DAY FOLLOWING A HUGE SNOWSTORM, I was walking down the street in the little town of Brenizer, Pennsylvania, where I lived, wearing only a pair of shorts and slippers when a car with an old man in the passenger seat pulled up beside me. "You want a ride?" came a voice. I pointed to my home, which was only about 70 yards away, and declined the offer. Then George Chaump greeted me and said that he would like to introduce coach Woody Hayes to me. Maaaann! Was I surprised and embarrassed. Coach Hayes must have thought I was a fool to be outside dressed the way I was.

My mother, Gladys Louise Skillings Dukes, had met coach Chaump before, but not coach Hayes. After introducing everyone, including my cousin, Curtis Clayton, back at the house, I began to settle down. However, to my immense surprise, coach Hayes asked, "Don't you have something to do, young man?" I told him that I was going to work out with Curtis but that it could wait.

"Well go do your workout, because I didn't come here to talk to you anyway. I came here to talk to your mother," he said. Still recovering from the shock of coach Hayes' bluntness, I reluctantly went to my workout.

Four hours later, I got home just as Mom and coach Hayes were finishing their conversation. He then turned to me and said, "You have a beautiful mother, son. Would you like to attend Ohio State University?"

With my mouth hanging to the floor, I answered, "Yeah, sure, of course." He then went on to say, "I won't promise you that you will start or even play

Vince Skillings was a three-year starter in the secondary.

at Ohio State, but I will promise you a fair chance to do so. I also guarantee that if you listen to me and our staff, you will get your degree."

Right there and then, I was sold on Ohio State, and I hadn't even talked to coach Hayes for more than three minutes total. I could have chosen from Syracuse, Boston College (which almost persuaded me to change my mind), Penn State, West Virginia, Pittsburgh, UCLA, and more, but coach Hayes was the only coach who seemed more interested in me as a person and not just another cog in the machinery of big-time college football.

Once on campus, Leon Ellison, Cal Murray, and I became known as the "Three Musketeers." Rarely did anyone see one of us without the other two somewhere close by. I will never forget the day the three of us were really depressed during preseason camp as freshmen. We were really homesick, so we went for a walk and ended up downtown at some hole-in-the-wall church. We all decided to give our life to Christ right then and there. We came back all fired up and elated with a new outlook on things.

Leon became like a brother to me. Leon felt he was not getting the playing time he deserved at defensive end, and we would always talk about it at our apartment. He would be so frustrated and disappointed, and yet he never complained. He just kept practicing hard trying to crack the starting lineup, and I really admired him for that.

239

Our families are very close to this day. He was the stabilizing force for me during my years at OSU. Ron Springs, my host during my official visit to Ohio State, also became a close friend. One day, Ron took me to his uncle's home, Spencer "Shade Tree" Brown. That is where I would meet his cousin Joyce. I immediately became enamored with Joyce, and we dated for the next three years before I foolishly ended our relationship. That became one of my biggest regrets.

On the field, Ron really carried us with his running ability. He was just one of those guys whom everyone looked up to.

Everyone who played for coach Hayes has some good stories, and one of mine is the funniest moment I remember. It was prior to a homecoming game. Coach Hayes called the second-team defense to go against the first-team offense. Well, all the defensive starters went to the visitors' sideline and sat down on these folding chairs that were set up. Man, why did we do that?

I didn't even notice coach Hayes leave the middle of the field. I just saw players falling over chairs and beating feet toward the open end of the stadium. There was coach Hayes running down the sideline, kicking over chairs, screaming, "Get up! Get up! This ain't no Goddamn country club!" Then he saw Al Washington still seated, and he picked up a chair and began chasing Al with it. Al's eyes nearly popped out of his head as he jumped up and took off running. Coach Hayes started throwing all the chairs into the stands, repeatedly screaming, "This is not a country club!" We were falling all over ourselves with laughter. Later, I often wondered how he didn't suffer a heart attack.

The 1980 Rose Bowl will be in my memory forever. The national championship was on the line and USC had such greats as Charles White, Anthony Munoz, Roy Foster, Ronnie Lott, Dennis Smith, and Marcus Allen. USC was supposed to crush us by 35 points, but we had them on the ropes until the final two minutes of the game. They scored on that final drive to beat us 17–16, and it just tore us apart. It was the first time that I had ever cried following a loss. Everyone was crying, from coaches to players. We knew we had that game. It was truly the toughest loss I ever experienced.

I've had a few regrets, like coach Hayes getting fired, the run-ins I had with coach Bruce, for which I apologized years later, and breaking up with Joyce. It was a prayer and dream of my mother's that at least one of her children graduate from college. I thank God that I did.

Coach Hayes was right—I earned my degree in 1982, and I discovered that when I did listen to him and the staff's advice (a lot of times I didn't), things went very well for me. Often during interviews with potential employers over the years, the fact that I played football at Ohio State for Woody Hayes would break the ice. That and my degree opened doors for me that I otherwise would have never had the chance to enter.

As I look back on it, we were all one big happy family.

Vince Skillings was drafted in the sixth round by the Dallas Cowboys in 1981.

TOM SKLADANY

1973–1976

GROWING UP IN BETHEL PARK, PENNSYLVANIA, I didn't even know where Ohio State was. All I knew then was Pitt football, or Notre Dame because they were on TV all the time. What's a Buckeye, I thought. I remember when George Chaump recruited me. He said, "Woody doesn't want you. I want you, but they don't want to give you a scholarship because there's never been a scholarship given to a punter at Ohio State."

So I took my visit to Ohio State and there were eighty-eight thousand fans at the game. I thought, "Wow!" But Woody told me this: "Now, we're probably not going to give you a scholarship, but I hear you kick pretty good, and if you come up here and if you do what coach Chaump says you can do, you may end up getting a scholarship."

At the same time, Notre Dame, Michigan, and Penn State were offering me full rides. So I told coach Chaump I wasn't coming, because I had offers with full scholarships. Finally, Woody told him, "If you think he can do it, then go ahead and give him our last scholarship."

Woody called up and told me, "Now son, we're going to give you a scholarship. Are you coming or not?" I told him I had one last visit to take, to Penn State. "You don't want to come here, son?" Woody asked me. "You better make up your mind."

I ended up signing the scholarship to become a Buckeye, and I was the first kicker to ever get one to Ohio State.

The first guy I met up there when I was getting recruited was Ken Kuhn. We were sitting at this bar near campus, and someone introduced me to him.

He reached over, and I thought he was going to shake my hand, but he took my glass of beer. He drained it, bit it, and chewed the glass. Blood was coming out of his mouth. That's my first impression of Ohio State—Ken Kuhn ate glass!

When I went out on that field for that first practice, there were seven punters and eight kickers. They were all walk-ons. I was thinking, "What did I get myself into?" Here I am the first scholarship punter and these senior walk-ons are pounding the ball past me. I knew I could punt, but it's different punting in front of Woody Hayes, Randy Gradishar, and John Hicks. I had the scholarship, but these other guys deserved it, I thought then.

It went down to the final week of camp, and Woody named me the starting punter, as a freshman. So I went out there for the first punt, in front of eighty-eight thousand people in the horseshoe, and I got a 41-yard fair catch. I ended up that year with 35 punts, 35 yards returned, and a 35-yard average. Everything was 35. I was last in the Big Ten, and I broke my leg in the Michigan game when I got clipped. I did lead in tackles on the kickoff team. When I didn't bomb it out of the end zone, I made the tackle. But Michigan sent a guy after me, and he clipped me from behind, broke my leg, and dislocated my ankle.

I remember Woody came up and asked, "Well, how is he?"

The trainers told him, "Coach, it's bad."

He said, "Well, check him out over there," meaning on the sideline.

I missed the Rose Bowl and had a cast up to my hip for two and a half months. I really think that's what made my leg stronger. My thigh grew an inch and three-quarters carrying that cast around campus. My leg got hard as a rock. That, and I worked my ass off that summer.

The next season, my first punt went off the side of my foot, but it rolled and ended up 61 yards. On the very next one, it was a 55-yard spiral for a fair catch. I led the nation in punting with a 46.7-yard average. From then on, I don't know if it was mental, all that work, or my leg, but I hit spirals the rest of my life. I made All-American as a sophomore and was on top of the world.

Until then, Woody didn't call me by name. He just called me, "Punter." As in, "Punter, get back here!" After I made All-American, it was "Tom."

I remember I hit a 59-yard field goal, which was the Big Ten record at that time [it remains the OSU record], and averaged 56 yards a punt—in the same game [at Illinois in 1975]. But Woody never really said, "Nice game." He was like my father that way: he never really complimented me, but it motivated

Tom Skladany averaged 42.7 yards per punt during his career and holds the school record with a 59-yard field goal.

me. And I noticed he would do it in the papers. He would say, "Archie Griffin is the best running back in the history of college football" or "That Skladany . . . you won't find a better punter." He'd tell you after your playing days—in front of other people, too. I guess he didn't want you to get fat-headed.

The guy was hilarious. He was the most intense, honest, hardworking guy there could ever be. Here's what I always told people about Woody Hayes: you were afraid of him as a freshman, you hated him as a sophomore, you liked him as a junior, and you loved him as a senior. He took you on an emotional roller coaster. Nobody would outwork him. You'd go in to work out for the summer at 7:00 A.M. and he'd still be on his couch from falling asleep at night with the projector on and he would have the same clothes on. He'd burn out four projectors a year.

I remember one time I went to be on *The Woody Hayes Show*. The image I have of that time is he was passed out between a Pepsi machine and a Coke machine in the lobby. I mean, he was sleeping with his tongue out drooling on his tie. He was absolutely beat. They had to wake him up five minutes before the show. He just wouldn't stop working.

And that's what he wanted us to do. Before my junior year, I developed a new practice routine. I went home and punted around a nine-hole golf course. I punted from the side of the number one tee; I would jog, pick it up, stop, and punt again. I would punt it to the green, go pick it up, and jog to the next tee. For 300 yards, you would have six punts, and all that running in between.

I always had fun before, during, or after practice at Ohio State. I made up these games, such as throwing golf balls out of the stadium. I could throw a golf ball from the block "O" at midfield right out of the stadium. All of the other guys thought it must not have been that hard, but nobody else could do it. I'd bet five bucks a man and get all warmed up, throw it out of there, and take the cash.

When it was cold, I led the punters and kickers into the locker room and we would be eating jelly doughnuts and drinking hot chocolate, because they didn't need us until the final 15 minutes of practice. At times, we were in there either studying, playing cards, gambling, eating. . . . This one time the trainer ran in and he was yelling my name. "Woody can't find you!" he said.

I went out of there running as fast as I could. I could hear Woody: "Where the hell is the punter?" Everybody was laughing because I had jelly all over my face. I stayed outside after that.

I was the goof-off, but that's how I got through it.

I remember we had this little party for Woody the year after he was fired. He didn't like that, but we all wanted it. Everybody put up 50 bucks and guys came from California, Texas, Kansas, everywhere. Bo came back and talked. I remember Woody telling Rex Kern, "Rex, I don't like the idea that you're spending money flying all the way from California for this party."

Woody was always worried about his guys.

If only I could bring back that time. It was the best four years you could ask for. I should have paid Ohio State. I had more fun than anyone could have. I went to three Rose Bowls, the Orange Bowl, the Japan Bowl, and the Hula Bowl. I've got six rings and six watches from Ohio State. I had the time of my life. And to think, while I was a senior in high school, I didn't even know where Ohio State was.

I wish all the fans could experience the feeling of running out of the tunnel in the "Shoe" after hearing the band come into the field before a game. You can't explain it with words. It is magical, intense, and overwhelming, and that is the exact moment when you know what being a Buckeye is all about.

Tom Skladany, team captain in 1976, became only the sixth Ohio State player to be named a three-time All-American. He played six seasons in the NFL with the Detroit Lions and the Philadelphia Eagles.

CHRIS WARD

1974–1977

IN 1969, I WAS JUST A VERY LARGE EIGHTH GRADER who held no great hope of ever really pursuing an athletic career of any type. Most of my coaches' reports were negative at best, but I improved as the years went on at Dayton's John H. Patterson High School, thanks to the coaching of Ken Amlin. And I developed dreams of playing college football.

I'll never forget the day that Wayne Woodrow Hayes visited my house to recruit me. He was so polite and demure that he just won my parents over right from the start. "We would really love to have Chris at Ohio State," he told them. "We will take care of him like our son. He's a fine young man, and he is exactly the type of young man we want at Ohio State. Can you get a commitment from him?"

My father said something like, "It's his decision," but I already knew I was going to Ohio State, anyway. All I did that day was commit to visit. I didn't want my dad to have to go more than 70 miles to see me play college football.

Anyway, because of Woody Hayes' visit, I became an instant celebrity at school. He was the greatest coach from the greatest school, The Ohio State University, visiting me!

When I arrived at Ohio State, it was a few years after freshmen became eligible, so my mind was on playing right away. And it was working out that way, too. I played in every game but didn't start until we had several tackles go down with injuries before the Michigan State game. I was going to get my first start. They were ranked high, and we were ranked number one and undefeated, and I was all pumped up for my first start. Then in practice, dis-

246

aster struck—I hurt my knee. It turned out to be an injury that was between operable and nonoperable.

So we beat Michigan and we were headed to the Rose Bowl, but I had this mobile cast on my knee and I was hobbling around. We were practicing in Columbus before the Rose Bowl, and it was raining so hard and it turned to ice. It was one of the worst ice storms we had ever had. Coach Hayes called me in and asked me, "Chris, how's that knee?" I said, "I don't know, Coach, I don't know, but it hurts."

We were leaving for California in three days, and the doctors didn't know what to do with me. "Chris, we think a lot of you, you know that," Woody told me. "But we're about to go to the Rose Bowl; do you want to go?"

Well, of course I did.

So coach Hayes got all excited and just said, "I'll tell you what the hell we are going to do, son. You are going to take that cast off right now. We are going to take you outside and you are going to run. If you can't run, we are operating first thing in the morning. If you can run, you are going to the Rose Bowl."

I said, "Coach, there's ice out there on the field and it's cold."

It didn't matter to coach Hayes—so I took the cast off and I ran like a gazelle.

247

Woody came in and told the doctors, "Chris is going to the Rose Bowl with us."

The man was a psychological genius. He really was. Anyway, I was fine after that.

I ended up having a great career at Ohio State and having the distinct pleasure of playing with the greatest athletes in my career—which spanned 10 pro training camps, four different teams, and 20 years—right there as a Buckeye. There were no finer teammates, talent, or players anywhere than what we had at Ohio State.

I would have been a four-year starter if it wasn't for that knee injury, and that's something I really take pride in. In four years, we were about 10 points from winning a couple of national championships. That 1975 team that lost to UCLA in the Rose Bowl could have beaten some pro teams. We had the very best players at every position. But it wasn't to be.

During my senior year, I was a finalist for the Heisman Trophy, and during my trip to New York, the president of the Downtown Athletic Club took me to lunch and told me, "We lobbied for you to be the first nonskilled player

Chris Ward, here blocking against Oklahoma in 1977, anchored the left tackle position for three seasons.

to win the Heisman Trophy. We really think you deserve it." Well, the Heisman went to Earl Campbell and I never won the Outland Trophy or Lombardi Award either, but I was an All-American. And I was and always will be a Buckeye.

As long as I live, I will always remember "Script Ohio" on a Saturday afternoon at Ohio Stadium. I love Ohio State, and I would do anything for that school. My heart will bleed scarlet and gray forever.

Chris Ward, a two-time All-American, played for the New York Jets, New Orleans Saints, and Miami Dolphins.

The
EIGHTIES

VAUGHN BROADNAX

1980–1983

WHEN I MADE THE DECISION TO ATTEND The Ohio State University, choosing the Buckeyes over Notre Dame, I had no idea what the future would bring. But I have never regretted that decision for even one day since.

I played with many great players and have so many fond memories and stories. You'll laugh at this one. Jay Holland was one of the finest athletes I have ever seen, but he just never seemed motivated. During a game against Northwestern, I noticed Jay was asleep on the bench. It was not uncommon for a player who doesn't play regularly to retreat to the bench, don a helmet, and catch some z's. Well, on this day, we were up by about 50 or 60 points so everyone was getting an opportunity to play. After a change of possession, Jay's number was called.

After someone woke him up, he immediately ran on the field and lined up at safety. Northwestern fired a pass downfield, and Jay intercepted it and returned it for a long gain. He then came off the field and everyone was congratulating him and he promptly found his seat on the bench. He went right back to sleep. True story.

I remember seeing Keith Byars showing up at camp as a freshman. I was amazed at how big he was and at some of the things he could do. A classmate of his was Pepper Johnson. I can honestly say that Pepper was the hardest-hitting and best linebacker I played against. I didn't like it because we had collisions on nearly every play in practice. William Roberts was the most graceful big guy I ever saw. My roommate my freshman year was Rowland Tatum. We called him the "Nicknamer" because he had a name for everyone.

Vaughn Broadnax, here carrying against Northwestern in 1983, was one of the most bruising blockers in Ohio State history.

Here's an example: "Misleading"—this player had huge biceps, but when he took off his shirt, it was quite apparent sit-ups were not his priority.

I guess I will be known for "the Block" in 1981 at Michigan. We were behind 9-7 late in the game, and we drove down the field with several key plays by Tim Spencer and Art Schlichter. When we got inside the 20, we knew Bobby Atha would nail the field goal, but we knew a touchdown would eliminate Michigan's winning with a field goal. In the huddle, Art called "Play Pass 28." The play is designed to attack the outside and force the defense to either stop the run or defend the pass. Michigan chose to defend the pass. I was blocking Carlton Rose; I just held my block and Carlton went down and tripped up two other defenders, allowing Art to scamper into the end zone. At that time, I didn't realize the impact of the play, but I do now all these years later. It was the result—a victory over Michigan.

The worst defeat I can recall didn't involve Michigan. In 1982 we played against a Stanford team that we had beaten a year earlier at Stanford. I had left that game unimpressed by John Elway. But a year later, we were leading and driving with about three minutes remaining and we turned the ball over. Elway then drove Stanford down the field to beat us in the final seconds. When I think of Elway and "the Drive," I don't think of the Browns versus the Broncos but of that drive that beat us in 1982.

That year we started 2–3 and there was some dissension and finger-pointing. Then we upset a heavily favored Illinois team and won the rest of the games. We beat an arrogant BYU team led by Steve Young, 47–17 in the Holiday Bowl, and I truly believe we were the best team in the country at season's end.

I can't begin to describe the range of emotions I experienced while sitting in the stands during that Fiesta Bowl for the 2002 national championship. To see the look of joy and pride in the faces of several of my ex-teammates brought tears to my eyes.

Everyone knows that The Ohio State University is my alma mater, and I still get so emotional when our alma mater is played at the end of each game.

How much does my alma mater mean to me? We named our daughter Carmen.

Vaughn Broadnax started at fullback in 1981, '82, and '83 and made one of the most famous blocks in school history.

KEITH BYARS

1982–1985

I WANT TO SAY IT WAS AN EASY DECISION to come to Ohio State, because when I was a young boy I watched all of the games on TV and I knew I wanted to play for Woody Hayes. But once I grew up and all the schools in the country started to recruit me, it was easy for me to get confused. I know I hated Michigan with a passion, but I actually went up there on a recruiting visit, met Bo, and thought, "This is not as bad as I thought it was." In the summer before my senior year, I went to Wilmington, Ohio, during the Bengals' summer camp and met with Archie Griffin. He told me, "If you are looking for a challenge and you want to be the best you can be and go against the topflight competition every week, you need to be at Ohio State." And I was from Dayton, so he told me, "All of the top running backs in Ohio stay in Ohio."

Pittsburgh was recruiting me pretty hard at the time, and Dan Marino was there, but I told Dan, "You have only one more year left when I get there." I wanted a great running back tradition, and when I added everything up, I knew I was making the right decision to come to Ohio State.

I also knew then that no one player was bigger than Ohio State, and that's a part of it that I really liked. I wanted to be a part of something big and something important.

Once I committed, during the OSU spring game prior to my freshman year, the coaches told me I would be rooming with a guy named Thomas Johnson. When we met that day, we really didn't need an introduction. We just walked up and started talking to each other like we had known each other for all of our lives—"What are you going to bring? You bring the TV, I'll bring the radio . . ."—and that's how it went for Pepper Johnson and me. We bonded right away, and he's been my best friend since.

When coaches put roommates together, it is a crapshoot of whether it will work out, but in all these years, we've never had a cross word between us. We thought an awful lot alike, and we had so many great conversations in that dorm room. When the going got tough, we wouldn't let each other quit. When he was down, I picked him up, and when I was down, he picked me up. And we still do that to this day. It really was like meeting a brother I never knew I had.

When I got to campus for summer camp, I was amazed at how fast the game was. Everybody was bigger and faster than what I was used to.

I remember this linebacker, Clarence "Curt" Curtis. On one of the first days of training camp we had to do weight testing, and he couldn't bench 225 pounds. A lot of the guys were standing around laughing. He jumped off the bench and got mad at them. He said something like, "It doesn't matter what you can lift, it matters how big your heart is." So we got out to practice, and I saw him pick up this 300-pound offensive lineman and toss him into the quarterback's lap. I thought, "He's got a point."

Then in the first scrimmage, I was supposed to block the inside linebacker, and I thought I knew where he was coming from. All of a sudden, Curt came rushing in from the outside and gave me a forearm shiver in the head. Now after this play, I was thinking I was really sweating pretty badly, but somebody came up to me and said, "Are you all right, because you are bleeding?" I had this big cut over my eye, and that was the first time I ever needed stitches.

I thought to myself, "Welcome to college football."

The first time I ever went to a college football game was the day I played in one. It was a dream come true. We were playing Baylor, and I was playing on the punt team. In camp, guys had told me what it would be like to run onto the field at the horseshoe in front of ninety thousand fans: "You wait, it will be unbelievable—your feet don't hit the ground." They were right— it was exactly that way.

Tim Spencer was All–Big Ten that year and a great back, so I played mostly on special teams as a freshman. I couldn't wait for my sophomore year. I wasn't nervous at all, just excited to get my opportunity. I worked hard and

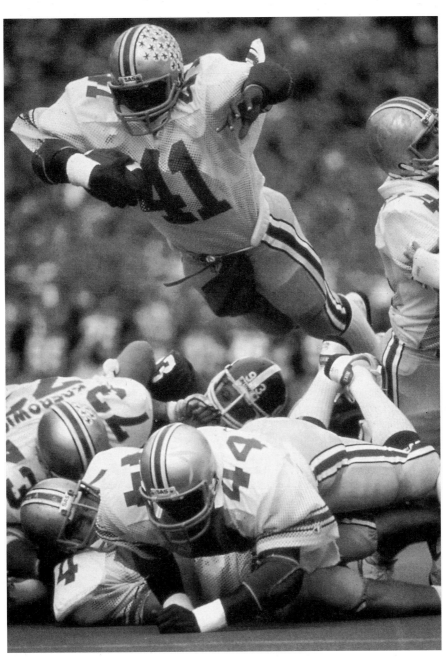

It seemed as if Keith Byars could do anything on the football field—including defying gravity against Michigan State in 1984.

tried to be the best I could be, and I took it very seriously. I had a real good sophomore year [1,199 yards rushing, 22 touchdowns] and made some All-American teams, but my goal in college was to be better than the year before each and every year. I wasn't shy about it—I wanted to win two Heisman Trophies.

Everybody always asks me about that Illinois game my junior year and the run without my shoe. Over the years, I figured there must have been more than one hundred thousand fans who were there that day, because more than that have claimed to be there to see it. I remember we got down 24–0 and I had fumbled. But when I scored, we all felt we were coming back, and that's when I told the TV cameras exactly that. I just said what the whole team believed.

On the [67-yard] run without my shoe, it was a simple draw designed to go left, but I saw a big hole on my right. I saw an opportunity to go for the home run. As I was going upfield, I made my last cut to the left, and my shoe started to come loose. I was about to lose it anyway, so I just kicked it off [at Illinois' 35-yard line]. Then I thought, "Now I had better run faster, because I don't want anybody to step on my foot." People still bring that play up when they meet me.

As a junior, it came together [1,764 yards, 24 touchdowns] for me, and I thought I really should have won the Heisman Trophy [Byars finished as the runner-up to Boston College's Doug Flutie].

Later in the NFL, I would ask Doug Flutie, "How's my trophy doing?" I should have won it, but things don't always work out the way you want them to.

Then I thought I would get another chance as a senior, but during camp before the season started, I was running when I made a cut, and I didn't hear anything, but I felt it. Something in my right foot wasn't right. I limped over to the trainer and told him we needed an X ray.

It was something doctors had never seen before, but in plain terms, I broke my foot. At that time, the doctors didn't feel it would keep me out all that long, and I tried to gut it out later, but I wasn't the same. Otherwise, I would have considered redshirting and coming back the next year.

It was very disappointing, but it really was a freak thing.

I didn't get the chance to go back to Ohio Stadium until I retired from the NFL, and I always told my wife, whom I didn't know in college, "You have got to go back to Ohio State with me. It is totally different from pro football." When I was inducted into the [OSU Athletic] Hall of Fame in 2000, my wife and kids went back with me. My kids got to come out onto the field with me, and it was a special moment. We took some pictures of everybody over by my tree at the Buckeye Grove.

You know, when you are 17 or 18 years old and you have to make the biggest decision of your life, it is very difficult to do. I believe I did it well, and I am so glad I came to Ohio State. I just think about all of the friends I have from my days there, and that is very special by itself. I knew back then it would impact me for the rest of my life, and it did. I made the right decision, and I enjoyed every minute of my college career.

Despite missing most of his senior season, Keith Byars finished his OSU career with 3,200 rushing yards—fourth on the all-time list. He scored 46 touchdowns—second all time behind Pete Johnson. Byars, who was the Big Ten MVP in 1984, played 14 seasons in the NFL.

CRIS CARTER

1984–1986

I HAD SO MANY CHOICES COMING OUT OF HIGH SCHOOL in Middletown, Ohio—I could have gone almost anywhere to play basketball and anywhere to play football. I had always considered basketball my first love, and my brother Butch played basketball at Indiana and had played with Isiah Thomas. My brother George played at Illinois State, and my brother John played at West Liberty. But one of my football coaches, Bill Conley, who's now at Ohio State, told me: "Cris, there are a lot of Isiah Thomases out there playing basketball, but there are not many tall receivers like you!"

I had decided to narrow it to five basketball schools and five football schools. Butch used to tell me, "Don't go to Ohio State. They never have thrown the football, and they never will."

Then one day, I came home and I was worn out from people asking me where I was headed to college. I sat down in the living room and told Mom, "Everybody is asking me where I am going and what I am going to do, but nobody ever asks you what you think. So, what do you think, Mom?"

She looked at me and said, "Son, I always had a dream that one of my boys would play football for the Buckeyes."

I also figured this out: there is a tremendous benefit to being an Ohio State alum and being in Ohio.

I knew right then what I had to do: I committed early—but part of the deal was that I could play basketball at Ohio State, too.

Chris Spielman committed early, too, and he and I helped recruit the rest of the class. We had the number one recruiting class in the country, and we had plans to win a national championship. There was Chris, Alex Higdon, William White, Tom Tupa, Greg Rogan . . . we knew we had an awesome class.

I remember when I first got to campus, Lenny Willis was finishing up his degree and he was playing in the NFL. I was basically a basketball player playing wide receiver, and he helped me out on my routes, but I almost left Ohio State a few days after I got there.

When I got there, there was the first team, the second team, and the scout team. All the freshmen were on the scout team. I told coach Bruce, "I am leaving school. You promised me a chance to make the varsity, and this is not what you had told me while you were recruiting me." He had told me, "If you don't start as a freshman, I would be surprised."

The next day, they moved Chris Spielman and me up to the third-string on the varsity. Now there really wasn't any third-string, just two spots—for me and Chris. I have to say that Jay Holland, Doug Smith, and Mike Lanese were guys who really helped me. They were receivers who were fighting for the same jobs, but they were very, very helpful. So was Mike Tomczak, who was a senior and the starting quarterback.

Now, I had seen the team come out of that tunnel a dozen times . . . with coach Bruce standing there in front and the police holding the team back. I just didn't know what it would be like to run onto that field. Literally, my feet didn't touch the ground that first time in my freshman season. It was so exciting. When I got into pro football, that feeling made me love Ohio State even more.

You wind up chasing that feeling again for the rest of your life.

I didn't start those first two games in '84, but I started against Iowa in the third game, and I was in there ever since.

That whole experience of playing in the Rose Bowl that year was very special. I had a pretty good game [nine receptions, a Rose Bowl–record 172 yards], and that was the first day I became convinced I would never play basketball again. I would just stick to football.

In practice, Keith Byars and I used to play these games to challenge me to do something no one else had ever done. We used to play catch near the sideline, and I would try to make one-handed catches and still keep my feet inbounds. So when people mention that one-handed catch I made along the sideline of the Citrus Bowl my sophomore year against BYU, that's where that comes from. I had made up my mind that is the type of

Cris Carter, an All-American in 1986, amazed opponents and his teammates with acrobatic receptions.

player I wanted to be. I didn't want to be average, or even good—I wanted to be great.

Still, I admit there were many times I was frustrated with our offense. It seemed it was always a struggle with the coaches to open it up a little and throw more. We would run on first down, run on second, and then try to throw to me on third-and-long. We didn't have the most sophisticated passing game in the world. It was frustrating for me.

I was close to most all of my teammates and especially those in my class, and that's why what happened before the 1987 season made it so tough. I was ruled ineligible [for dealing with an agent], and it crushed me. We were pointing everything toward that senior year, and we were all coming back. We were going to be good, and we knew we were going to be good. Everybody else knew it, too.

When the ruling came down from the NCAA, and then [OSU athletic director] Rick Bay said, "Cris Carter will never wear an Ohio State uniform again," I had only one option, and that was to apply for the NFL draft. I didn't want to leave; I wanted to file that appeal, but Ohio State did not want to do that. I was upset at myself. Given what I knew about athletics, I didn't have to do what I did to get into that predicament.

I admit that initially I was a little bitter, and of course, my teammates were mad at me. The most vocal one of all was Chris Spielman. He is a no-nonsense kind of guy who does the right thing. He had a few choice words for me, and I understood that. I really did. I respected him so much.

After that, I just had to withdraw from school and leave Columbus. It was on every TV station, every radio station, wherever I went in town. Then all of those things just wore that '87 team out. We didn't have an offensive leader that [quarterback] Tom Tupa needed. I faced the question that if that wouldn't have happened to me, we wouldn't have had a bad year, and Earle wouldn't have been fired. I had to live with that, but I do know something about Ohio State, and Bill Miles told me, "Hey, every coach who ever worked here has been fired."

I still have to say that playing at Ohio State was a great experience.

I feel some relief that people have forgotten what happened as the years go by. Earlier in my pro career, I still caught flak for it, and I had stayed away from Ohio State for a few years because of the emotion and frustration people showed to me. I always wanted to make those fans cheer for me, and if they did, I enjoyed it so much.

It is the truth to say that I always have been in pursuit of making all Buckeyes proud of me. Not everyone has that opportunity to put on that helmet and wear those Buckeye leaves. I have no regrets about my choice to play for Ohio State, and I will always have a deep fondness for the Buckeyes.

Cris Carter, who recorded 168 receptions in his three-year Ohio State career, played for the Philadelphia Eagles, Minnesota Vikings, and Miami Dolphins. He ranks second in NFL history in receptions and touchdown receptions, behind Jerry Rice, and he likely will become the sixth Ohio State player elected to the Pro Football Hall of Fame.

GLEN COBB

1979–1982

As it turned out, I didn't get to play for coach Hayes, but I have a story that I love to tell about him. During my senior year in high school, I was invited to watch the team practice in preparation for the Gator Bowl versus Clemson. It was a cold, wet December day, and the team was still in Ohio. The practice was being held in the horseshoe, and not many recruits were there that day. Anyhow, I was standing along the sideline when coach Hayes motioned for me to come over to him. At the time, the team was broken out into individual position groups doing drills.

When I reached coach Hayes, he asked, "Son, do you see those linebackers over there?"

I replied, "Yeah."

"No, you will respond by saying, 'Yes, sir.'"

I corrected myself: "Yes, sir."

"Son, I want you to watch those linebackers today. You watch them. If after the end of practice you think you can play alongside them, then I'll give you a scholarship. If you don't, then get back on I-71 South, and go back down to the farm and stay there!"

"Yes, sir."

I trotted off and my thoughts turned to farm life. It's a pretty good life really. I can do that, I thought. Understand, the mind-set I had was that it was very intimidating. I didn't think I could compete academically or athletically. I remember that during that same visit, I watched a tape of the

264

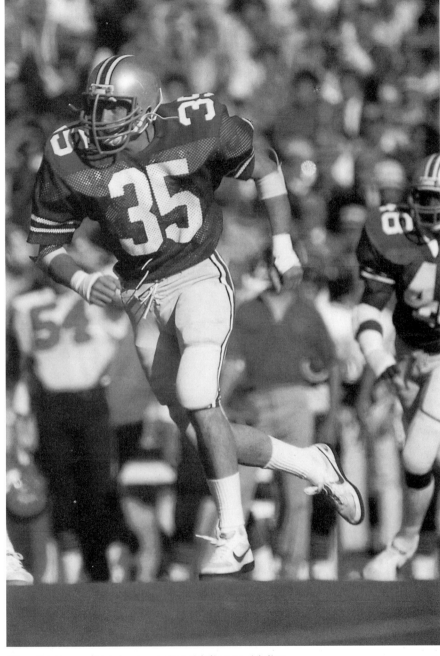

Glen Cobb was at his best running sideline to sideline.

previous season's highlights and said to myself, "There is no way you can compete at this level." The whole Ohio State thing was out of my league. However, I really believe that if God wants a person somewhere, He will provide a way.

As you know, that Gator Bowl would turn out to be coach Hayes' final game, and I never got to play for him. But I did become a Buckeye the following season.

My first year, the freshmen came in early prior to two-a-days. We had three practices without pads. I remember thinking, "This isn't so bad." Then came the upperclassmen. We put the pads on and went full contact. Dennis Fryzel was our linebackers coach, and you will not find a more colorful and excitable man. The very first contact drill he put us through was a tackling drill. One player runs the ball, the other tackles. Nothing fancy, but good old-fashioned smash-mouth football. To ensure that contact will occur, the runner must run straight ahead inside of two cones spread a few yards apart. This doesn't allow for much deviation east or west. Well, I had a crack at it both ways. First, I ran the ball and was tackled. No big deal. Then I tackled one of my fellow linebackers. It wasn't pretty, but I got him down somehow. Then we started on the second round. This time I faced Al Washington, who was 6'5" and weighed about 260 pounds. I was considerably smaller and weighed 210 pounds soaking wet. I took off with the ball, of course running straight up not knowing any better. Al, I would say, put a pasting on me the likes of which I had never seen nor felt before. When I got up, my face mask was broken in three places.

266

I can say that it never happened before, and it never happened again. Keep in mind, this was my very first contact drill at Ohio State. This was very entertaining to the upperclassmen, and I think it accomplished the initiation that coach Fryzel wanted. "Welcome to the Big Ten," he said.

Who was the toughest player I ever played with? No doubt here, it was Art Schlichter. I saw him time and again take substantial pounding as a freshman, especially in the Penn State game [a 19–0 loss in 1978] played in the Shoe. Penn State All-Americans Matt Millen and Bruce Clark firmly planted their helmets in his chest all day long. Although he wavered, he still got up. Coach Bruce was fond of saying, "When you get knocked down, get up." Art carried this to the max in that game. During our high school days at Miami Trace and later at Ohio State, I saw him get hit with the best of them. He was one tough amigo on the field.

I have to say that coach Bruce was a man of integrity. Yes, he wanted to win with the best of them. However, he parted ways with coaches at some other institutions in this: he wanted to win the right way—without cheating. He spoke of integrity and its importance often. He spoke often about how a man is known by his friends, so be careful with whom you associate. He spoke about life after football, and the need to grasp the bigger picture. He had a passion for football, and he was tireless in his work habits and very committed to the process. He was always mindful of the need to outwork your opponent and the values of hard work. I have the greatest respect for the man. He was a father figure to me at Ohio State and helped me even beyond my days on the gridiron. He took a personal interest in his players. Coach Tressel is fond of saying, "People don't care how much you know, until they know how much you care." To me, Earle Bruce demonstrated the right balance of compassion and competition. I am grateful to have played for the man and know that The Ohio State University was a better place with him during his time as head coach.

You need friends to go through college, and some of my teammates were my best friends—guys like Joe Berner, Dave Medich, and Ray Myers. You won't find them in the record books or in the OSU Hall of Fame. However, they will always be in my memories because they made a big, sometimes impersonal institution such as Ohio State feel more like home. In reality, it is not the institution that you remember the most, it's the people. Without friends, this world is a lonely place. But Ohio State felt like home because of them and many others.

It is natural to thank your coaches and teammates for getting you through, but my adviser, Neil Andrew, was truly an inspiration to me. I can recall first meeting Neil on my official visit as a senior in high school. I have to say that Neil helped me for four years and was instrumental in helping me graduate on time with a degree in park and recreation management. I am just glad I didn't go back to the farm and stay there. I went to Ohio State, played football, learned countless valuable lessons about life, and earned my degree.

267

Glen Cobb, who recorded 336 tackles in his career, which is eighth on Ohio State's all-time list, was a two-time team captain (1981 and '82).

JUDD GROZA

1980–1984

"And lead us not into temptation, but deliver us from evil. Amen."

There was a pause. The silence was then shattered by a voice from the back of the room. "Let's go out there and kick some ass." This one phrase seemed to trigger a frenzy among all of the players who were anxiously awaiting the race onto the field. This, my first encounter at Ohio Stadium, was to be an experience I would never forget.

As the team filed into the hallway, which led to the tunnel, I was completely surrounded by scarlet and gray. The players' uniforms and coaches' outfits were proudly displaying Ohio State's colors. I was in the middle of a giant mass of players. As the mob slowly moved toward the tunnel's opening, the sweat began to drip down my face, and the smell of athletic tape, perspiration, and the stick-gum that receivers had spread on their hands filled the air. My heart began to throb upon seeing the light from the outside. I heard a voice, a coach's voice, yell "Let's go!"

It was like running through a human funnel that emptied onto the field. As soon as my feet hit the turf, the roar of the fans rose to a deafening pitch. The team began to cluster into the traditional huddle with players climbing, jumping, and piling onto each other. At that moment, I was so overwhelmed by emotion—excitement, fear, and joy—that I felt like bursting into tears.

As the other team's kicker placed the football onto the tee, I could hear the marching band playing "Across the Field," and it sent chills racing down my of our receiver. Almost instantly, shoulder pads were hitting shoulder pads and helmets were banging helmets. The ball carrier was finally tackled, but after making good yardage. The wedge had done its job.

As the game was coming to an end, I stood and watched our offense manipulate its way down the field. I was suddenly grabbed by coach Bruce and instructed: "Take this play in, 'Fly right 20.'" I ran onto the field as fast as I could and headed for the huddle. I relayed the play to Art Schlichter, the quarterback, and he took over from there. The huddle broke, and as I got down in my stance for the first time, I studied the defensive player opposite me. I could tell he was strong from the thickness of his arms and legs. He was big, and I knew it would be difficult to block him.

"Set, blue 20, blue 20, set, set," Art shouted. The ball was snapped and I exploded out of my crouched position into the defensive player in front of me. I met him at full speed, cracking him hard. As I drove my legs harder, I could hear the roar of the fans get stronger. Our running back had gained a first down. I was overwhelmed by a feeling of satisfaction, of being part of a perfectly executed play. The final gun sounded and the game belonged to the Buckeyes.

That night, as I lay in bed, I found it hard to sleep. Even though the room was dark and my eyes closed, I could still see the scarlet and gray that had surrounded me in the tunnel. I could still smell the athletic tape, perspiration, and stick-gum. My heartbeat made the sheets jump as I lay there remembering the roar of the fans, the marching band, and the times I was on the field.

I was proud to be a Buckeye, I had survived my first encounter in Ohio Stadium, and I knew it was an experience I would never forget.

You have just read an essay that I wrote for my freshman English class at Ohio State on November 20, 1980.

Some of those memories now make the hairs on my neck stick up. I even appreciate the memories of two-a-day practices and wind sprints. I underwent two surgeries [knee and back], and I went through many ups and downs, and many times I felt like quitting. At that time, I remember wondering if playing football was worth all the trials and tribulations. I now realize it was well worth it. Not everyone gets the chance to be a Buckeye football player. It is a tremendous privilege to wear the scarlet and gray.

I grew up in Berea, Ohio, as the youngest son of Lou "the Toe" Groza. He was a legendary football player, but he was an even better dad. I miss him dearly. The Grozas and the Tressel family were close friends in Berea. Lee Tressel, of course, was the great coach at Baldwin-Wallace, and by now everybody in Ohio knows his son Jim. "J.T."—coach Tressel's nickname back then—shagged footballs with me and my brothers when Dad practiced

270

Judd Groza signals a touchdown against Indiana in 1984.

kicking at Berea High School. J.T. was then the star quarterback at Berea High, and my oldest brother, Jeff, was the tight end. Jeff would tell me how J.T. would memorize the opponents' defenses and call his own plays at the line of scrimmage. He was a true student of the game, even at such a young age, and he also was a great student in the classroom.

I had the honor of having J.T. as my T-ball coach, and the thing I remember is that he made every player on the team feel important, regardless of their skill. He made it fun for everyone, and he was a great role model. He had recruited me to play football while he was an assistant at Miami of Ohio, and later our paths crossed when he came to Ohio State as an assistant under Earle Bruce.

It was my final year as a Buckeye, and I knew then that eventually he was going on to bigger and better things. It really was his destiny. I am confident that "the Toe," coach Lee Tressel, and Eloise are all looking down from heaven on J.T. and they are smiling.

Judd Groza, son of NFL great Lou Groza, was named to the Academic All–Big Ten team in 1984.

DEREK ISAMAN

1985–1987, 1989

I CAN HONESTLY SAY THAT PLAYING FOOTBALL AT OSU was the best time of my life. I can remember a certain Monday practice just like it was yesterday. . . .

I had a rough year my junior year. I was injured during two-a-days and had lost my starting linebacker job to Mike McCray, who played excellent all season and deserved to start. I'll never forget Monday's prepractice meeting before the Michigan game. Coach Bruce stood before us and announced, "I have been let go by the university." As tears ran down his face, he told us it was not going to affect our determination, desire, and willingness to play error-free football. "This is the most important game in your entire life," he said. "The school up North is good, but they're not great." His face was getting red, and the tears were streaming down his face. "Strap on your helmets, boys, because there is no game like this one, and we'll be flying around the field and cracking heads. This will be the hardest-hitting game of your lives. We are going to go up to Michigan, and we are going to kick their ass!"

We were ready to play Michigan on that Monday. I was moved to inside linebacker next to Chris Spielman, and I was starting that week. (By the way, Chris was one tough son of a bitch. He slept and ate OSU football, and nobody matched his determination, hard work, and effort.)

At practice that day, as we were beginning a 7-on-7 drill, I looked up and saw coach Bruce with this big grin on his face, looking right at me. Here I was starting the Michigan game in coach Bruce's last game as the OSU head

Derek Isaman was one of the toughest Buckeyes—on the field or in the ring.

coach. What an honor it was. Joe Staysniak had purchased headbands for the whole team with "Earle" written on each. We thought it was a great idea to honor a wonderful coach and a good man.

As everyone knows, we were a big underdog, but we went out and won the game [23–20]—it was awesome to win it for coach Bruce.

We had good times off the field, too. Like the night at the Cotton Bowl a year earlier when we were facing an 11:00 P.M. curfew. A few of us probably had a few too many beers, and it got to be 10:30. We had Jeff Uhlenhake's dad's car, and we made a wrong turn and got lost trying to find our hotel. We exited the ramp at about 50 mph, lost control of the car, and jumped the curb. We broke the front axle and had about 15 minutes until our curfew. The clock was ticking, but we persevered and continued driving on a wobbly wheel at 15 mph and made it with just a few minutes to spare. Then we beat Texas A&M.

I took the 1988 season off when John Cooper came in so I could try out for the U.S. Olympic boxing team. I went on to win the 1988 National Golden Gloves and beat Tommy Morrison. But in the Olympic trials, I was defeated by Mike Bent, who later won the heavyweight title by knocking out Morrison. It was a long, tough year. After training and being in the boxing ring with the best fighters in the world like Riddick Bowe, Evander Holyfield, Ray Mercer, and Mike Tyson, I was ready to kick some ass on the football field. So I called coach Cooper and he had held my scholarship. He welcomed me back.

It was such an honor to be named captain of the 1989 team. It means so much when it comes from your peers. We didn't have much talent that year, so we weren't great but good. We probably had the worst defense in the league, but we won games [the '89 team finished 8–4].

I had broken my thumb against Iowa, and I needed surgery. After the operation, they said I might have a chance to play in the Michigan game. Little did they know that nothing was going to keep me out of that game. They put a soft cast on it, and the doctors asked if it hurt. I said no, but it was killing me. The pain was like nothing I could describe. It was the most pain I had ever endured, but I was not coming off the field against Michigan. I would come to the sideline and go sit down near the end of the bench as my thumb throbbed uncontrollably.

After the game, I had turf burns head to toe. I was beat to a pulp, and my thumb was about to fall off. I guess you could say I truly had a dislike for Michigan. I took it personal.

That's another reason why I love coach Tressel. He brought back the tradition. He's beaten Michigan.

I am still so proud to be part of that tradition. I am so proud to be a Buckeye.

Derek Isaman, who started three years (1986, '87, and '89) at linebacker, was named MVP of the 1989 team.

THOMAS "PEPPER" JOHNSON

1982–1985

I'LL BE HONEST—OHIO STATE REALLY DIDN'T do a good job of recruiting me. In fact, it was kind of a bad recruiting process and the worst visit I had out of any of them. I was considering Arizona State, Minnesota, Michigan, and Michigan State, but I had always loved the tradition of Ohio State, even while growing up in Detroit.

When I visited, Earle Bruce was visiting with other recruits and then had to go somewhere, and I never even got to meet him. My hosts that day were William Roberts and Doug Hill. They just told me, "It is best to see Ohio State for yourself. So go walk around campus, get a feel for the place, and we'll be here if you have any questions." They really thought that this place would sell itself. But it sort of made me mad that coach Bruce didn't see me, and I started thinking I had a point to prove. But when I visited Michigan, it seemed there was a lot of animosity among the players. They just didn't seem to get along that well, and I think they may have been recruiting me as a tight end.

Despite the foul-up on my visit, I started thinking Ohio State was the best place for me. It wasn't so far that my family couldn't come see me play. So I signed without ever meeting the head coach, and anybody will tell you that is very unusual. My life changed during the spring Scarlet and Gray Game in 1982. Not only was that the first time I met coach Bruce, but coach [Bill]

Miles told me I would be rooming with some guy named Keith Byars. The first time I saw him that day, he was wading through a lot of people, and I knew that must be Keith. He saw me too, and he knew his roommate was named Thomas Johnson, but he thought that must be a white guy. He walked up to me and asked, "Thomas?" I said, "Yeah, just call me Pepper."

From that day forward, we became very close. We really became just like brothers. As I write this, I know he's somewhere in South Florida on the golf course.

I remember the day my mother and sister dropped me off that fall in Columbus. They were about to cry, but I felt very comfortable at Ohio State from the beginning.

We had to pass a 12-minute run where the linebackers had to finish seven laps. I had trained all summer for that thing. That's all I thought about, but I misunderstood what we had to do. I thought you just had to finish the seven laps within that time and that would be that. I didn't realize you had to finish the 12 minutes no matter what. All anybody talked about back then when it came to the 12-minute run was Glen Cobb. They talked about how nobody could beat him. They said he was half human, half horse when it came to that run. So I heard Earle's whistle and I took off like a bat out of hell. I could even hear the trainers standing around the track saying, "He'll never keep up that pace." I was leading this thing and I was beating Glen by about half of a lap, and I finished my seventh lap, sprinting to the finish. I broke it down and stopped but everybody started screaming. I was waving, accepting what I thought was their congratulations. I even got a quick drink of water. But they were screaming because I had stopped. I didn't know you had to run the whole 12 minutes. Earle was going crazy, hollering at me. There went Glen, running right by me. Have you ever tried to restart running after you had stopped? It's not easy, but I took off and tried to catch Glen. Finally, they blew the whistle as Glen made his eight laps and I was about 10 or 15 yards from the line. I was so disappointed.

That very first practice, I experienced a real eye-opener. Shaun Gayle was one of our hardest hitters on defense, and the offense ran a toss play with Tim Spencer. Shaun came up for support to make the tackle, and Vaughn Broadnax led the blocking ahead of Tim. Vaughn and Shaun met head-on and wow! . . . the collision was huge. They hit each other so hard, I could feel it. They got up, patted each other on the back, and went back to the huddle. I tightened my chin strap and told myself, "Welcome to college football."

I came from a Detroit public school where we would be happy if we had 250 people in the crowd for one of our games. All the stories I had heard

278

Pepper Johnson was one of the hardest-hitting linebackers in Buckeye history.

about running out of that tunnel before a game for the first time were true. That is a highlight of "the shoe" for everyone who has ever played there. Still today, after all these years, it remains my ultimate feeling. I just can't imagine anyone not enjoying it. I was near the front and I sprinted over to the bench. I really don't remember my feet touching the ground that first time. I got over there, and I remember seeing guys flipping over from the top and then winding up on the bottom of the pile.

My first game action came on kickoff returns and coverage. Keith and I both got our first action that way. The thing that was important to me was getting Buckeye leaves, and if you made a tackle on the kickoff team inside the other team's 20-yard line, you got a leaf. I played behind Marcus Marek at linebacker, so that was the only way for me to get a Buckeye leaf my freshman year. That's what I took pride in, and I think we led the nation in kickoff return average that season. Keith returned kickoffs, and we still take pride in that. In my first game against Michigan, I tackled Anthony Carter on a kickoff inside the 20. That was huge.

The next few years, it didn't really matter to me when I was named All–Big Ten and All-American. It really didn't. I never really liked individual honors like that. I took more pride in receiving Buckeye leaves and being named the team's "Defensive Player of the Week." I had been voted captain for my junior and senior years, and to be recognized by your peers like that, no All-American team can match that. It's how you play in the eyes of your peers and what type of person you are for them . . . that's the stuff that matters and that's what sticks with me now.

As a captain, I felt responsibility, too. I remember when two of our starters, Rory Graves and Terry White, got suspended before my final home game for doing something really stupid. We lost to Wisconsin 12–7, and the next day we had a team meeting. They had to hold me back from putting my hands around one of those guys' necks. I was about as mad as I could get. Who wanted to lose their final home game? Either one of them could have made the plays to make the difference to win that game.

Before the Michigan game my junior year, Woody Hayes came to the captain's table and I got to sit next to him. Woody and I were sitting there talking, and he was telling me all about how good these cinnamon rolls were. He always loved those cinnamon rolls from the golf course, and he was telling me how to put a little butter on them and how to eat them. The next year, he sat next to me again and we had the same conversation. Now I looked out and saw 100 guys looking up at me and Woody talking together. They were all wondering what we were talking about, because it was an intense conversation. But they had no idea that it was all about cinnamon rolls. That was one of those "Call Mom and tell her what you did today" type of deals.

I remember when he walked in to give us a talk before a Michigan game. You know, we respected coach Bruce and listened to coach Bruce, but when Woody came into the room, every set of eyes looked straight at him. People sat up in their chairs. You could just feel it. He was just awesome and people knew it. Nobody even looked off to the side. Nobody fiddled with a watch or pen or anything. I thought, "Man, why wasn't I born four or five years earlier so I could have played for this man?"

The thing Woody told us was how to be a real football player. He told us he hated to see a guy miss an interception and then pound his fist on the ground or look at his hands like his hands let him down. Just because of what Woody said, I never did that after that, even in the NFL. I never looked at my hands if I dropped a pass. I tell my son that today. There's no need to do it.

One thing Keith and I never did in all those practices was hit each other. I never tackled him, he never blocked me, and it drove coach Bruce crazy. Finally, in our final spring game, he put us on opposite sides and Keith cut off the tackle on one play. I just blew him up. So that night at dinner, coach Bruce must have played that 10 times on the film. (Keith got me back later in the NFL during a Giants-Eagles game when I was chasing Randall Cunningham.)

I am coaching today, and I tell everybody about what I experienced at Ohio State. If I had to do it all over again, I would. Not a doubt about it. Not a hesitation. I loved every moment I was there, the good times and bad times. It was a great experience.

Pepper Johnson, who recorded 379 tackles in his Ohio State career, played on two Super Bowl championship teams in his seven seasons with the New York Giants. He also played with the Cleveland Browns, Detroit Lions, and New York Jets.

JOHN KACHERSKI

1987–1988, 1991

I HOPE MY STORY SERVES AS A LESSON in perseverance. After four years of high school in Riverhead, New York, I was short the credits I needed to graduate, and I had no eligibility remaining to play football. My dream of playing college football at Ohio State was fading fast, so I enrolled at Milford Academy, a prep school, in Milford, Connecticut. After two seasons at Milford Academy, I earned my diploma and the necessary grade point average and SAT scores needed to become eligible. I returned to Riverhead to pursue my dream—I prepared a highlight film and sent a copy to Ohio State. A few days later, I received a call that would change my life forever.

While at Milford, I remember watching the Buckeyes play Alabama in the 1986 Kickoff Classic. I was impressed by their hard-hitting defense and how they played with reckless abandon. I took it upon myself to learn about the rich tradition and what it meant to play football at Ohio State. I took my recruiting visit in January 1987, weeks after they defeated Texas A&M in the Cotton Bowl, and I had the privilege of meeting coach Hayes while I was having lunch with coach Bruce. Coach Hayes told me that playing football at Ohio State was an honor and that a degree from the university could change my life.

The player who cemented my decision to choose Ohio State was Chris Spielman. Unlike other recruiting visits, where recruits were wined and dined and shown campus nightlife, Chris took me back to his apartment to eat pizza and watch game film. Right then and there, I began to understand that football at Ohio State was more than just a game—it was a way of life.

John Kacherski was named
captain of the 1991 team.

I enrolled in 1987, just in time for spring football. After opening the season with wins at home against West Virginia and Oregon, we traveled to Baton Rouge to play LSU. It was a hard-fought game that ended in a 13–13 tie. In the locker room after the game, I witnessed players and coaches crying. It was then that I understood that the Ohio State Buckeyes go into every battle expecting to win, and that is the cornerstone of the tradition.

The most memorable game for me, emotionally, was the Michigan game that season. Coach Bruce informed us on Monday before the game that he had been fired and that game would be his last at Ohio State. In the locker room before the game, he said he appreciated us wanting to win for him but that we should win this game for the seniors and for what it means to the tradition at Ohio State. Losing that day was not an option, and we defeated Michigan 23–20.

The next season, I moved to outside linebacker and was determined to make my mark on OSU football. A large part of my success is credited to my position coach, Fred Pagac. Coach Pagac had the ability to make average players good and good players great. He embraced the tradition and taught us to play with passion and emotion. More important, he taught his players the responsibility of playing at Ohio State and the character needed to be successful off the field.

283

Coach Cooper's era began with a resounding victory over Syracuse—when I would make my first start. I remember staying at the hotel the night before the game, and I was so excited that I couldn't sleep. It was similar to the feelings I had when I was a kid on Christmas Eve! The morning of the game, you could feel the excitement as fans welcomed the buses with loud cheers of "Let's Go Bucks!"

Two weeks later, against LSU, we were losing 33–27 with less than two minutes remaining. LSU had the ball and we had two timeouts left. I remember that the noise was deafening. Their third-down pass sailed out of bounds, and on fourth down, they opted to take a safety. After the free kick, Greg Frey hit Bobby Olive for the winning touchdown. The stadium erupted as we watched the fans tear down the goal posts.

One of my best games at Ohio State was against Iowa in 1988. We were playing in Iowa City on a cold and rainy Saturday in November. I hurt my hand in a pregame pass rushing drill. I remember coach Pagac riding me before the game, asking me if I wanted him to kiss it and make it feel better. It was his tough love that made him so effective. I had three sacks, but we tied 24–24. I later found out my hand was broken.

One of the most difficult times for me began in 1989, when I sustained a serious knee injury in the spring. I was forced to sit out the entire season while rehabilitating. It was the first time in my career that I would miss a game, let alone an entire season. I returned to the field in 1990 determined to win back my starting linebacker spot. But a pure freshman, Alonzo Spellman, had stepped into my spot and had an outstanding season. Fortunately for me, Alonzo began looking more like a defensive end rather than an outside linebacker. By the start of the 1990 season, Alonzo was 6′6″ and weighed 285 pounds.

We opened the 1990 season against Texas Tech. I had two sacks in the first quarter only to reinjure my knee before the half. Once again, I was forced to sit out the entire season.

After another year of hard work and rehabilitation, I returned in 1991 for my final season, and my teammates rewarded my determination with one of the greatest honors possible at Ohio State: I was elected a captain, along with Scott Graham and Carlos Snow.

Playing football at Ohio State was an incredible experience for me. I feel I contributed a small amount to the great tradition, but I know I received much more in return. I completed my degree and graduated in 1992, which is one of my most satisfying accomplishments. The tradition at Ohio State taught me to set high goals and to expect to be successful. Facing my injuries and how I rebounded from them taught me how to deal with, and overcome, adversity. As I look back at my time at Ohio State, I am humbled by my good fortune. I met my wife, Courtney, and we have two wonderful boys. We moved back to Columbus in 2002 just to be closer to the program and to be part of the Buckeye community.

I was never more proud than when I was watching the 2002 Buckeyes win the national title. Coach Tressel has embraced our great tradition and instilled the character in his players, which is what makes Buckeyes great off the field. The 2002 national title was most deserved by a program that is larger than one player. The program has earned its place as one of the best in college football.

Coach Hayes was correct: it is an honor to play football at Ohio State.

In 1988, John Kacherski set a then–Big Ten record for the most sacks in a season with nine.

MIKE LANESE

1982–1985

I WOULD LIKE TO SAY I HAD A REALLY GOOD REASON for selecting Ohio State over Michigan. I didn't. Several schools recruited me, but from the beginning I knew it would be a toss-up between spending the next four years in Columbus or Ann Arbor. I researched each school's academics, football program, and a category I just called intangibles. No matter how I examined the data, I couldn't distinguish between the two. Michigan had been stealing guys from the Cleveland area for a few years, and several of my friends in high school were big Wolverine fans. So early on, I probably leaned toward Michigan.

I struggled with the decision for a few weeks. But as the signing date drew near, I woke up one cold February morning from a fitful sleep and, almost unconsciously, I said aloud, "I am going to Ohio State." Call it an epiphany. Call it an attack of prospective common sense. Call it what you will, but then and there I committed to be a Buckeye for the rest of my life.

It was the most important decision I ever made, and it was clearly one of the best.

That's not to say my Ohio State career started out all peaches and cream. I was an all-state tailback at Mayfield High School and wanted to play tailback in college. Coach Bruce promised that I would get a shot at playing tailback. He kept his word. The problem was that he also recruited four other all-state tailbacks, three from Ohio and one from Tennessee.

One of the three from Ohio was a guy called Keith Byars. He looked like a fullback to me, but coach Bruce promised him a shot at tailback, too. As summer camp began for freshmen, it was pretty obvious that Keith was a man among boys. Keith saw playing time as a freshman while I rode the bench. During the week, I played scout-team tailback, with my 6′0″, 185-pound frame getting beaten up on a regular basis by the likes of Marcus Marek. At the end of my freshman year, coach Bruce asked if I wanted to make the switch to flanker. The hardhead that I was, I said no. But midway through my sophomore year I had another one of those epiphanies. Barring a pretty significant growth spurt, I concluded that if I wanted to play, I would have to find a different position. So I made the switch to flanker.

I could always catch the ball pretty well, so the transition to flanker was pretty natural athletically. But emotionally, I felt as if I should be watching the game from the stands. A tailback, especially at Ohio State, is a large part of the game. Sometimes he is the whole game. Wide receivers can go a whole game without getting so much as a grass stain. I struggled and played little my sophomore year. I never lost confidence in my ability, but something was missing. Little did I know that something was Cris Carter.

In the summer before my junior year, I decided to take a summer class and stay in Columbus to work out. The quarterbacks/receivers coach at the time, Jim Tressel (whatever happened to him?), asked if I would consider taking on a roommate. I had a feeling I was being set up, and I really liked living alone. So I said no. But coach Tress persisted, and I wound up with Cris as a roommate. He was, in a word, unique. He is one of those guys who just lights up a room. When coach Tress asked me how things were going, I just shook my head and asked, "Who is this guy?" Even John Bozick, our equipment manager, liked him. And he hated all freshmen.

I think coach Tress thought I would be able to become something of a moderating influence on Cris, but it was Cris who ended up influencing me. When summer camp started in 1984, things just clicked for me as a receiver. No more doubt, no more second thoughts. I enjoyed playing wide receiver. I enjoyed playing, period. After being written off in the preseason, the Ohio State receiving corps ended up making a pretty respectable contribution to the 1984 Big Ten championship season.

Despite the success I had as a receiver, people remember me for one catch. During the Michigan game in 1984, I fumbled a punt just before the half. But I came back in the fourth quarter to make a big catch on a third-and-long that kept a drive alive. We went on to win 21–6, and I was named the Chevrolet MVP for the game. To this day, little old ladies come up to me and

Mike Lanese was a winner on the field and a champion in the classroom.

say, "I remember that catch you made against Michigan. . . ." I guess there are worse things to be remembered for.

Ohio State fans are, literally, everywhere. I've had the good fortune to travel around the world, and whether it's Singapore or Shanghai, Mombassa or Mexico City, I've run into people who love Ohio State. It's pretty humbling, really. They don't always know the names or faces of the legends, and some have never actually seen a game, but many can hum the fight song or "Carmen, Ohio" as well as anyone in Ohio Stadium.

Three things distinguish the Ohio State program from the rest: first, Ohio State is a world-class university. It's one of the few universities in the country that offers a truly overwhelming array of opportunities and challenges. Ohio State is a place where you can be intellectually curious, where you can think about yourself and your place in the world. Given Ohio State's size, comprehensiveness, and diversity, I can think of no better place for a young student-athlete to define the parameters of his or her intellectual experience.

Second, the Ohio State program embodies the no-nonsense, Midwestern work ethic. No frills. No glitz or glamour. Just a bunch of tough coaches, players, equipment guys, and trainers. It's no surprise that a guy like Earle Bruce would find success at Ohio State. Earle was a football coach. He didn't care about image. He just wanted to line his team up against our opponent and play clean, hard football. He treated his players fairly and made sure that we kept our perspective. During one practice, for example, after returning from my first Rhodes Scholarship interview, he wanted to make sure I was still thinking about football. We were running passing drills and I ran the wrong route on a play. As I jogged back to the huddle, he yelled to the rest of the offense, "He has to be the dumbest guy I ever coached!" That was Earle. No slack. Just do the right thing all the time.

Third, the Ohio State program is about winning. Win fairly. Win with class. But win. We had a team full of guys who wanted to win, but I can't think of anyone who wanted to win more than Keith Byars. I've never met anyone with a more competitive spirit. There were games where he would just wear down the defense with his combination of speed and strength. And I saw him play with pain, too. During one game, I saw him come back to the huddle a little wobbly. He was bleeding from his mouth and nose. I told him to take a blow for a play so he could gather himself. But he wouldn't leave the field. During another, he knocked a linebacker from Purdue out cold. The biggest frustration of my career was seeing him robbed of the Heisman in 1984.

As the years go by, I forget the scores and statistics. I even forget a few of the names and faces. But I take a piece of Ohio State with me wherever I go. Whether it was as a naval officer 10 years ago or now as a banker, I often think back to that cold day in February when I made a commitment to become a Buckeye. It made all the difference in my life.

Tradition is the glue that keeps the Ohio State program together, Despite the coaching changes, despite the player transition, through the good times and bad times, it is the tradition built over the past 100 years that remains and sustains the program. I am honored to be a part of it.

288

Mike Lanese, a team captain in 1985, earned a Rhodes Scholarship and was a two-time Academic All-American.

KIRK LOWDERMILK

1981–1984

IT WAS A GOOD THING THAT I WAS A PRETTY FAIR WRESTLER, or I don't think I would have ended up at Ohio State. I was from Salem, Ohio, and I didn't get recruited by the big schools—just Toledo and Cincinnati. I was kind of what they call a potluck guy, but I went down to the state wrestling tournament and I beat two guys that were headed to play football at big schools. Mike Golic would go on to Notre Dame, and Dave Crecelius would head to Ohio State.

I won the heavyweight division, and the next day I met with coach Bruce. He offered me a scholarship and said, "Go home and think about it."

I told him, "What's there to think about? I will sign it right now." There was no question where I wanted to go. I always wanted to play at Ohio State.

Once I was there, I remember getting to play just one play at our first scrimmage and it motivated me. I was really broken-hearted. I just decided that was it—I was not going to sit on the bench for four years. I would do anything to get on that field, and that's how I got my letter as a freshman— I was on the kickoff team.

You'll never forget that first time you run onto that field in front of ninety thousand fans. Really, it's a cliché, but your feet don't touch the ground. On my very first play as a Buckeye, I hurt my knee. My foot just got stuck on the artificial turf, but I didn't want to tell anybody, because I didn't want them taking me out of the game.

The Michigan game of my freshman year was one of the most exciting games [a 14–9 OSU victory] of my whole career. I can still see Vaughn

289

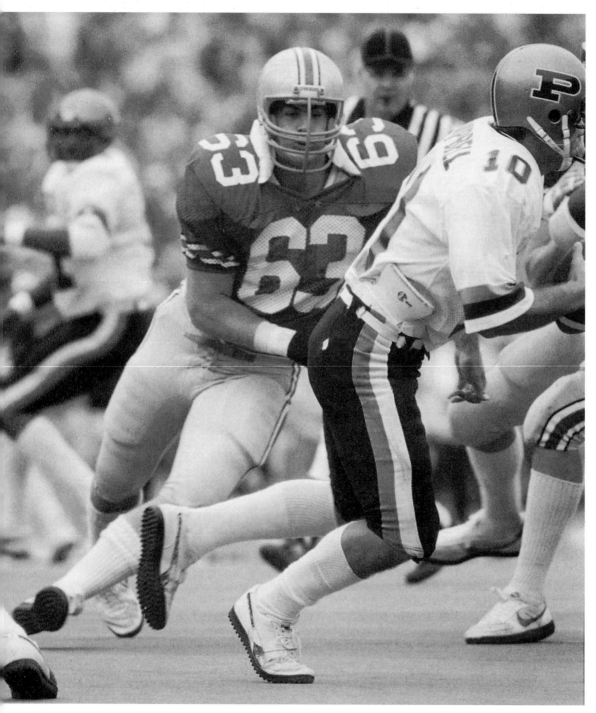

Kirk Lowdermilk, here blocking against Purdue in 1982, was All–Big Ten in 1984.

Broadnax making that block for Art Schlichter. That was just an awesome game.

My sophomore year, they moved me to defense. I was too slow to play defense, but I was getting playing time and that is what mattered to me. I backed up Spencer Nelms at nose guard. I remember during that Florida State game [a 34–17 loss], I got a deep thigh bruise and Dr. Murphy gave me a shot right on the bruise. I walked out of the locker room and passed out. The following spring, they moved me back to left guard. Hey, I just wanted on the field. Then I played center for my senior year.

The game everybody remembers in 1984 was the Illinois game when Keith [Byars] turned it on. We got down 24–0 and I could tell from looking at Keith in the huddle that he was ready to do something. He scored, came back to the bench and the TV cameras were on him, and he said, "We're coming back, baby, we're coming back!" I was standing right next to him when he said it.

He brought us back, and everybody remembers him losing his shoe on that long run. That was such an amazing game [a 45–38 Ohio State victory].

I have to say that Keith, John Frank, and Pepper Johnson were my favorite players, and it wasn't so much because they were good, it was because they were tough, they practiced hard, and they were physical each and every day. They were first-class people.

Later, at Wisconsin, I broke my fibula in my left leg, making the rest of the season very disappointing. We beat Michigan, and I got in for a charity play just to say I played, but it hurt so much to be injured when I wanted to be on the field with my teammates. My senior year and I couldn't play against Michigan . . . that hurt more than any broken leg.

We were 3–1 against Michigan, which means I have three pairs of gold pants. I gave them to my mom, my sister, and my wife. They wear them on a chain.

Once we went to the Rose Bowl, nothing was going to keep me out of that game. I knew I couldn't do any more damage, so I played the whole game. We drove it right down the field on that first drive, missed a field goal, and ended up losing to USC 20–17. I really believe that we were the better team and that is one game we never should have lost. Plus, it was my final game, and it was tough leaving the field. I loved being a Buckeye, and I can still remember sitting in that locker room, in no big hurry to take off the uniform. I remember coach [Fred] Pagac coming over and giving me a hug. It's very sad when it all ends.

I will never have a bad word to say about coach Bruce. I think back to what he used to preach to us and how it all makes sense now. I remember how he used to get fired up and he would pound his index finger on the desk. . . . I don't know how he didn't dislocate it. The guy loved his players. The time Curt Curtis put his foot through the glass door at the French Field House, nearly slicing his calf off, coach Bruce was crushed. It ruined the guy's career, and coach Bruce was crying for him. I don't think President Ed Jennings ever understood what that man did for the university. His firing a few years later was a black eye for the university, and I really believe he deserved better.

I told my daughter, who's a good athlete, that she will like college ball so much better than high school for one big reason—everybody is there for the same reason. They are there to get better and compete. The intensity in our practices was unreal. The game was the easy part, but the part I really liked was the work in practice. We would work hard in practice, compete against each other, and then go have a beer together.

We ended up with two Big Ten titles and a Rose Bowl trip, but I would have liked to win a national championship.

Because of my NFL career, I didn't get to go to a Buckeyes game in Ohio Stadium until 1998, and I was just mesmerized when the band came down the tunnel. You know, that's something you don't get to see when you are a player. Man, I almost got emotional. I was just stunned. It really makes the hair on your neck stand up. It never gets old. Those are the things that make Ohio State really special.

Kirk Lowdermilk, a team captain in 1984, became one of the NFL's best centers in eight seasons with the Minnesota Vikings.

MARCUS MAREK

1979–1982

At first, I was recruited by Woody Hayes, but that was December of 1978, three weeks before the Gator Bowl incident. He pulled his chair up to mine, and he was about three inches from my face when he told me, "You are an Ohio boy and you are coming to Ohio State!" I grew up in Masury, Ohio, near Youngstown and the Pennsylvania border. Once Earle Bruce was named head coach, he and two assistants—Dennis Fryzel and Glen Mason—came to see me. I was playing a pickup basketball game, and I didn't talk to them until the game was over. I guess that didn't sit well with Earle. He told the other coaches that showed a lack of respect on my part, but it was a close game and we were playing to 15 and I didn't want to lose.

Fortunately, it didn't end up costing me the chance to go to Ohio State.

I can still picture the day my dad dropped me off. I had reservations about whether I could even play there. I weighed 198 pounds soaking wet, and when Dad drove me down there, we didn't say much in the car. Dad was a no-nonsense guy who had dropped out of school in the ninth or tenth grade to help support his family by working at the mill. We got to campus that day, and he got my bags and put them down on the curb. He shook my hand and said, "Good luck and do your best," and he drove away. I think I had tears in my eyes as he drove away.

I was in awe of the university, and I was ready to pack up and come home in those first few days on campus. Everybody was a high school star, and you felt you were just a number. Jeff Gottron was a walk-on, and he and I would play backgammon in between practices in that first camp. We both had

Marcus Marek ranks third in unassisted tackles, first in assisted tackles, and first in total tackles on the Ohio State career list.

sweethearts back home, and we both were homesick. But they gave me [Tom] Cousineau's No. 36 and Jeff had "B-147," so it could have been worse. I remember the coach at Youngstown State once told me, "If it doesn't work out down there, you'll always have a place here." I thought about that a little.

We had our first scrimmage and I just ran around and made tackles, trying as hard as I could.

In that first game against Syracuse, I played on special teams, and in the second quarter, Tony Megaro went down with a knee injury. I was behind him on the depth chart, but I really thought I was the third-team linebacker until I heard my name called. As I ran onto the field, it was almost as if I could hear eighty-eight thousand people turning the page in their programs to see who the hell this kid was. On that first play, they ran right at me, but somebody forgot to block me and I tackled the guy for a one-yard loss.

The great thing was the fact that as Tony rehabbed his knee for three or four weeks, he was right there helping me out. He was teaching me, standing right behind me. That year was pretty special because we had a real good team. I went into every game nervous, but it wasn't because I was afraid of the guy across from me. I just didn't want to look bad or get beat and have it show up on film in front of my teammates. I always had that fear of somebody making me look bad.

As a freshman, I made three tackles on that goal-line stand we had up at Michigan. It was their first drive, and they went right down the field, but they went for it on fourth down, running an option, and I made the tackle. I'll never forget that day [an 18–15 OSU victory], because it was so loud we couldn't hear each other in the huddle.

At the Rose Bowl, it was a business trip for us. We were out there to accomplish one thing, and we were totally focused on it. We actually were just a few minutes away from being national champs [leading USC 16–10]. I remember that I couldn't even see Charles White in the backfield behind those linemen because he was shorter than everybody else. All these years later, I may think, "If I could have made one more play, or stopped the ball . . ." What I remember is how close we were.

During my sophomore year, I remember walking across the campus and Woody Hayes and I were on the same path. I was thinking, "He won't remember who I am." Not only did he remember, he remembered my parents' names and one of my friends from high school. "Didn't you have a friend who was going to Allegheny College?" he asked. He never forgot people.

It is an honor today to hold the career tackling record. Records are made to be broken, but somebody would have to average about 12 tackles per game for four years. I was just fortunate that I never got injured.

I have no regrets. I made the best of what talent I had, and playing at Ohio State those four years was like a dream come true for me. That Ohio State atmosphere drove me to play. It drove me to want to be a good player. When I went back to a game for the first time, I gave my ticket to someone else and just tailgated and watched the band come across the street from St. John Arena. I loved the festivities of it all, and it really was the first time I got to experience it. Those were all things I never saw before.

Ohio State is unlike any other school. It is an amazing place, and game day at Ohio Stadium is an amazing day. Everybody is wearing scarlet and gray.

Everybody is there to support the Buckeyes. When I took my wife back the first time, we stayed at the Holiday Inn on Lane Avenue. An hour before the game, I said, "We had better get walking." She said, "What do you mean? The stadium is right there. It won't take that long." We started to walk, and I left with one beer in my hand. By the time I got over past St. John Arena, I had guys shoving beers at me and telling me how much I meant to them. I think I ended up with a 12-pack, but it really gave me an idea of how great the fans are.

I look back now and I can really sense how important being a Buckeye is to me.

Marcus Marek, Ohio State's all-time leader in tackles with 572, played three seasons in the United States Football League and one in the Canadian Football League.

CARLOS SNOW

1987–1989, 1991

I CAME FROM A SMALL HIGH SCHOOL in Cincinnati by the name of C.A.P.E.—Cincinnati Academy of Physical Education. We were playing in our most intense rivalry game against Ironton, and even though we lost on the scoreboard, I knew I had left everything on the field that day. All that summer conditioning, spring ball, weight lifting, determination, heart, and soul were left on the field in that game. I was lying on the ground after the game and I asked God, "Where did I go wrong? What could I have done better to help our team win?"

A voice spoke over me and it said, "Your grade was 99 percent. It would have been 100, but I never give perfect scores, little man." That voice was Earle Bruce's. He then said, "You are the kind of athlete we would love to have at The Ohio State University."

From that moment, I knew I was a Buckeye!

I was 5′7″ and 190 pounds, and because of my size, the odds were against me. But coach Bruce realized the size of my heart. I got the starting job during my freshman season, beating out guys that I had looked up to for years, but fumbling was a big problem for me in college because of the tight-fitting jerseys. I can honestly say that, because I never fumbled in high school.

During one hot summer practice, we were doing live goal-line hitting, and I was introduced to the difference between high school and college football.

The play called was "22 sprint draw." As I got the ball and saw the hole open up, I went through it and suddenly I ran into a brick wall. I had never been hit so hard in my entire sports life. To this day, I can still say that. The hit was so hard that I still have visions of it in my sleep. Mr. Chris Spielman was on the other end of that hit. His helmet hit smack in the middle of my chest, snot flew from my nose, and the pads came out of my helmet. My shoulder pads came undone, and my shoulder popped out of place. To add insult to my injuries, he spit tobacco juice right between my eyes.

"Welcome to Ohio State football," he said.

That man was a great, great player.

The greatest game we ever played in was against Michigan at the "Big House" in 1987. I think we were down by three points and Chris was playing the game of his life—he must have had 18 solo tackles at the half. I heard Earle calling for the "little guy." He said. "Put him in right now!"

When I got that call, I almost threw up my breakfast. He put me in the biggest game of the year, and here I was a freshman. He didn't know if I would hold onto the ball or fumble and let the whole team down. Tom Tupa called the play, and it was a pass. I was the number three read on the play, so I figured I wasn't going to get the ball. I ran my route to about four yards from the sideline, and I turned and saw the ball coming. It was coming in a hurry, and I was thinking, "Don't drop it!" Seventy yards later, I was in the end zone. It was the greatest feeling in the world to me.

We went on to win that game, which was coach Bruce's final game.

At the Columbus Touchdown Club's award banquet, I met Woody Hayes the year before he died. He had told me, "Run tough and run fast!" and that's what I was thinking about on that long run to the end zone in the Big House.

When you walk into my mother's house today, the first picture you see is that of Woody and me shaking hands.

I was always proud to wear the scarlet and gray. My one regret is that I didn't finish school because I put all my eggs into one basket. That would be the advice I would give to all the current and future Buckeyes: whatever you do on the field—finish, finish, finish school, so that life after football can be what you want it to be.

I will always love the Buckeyes!

Carlos Snow led Ohio State in rushing in 1988, '89, and '91. He finished with 2,974 rushing yards—sixth on OSU's all-time list.

Carlos Snow bursts upfield during the Indiana game in 1989.

CHRIS SPIELMAN

1984–1987

WHEN I WAS A KID AND I PLAYED WITH MY G.I. JOES, I didn't play army like all the other kids. I lined them up on each side and played a football game with them. I was a coach's son, and from an early age, I loved the game and studied the game so that I could be the best I could be.

In deciding where to attend college, I was torn between Ohio State and Michigan. I thought the two schools mirrored each other, but I was an Ohio kid, and once I got through all the fluff of everybody telling me how much they wanted me and how much they loved me, I knew where I had to go. At that time, the governor was calling my house. I came home from a recruiting trip to Miami, and I went through Dayton, and there were a bunch of people there with Buckeye signs for me to see. I always tried to keep it all in perspective and enjoy the process, and I look back on it with fondness now. I remember meeting with coach Hayes in his office, and we talked about history some. Here's one thing he told me: "Learn to speak a foreign language—it will help you later." When I first met him, I was eight or nine years old and we were in a Bob Evans in Canton. He was recruiting Ray Ellis at the time, and they were there. My dad was a high school coach and he knew Ray, so we went over and met him.

People have asked me if I wish I had been born earlier so I could have played for him, but I don't. That wasn't my time or my destiny. When I signed with Ohio State, I knew coach Bruce was like what I try to be: what you see is what you get. He was passionate about Ohio State, too. He told me I would have a chance to earn a starting job as a freshman, and he was true to his word.

On that first day we were in pads, I just tried running around and making a lot of plays. After the scrimmage, I was named the starting linebacker. Then I hurt my ankle and I wasn't able to start the first game against Oregon State. Now that drove me crazy. I had a goal to start for Ohio State as a freshman, and I was frustrated. But I got in the game in the second half, and I started after that.

Being new to college, football was the easy part for me. Being a coach's son, I always connected with the mental part of the game. I saw the advantage I would get if I learned what everybody's job was on the field—knowing where they were and what they were doing. As I got older, I just elevated that to college. I know I was focused about it.

My wife was my high school sweetheart, and she went to Ohio State, too. She was in a sorority, and when they had their functions, other guys would ask me, "Don't you want to be over there with her?" I said, "Hey, I trust her. She has her thing and I have mine." Mine was to focus on my goals—going to school, playing football, and maybe going to the NFL later. Let me put it this way, they didn't let me host many recruits, because they didn't want them hosted by a hermit.

Anyway, in that second half of the Oregon State game, I made plays and it validated that I could play at this level. We went on to beat Michigan to go to the Rose Bowl my freshman year. I was 18 and playing in the Rose Bowl, and we should have beaten USC that day. You always have that sense that you will get back there, but it didn't work out for us.

The next year, losing to Wisconsin at home irks me still. Losing at Michigan doesn't sit well, either. Then we had a great game plan in the Citrus Bowl and we played a 3-5 defense against Robbie Bosco and BYU. To start my junior year, we lost the Kickoff Classic, lost at Washington, and then we ran off nine wins in a row. We had a chance to beat Michigan, and that was a bitter loss. The best overall game I had been a part of was the Cotton Bowl against Texas A&M. They had three or four number one draft picks on that team, and everybody in Texas thought they were going to blow us out. I remember sitting in a press conference before the game and asking, "What are we? I mean, hey, we're Ohio State." It seemed nobody gave us a chance, but we won that game quite handily [28–12]. I remember that coach Bruce almost went to Arizona after that game.

Before my senior season, things didn't go right. We lost Cris Carter [ruled ineligible by the NCAA], and we never overcame that. With him, we lost a lot of our offense. When I look back at that whole ordeal now, the great

Chris Spielman possessed unmatched intensity and desire.

thing that came from it is how Cris turned his life around. He is a team guy, he learned from it, and he paid his consequences. He was the ultimate competitor, and he would be the first guy I would take if I were choosing sides. I do respect him very much.

In the end, I feel responsible for what happened to coach Bruce. Losing to Iowa in our last home game was the toughest loss. We had the game won, but they hit Marv Cook on a pass and they scored to beat us [29–27]. It was unprecedented for a coach to get fired before the Michigan game, and it was disturbing to me to say the least, but I was in awe of the way coach Bruce handled himself throughout that last week. He put his feelings of rejection aside and got us ready to play. One of my fondest memories was from Senior Tackle on that Thursday. He had broken his leg in college and never got to do Senior Tackle. I introduced him that night, and he was the last guy to do Senior Tackle. He went down there and hit the sled, and I realized how much it meant to him. Then before the game, we broke out those "Earle" headbands and he was surprised at that. After we won [23–20], we carried him off the field, but I didn't participate in the team celebration much. I just sat back and watched him.

When I look back on it, I am really privileged and honored to have played football at Ohio State. All I wanted to do was represent the tradition before me and after me in the best way possible. Ohio State is a living, breathing entity. It becomes a part of you. I am humbled by my experiences there. I have this radio show in Columbus, and I once said, "Our goal is not to be good, it is to be great" and fans called in questioning me, saying, "You expect too much from these kids. You put too much pressure on them."

Pressure is your friend. Being a former player, I believe this is the standard that was set before us, and this is the standard we must uphold. That will never change. We must keep our standards high. That is what Ohio State is all about. I can honestly say that I am very glad I was able to represent this university, and I worked hard to represent it in the right way.

Chris Spielman, who finished his career with 546 tackles, made a school-record 29 tackles (tying Tom Cousineau for a single-game high) against Michigan in 1986. He was named All–Big Ten three times and was an All-American in 1986 and '87 and a team captain in '87. He also won the Lombardi Award in '87. He played 12 seasons in the NFL.

MIKE TOMCZAK

1981–1984

I'LL NEVER FORGET THE FIRST DAY I had set foot on campus as an Ohio State freshman. We were in training camp, and Jim Lachey and I were walking down Woody Hayes Drive toward High Street. Who's coming the other way? It was Woody himself. He stopped us, and the thing that shocked us was that he knew everything about us—our parents' names and about our coaches. He told us how important an education was, and we listened intently. It was a unique experience.

I started to learn the tradition at Ohio State from the previous summer when I attended the football camp there. Growing up south of Chicago, I was named Player of the Year in the state of Illinois, and I was being recruited by Michigan, Notre Dame, UCLA, and Wake Forest. But I was sold on Ohio State for so many reasons, and I couldn't wait to become a Buckeye.

When I got on campus, there were six quarterbacks in my class, and of course, Art Schlichter had one more season as the starter.

But I wasn't afraid of competition, and I didn't take a redshirt season. I ended up as the third-string quarterback that season, and I traveled to all of the games. I will never forget that Michigan game of my freshman season when Vaughn Broadnax made the big block and Art worked his way into the end zone. Those guys, along with Marcus Marek, Glen Cobb, Gary Williams, and all the upperclassmen, were larger than life to me. Art was like an icon, more so then than anybody is right now. He just looked like a quarterback, on and off the field.

I learned about adversity right away as a sophomore. We started pretty well and beat Baylor and Michigan State, and we had Stanford beat in the third game. We were ahead and moving down to about their 35 late in the game. I threw a pass I shouldn't have thrown, and it got intercepted. John Elway then led Stanford to the winning score in the final seconds, and we had a lot of upset people after that game. We lost to Florida State and got beat by Wisconsin 6–0. I was benched. Everyone is affected by an Ohio State loss, but when you lose three in a row . . . it got really bad.

That whole thing put me into a shell. I was still a young kid and I wanted to prove people wrong, and as everybody knows, the media can be pretty tough in Columbus. We went to Illinois, and that was my home-state team. I wanted to go back and prove that I could do the job. I give coach Bruce credit because he threw me back in there and gave me another chance like he said he would. We beat Illinois 26–21 and won the rest of our games.

Earle was old school. He was very prepared, very disciplined, and very organized. I remember that during my sophomore year, we would have breakfast together twice a week at the Holiday Inn just to get to know each other and get on the same page.

The next year, in the season's second game, we beat Oklahoma on the road in one of the most physical games I ever played. I remember the big talk all week would be whether John Frank would play because of the Jewish holiday, but John played and had a huge game. We were the underdog that day, and we just physically dominated them. Our defense beat up Marcus Dupree so badly that he didn't play in the second half. I cramped up and spent the night in the hospital. Emotionally and physically, we were drained, and I think that is one reason we lost to Iowa the next week.

I went through my share of adversity the next year. In the spring game after my junior season, I was running the option when I got hit high by Pepper Johnson and low by Dave Morrill. I knew my leg was broken right away. It was just one of those things. Some doctors said that was the end of my career, and coach Bruce wanted me to redshirt my senior year, but I said, "No, I am going out with my class."

It was a long road to recovery. I didn't start the opener my senior year, but that was the last game I missed.

At the end of my career, I had three pairs of gold pants from beating Michigan, and I have to say that beating them up there was the ultimate.

305

306

Mike Tomczak
rebounded from a
broken leg to lead
the 1984 Buckeyes
to the Rose Bowl.

They were always very clean, hard-hitting football games. We used to stay outside of Ann Arbor in some little dumpy hotel, and our locker room there would have a single nail sticking out of the wall with your number above it. Those are the types of things you remember.

I thoroughly believed it was a privilege to play at Ohio State. In turn, I tried to do my best to uphold the rich tradition we have, on and off the field. I care about that school, and I do bleed scarlet and gray. A lot of people mature during adolescence, but I grew up between the ages of 17 and 21 and Ohio State allowed me to do that.

After my second year in the NFL, I decided to endow a scholarship. Jim Lachey did the same thing, and our goal was to get many others to do it, too. I decided I wanted to pay forward, since I couldn't pay back.

At the Fiesta Bowl in 2002, I was watching practice on the Wednesday before the game, and as a past captain, I almost felt a sense of duty to address the team. I just told them, "The world is betting against you. Write down your goal. Write down 'national champions.'"

Before the game that night, four or five players came up to me on the sideline and said they had written it down, and I thought it would have been neat if my speech touched just one guy. But that's what Ohio State is all about. The most wonderful guys I ever met in my life were my teammates at Ohio State. What you come to understand is that the people who played before you, and after you, are all part of the family.

Mike Tomczak played 17 seasons in the NFL—with the Chicago Bears, Green Bay Packers, Cleveland Browns, Pittsburgh Steelers, and Detroit Lions.

JEFF UHLENHAKE

1985–1988

Playing football at OSU has had a profound effect on my life through the connections I've made. Everyone knows that Ohio State football is always a topic of conversation at any Ohio workplace, and when people know you played football at Ohio State, they want to know all about it.

The games I remember most, of course, are the Michigan games. I am proud to say they also were my very best. The Michigan loss in 1986 when we missed a field goal with a minute left to go, and we would have gone to the Rose Bowl, would have to be the most disappointing game I played in.

A year later, the Michigan win in Earle Bruce's last game was the most enjoyable. It was a great way to send off most of the coaching staff that recruited me.

Being a captain in 1988, I had the honor to give a rousing speech at the pregame meal before the Michigan game. It worked so well—we were behind 20–0 at halftime. But we came back to lose a close one 34–31. That was the last of my pregame speeches.

The bowl games were great—no school, gifts, spending money, almost like playing in the pros. The one I remember most was beating heavily favored Texas A&M in the 1987 Cotton Bowl. That was an awesome experience because they were supposed to drill us in their home state.

That reminds me of the greatest players I played with: Chris Spielman and Cris Carter. Chris Spielman's hard work and dedication was second to none. I remember Chris, as a freshman in the Rose Bowl game against USC, flipping over a blocker and making the tackle. It was an awesome play. Cris

Jeff Uhlenhake was a mainstay on the offensive line from 1985 to 1988, starting at guard and center for four seasons.

Carter made a one-handed catch against BYU in the Citrus Bowl, and he managed to keep one foot in bounds (of course, everyone saw him make many one-handed catches and get two feet in bounds in the NFL). They were two of the greatest players making great plays.

Maybe you've heard of my favorite coach at OSU. His name was Jim Tressel [an assistant in 1983–85]. Steve Devine, Bob Palcic, and Fred Pagac were great to be around, too. Steve was very funny and always made meetings enjoyable. I roomed with Fred Pagac's nephew, and we would visit his house, and his wife "Bernie" treated us like her own.

One funny moment with Bob Palcic was in 1986 when we played at Washington. We came in at halftime and we were getting our butts kicked. We were sitting there waiting for our ass-chewing when a loud shriek shot throughout the locker room. We thought someone had broken their leg or something, but coach Palcic got his finger stuck in the door. You would have thought someone would had to have died from that yelp.

Anyway, it gave us something to laugh about on the five-hour airplane ride home after getting drilled by the Huskies.

All three children in my family have graduated from OSU. I feel as though everyone in Ohio and all the alumni throughout the world can take pride in Ohio State.

The pride exhibited in Arizona during the Fiesta Bowl game against Miami—I do not believe has ever been matched by any school, including Notre Dame. Sitting in the upper deck at the Fiesta Bowl with many players I played with, and who played before and after me as well, brought so much satisfaction and pride.

Any Ohio State recruit will know they are part of a loving, supportive family. With that family comes responsibility and accountability. The returns from practice, study, social life, and especially the games will be your rewards for everything you are willing to invest.

The bonds made between football players are made great by the brutal nature of the sport. Just know that all Buckeyes past and present are fighting the battles along with you.

I chose Ohio State because they offered me a scholarship, but I became and I am a Buckeye!

Jeff Uhlenhake, a guard, was All–Big Ten in 1986 and the MVP of the '88 team.

The
NINETIES

EDDIE GEORGE

1992–1995

I WASN'T RECRUITED MUCH DURING MY SENIOR YEAR of high school. As a matter of fact, no big schools were interested in me. I had a good year at Fork Union Military in Virginia, and all of a sudden I started to gain the attention of schools like Louisville, BYU, Virginia, and Virginia Tech. I had a friend who was on the Ohio State training staff, and he had told the coaches, "Here's a guy you need to look at."

They told him to have me send a tape. I did. They liked what they saw and wanted another one. I sent it. The next thing I knew, I was coming out to Columbus for a visit.

Right away, I was very impressed by the environment. The tradition at Ohio State just blew me away. It was all I had ever wanted. Coach Cooper, my mom, and I were standing by the Buckeye Grove where the trees are planted for the All-Americans, and I committed right there on the spot.

It is not a stretch to say that I dreamed of becoming an All-American and having my own tree in the Buckeye Grove.

I got there in time for spring practice in '92, and my first thought was, "I've never seen linebackers, running backs, and defensive backs this big." I was overwhelmed.

There were ups and downs right away. I scored three touchdowns against Syracuse [a 35–12 win] on national television. Then two weeks later, I fumbled twice and we lost a close game to Illinois [18–16] at Ohio Stadium. Those fumbles . . . that is what I became known for. I was just finding my niche as a short-yardage specialist, and then that happened. It really set me back. I was embarrassed by the fumbles, and we lost the game, really because of my fumbles. At that time, I was very disappointed and frustrated.

That was the crossroads for me. I could have let it get me down and not bounced back, but I decided to work harder and never let it happen again. Raymont Harris told me at the time, "It happens. Fumbles are part of the game, but your character will be revealed by how you respond to it."

He also told me what I needed to work on—I was running right away and not letting the play develop in front of me, and I needed to work on my speed.

Still, I never got another real opportunity until my junior year, but it was bittersweet because Raymont was having an outstanding season in '93. I wanted to play, but he was my best friend I had just had to step back and support him.

I felt I had a very good junior season [1,442 yards], but nobody around the country really knew anything about me. I wasn't breaking off the big runs, but I did have a 76-yard run that season. We were 9–4 and sort of rebuilding.

That next summer, my thought process was that we had the components to compete for a national championship. I thought I had the opportunity to be mentioned for an All-American team, and we were motivated as a team to do something special. We had gotten beat 63–14 at Penn State the year before, and that lingered with all of us. I pretty much worked nonstop and had extra workouts after practice. I had dotted every *I* and crossed every *T*.

We really had a hell of a camp. On offense we had Bobby Hoying, Terry Glenn, and Orlando Pace, and our defense was improving every day.

When we played Boston College at the Meadowlands in the Kickoff Classic of '95, we visited the Downtown Athletic Club and I noticed all the pictures of Heisman winners, like Billy Sims, O. J. Simpson, Hopalong, and Archie. I felt it was an honor just to be in that room. Then somebody took a picture of me with the Heisman Trophy. I thought to myself, "I'll be back to pick this up later in the season." Of course, I didn't say that out loud, but I did think that.

A few weeks later, we played Washington at home, and they had beaten us in a physical game up there the year before. They really let us know about it, too. I remember that this time around, I was getting into the secondary quite a bit and it was my first 200-yard game [212 yards]. That is the first time I heard the chant, "Eddie, Eddie!" at the stadium. It was overwhelming . . . just quite a thrill for me.

313

Eddie George cuts through a hole during the Buckeyes' 45–26 win over Notre Dame in 1995.

Another game I certainly remember was facing Illinois. They had beaten us in '92 and in '94, and they started to say they owned us in our house. I just felt a personal challenge to take it to them. The weather wasn't very good, and I knew we would run the ball that day. I remember looking up at the scoreboard, and I had 188 yards at the half and thought, "Whoa, this is getting out of control now." I broke the [OSU single-game rushing] record sometime in the fourth quarter on a simple draw for 13 or 14 yards. I really had no idea how many yards I had [314 on 36 carries].

It was that night that I had heard people talk about me and the Heisman Trophy in the same sentence.

A month later, I headed to New York for the presentation and really didn't know what would happen. I figured it came down to me, [Florida's] Danny Wuerffel, and [Nebraska's] Tommie Frazier. Archie had told me just to enjoy the moment, and that's what I planned to do, but when they announced the winner, my life really changed at that point.

I studied the Heisman history and its history at Ohio State, and I understand the fraternity that you join when you win it. It is such an honor, and I am happy I get to represent the Buckeyes in that manner.

As I look back at my entire career, it is an amazing story—how it started and how it ended.

Recently, they retired my No. 27, and it was the greatest honor of all. A lot of people told me I would never reach this level, but I did it. It's funny, but when I came to Ohio State, I wanted to wear No. 20 or No. 6, but they both were taken, so they asked me to choose between 38 and 27, and now that number is retired. It really put a closure to my career.

Being part of the Buckeye family is very, very special to me. The guys who played in the fifties support the guys who played in the nineties and so on. I can't walk through an airport anywhere without seeing somebody wearing an Ohio State hat. The support is everywhere, and I can say that Ohio State ranks supreme in my mind.

Eddie George, who gained a school-record 1,927 yards and scored 24 touchdowns in 1995, fulfilled his dream of being named an All-American en route to becoming Ohio State's sixth Heisman Trophy winner. He was selected in the first round of the 1996 NFL draft by the Houston Oilers (now the Tennessee Titans).

JOE GERMAINE

1996–1998

FOR A WHOLE YEAR, MY FAMILY KEPT THE TAPE of the message. It was John Cooper's voice. He had called my home, but we were out, and he just said, "Joe, just cancel all your recruiting trips . . . we want you to be a Buckeye." It was fun for me and my family to replay it and hear those words over and over again.

I was from Phoenix, and I had played one year at Scottsdale Community College, and I had set several junior-college passing records. One game against Arizona Western, I completed 49 of 60 for more than 600 yards, and we really couldn't figure out why I didn't have more offers. I visited Wyoming and Nevada-Reno, but Arizona State and the University of Arizona told me I could walk on. To this day, my family still wonders about it.

Then Larry Coker from Ohio State recruited me. He was the defensive backs coach at the time and then he got appointed quarterbacks coach, so I was really excited about that. But suddenly, he left for Miami [to become offensive coordinator] and I remember talking to him over the phone, asking him, "What am I going to do now?" He said, "Joe, you need to be a Buckeye."

I never second-guessed my decision once I got to Ohio State in 1995. Walt Harris had arrived as quarterbacks coach after coach Coker left, and I have to credit coach Harris with my development. Bobby Hoying had a great year at quarterback while I redshirted, and I feel that year helped prepare me for the next three.

Right away, I really liked the campus. Those old stone and brick buildings with so much history . . . being from Arizona, I loved how green everything was. Believe it or not, I always liked the winter—I really thought the cold and snow were great.

During my redshirt year, before practice one Friday, President Clinton was giving a speech across the street at the Fawcett Center. Somebody came in and mentioned to us that the president would be driving down Olentangy River Road and we could walk out to greet him. We were strictly told not to bring anything with us. Later, somebody announced that he was leaving the Fawcett Center and now was our chance. In a hurry, we left the Woody Hayes Center and we were walking out to the street. I realized then that I had a football in my hands, so I tucked it under my shirt. Well, we lined up along the street and the president got out of the motorcade and started to shake our hands. I didn't know what do with this football, but I pulled it out and all of a sudden there were three Secret Service guys in my face. The president said, "Oh, you want me to sign that?" He signed it, and then Al Gore signed it, too. I later gave it to my roommate in Morrill Tower.

That following spring, Bobby Hoying was gone, so the quarterbacking job was down to me, Stanley Jackson, and Mark Garcia, another junior-college transfer whom coach Harris had recruited personally. I think that is the time I really progressed, even though I was getting two repetitions to their four.

At the spring game, it turned out that the last rotation of the game was my turn. We drove down to the 5-yard line, and we had time left for one play. I threw this fade to Dee Miller, and he kept his feet in bounds and made the catch in the corner of the end zone. That sort of got the ball rolling for my career.

Mark Garcia had injured his knee, so he would miss the whole season. Then, as everybody knows, Stanley Jackson and I rotated for the next two seasons. There wasn't a set time when I would come in, and I definitely would have liked to have played more, but I didn't want to start any controversy. And there wasn't any, as far as the team was concerned. There was competition, but we got along fine. The coaches told us in camp, "Whoever separates himself from the other will get to play." I guess they really didn't think anybody stood out, so they just decided to play both of us.

I was never sure what the fans thought back then, if they ever favored one over the other, but I did receive a lot of support. The Ohio State fans were

Joe Germaine looks downfield against Minnesota in 1998.

just great to me. All the same, I wonder what I would have done if I would
have played more. For example, against Wisconsin, we were behind in the
third quarter, and I threw an out route to Dimitrious Stanley, who made a
guy miss and turned it into a touchdown. "Now we're rolling," I thought.

But I got taken out, and I didn't play the rest of the game.

As the year went on and we won each game, I was keeping track of the
Pac-10, and I knew that ASU was having a good year. I kept thinking that it
would be ironic if we played my hometown team in the Rose Bowl. It
couldn't have worked out any better.

The week we clinched the Big Ten, we played at Indiana. It had been so
many years since Ohio State had played in a Rose Bowl, and there was a lot
of pressure. Late in the game, we were leading Indiana in a close game
[20–17], and I remember Matt Keller and I fumbling the exchange on a handoff. I remember diving on the ball and all these linemen and linebackers
landed on me. One of them told me, "Man, you guys are losing it."

A couple of plays later, Andy Katzenmoyer caused a fumble that Matt
Finkes picked up and ran into the end zone to clinch it.

Even though we lost to Michigan the next week, we still went to the Rose
Bowl to play Arizona State. Their quarterback, Jake Plummer, scrambled for
that touchdown to put us behind 17–14, and there was just a little more than
a minute [1:40] remaining.

The coaches had to make a decision about who was going to go in at quarterback. Later, I had heard the story: Mike Jacobs was the acting offensive
coordinator, because coach Harris had already accepted the Pittsburgh job,
but he had stayed to coach us through the Rose Bowl. When they came to
deciding who would go in on that final drive, there was dead silence. Coach
Jacobs didn't say anything. Finally, coach Harris told them, "We've got to go
with Germaine."

They just pointed to me and said, "Get out there."

We had practiced that two-minute drill each Friday all year. I got into the
huddle and there wasn't a lot of talking. We just weren't going to let the game
end like that. We had good field position to start, at the 35-yard line. We hit
a couple of crucial third-and-longs, and then came the big play. We were on
the 5-yard line, and we sent Dimitrious Stanley to the slot on the right and
David Boston out wide to the right. The primary receiver was supposed to
be Dimitrious, who would run a corner route. David would run inside on a

319

hitch and then back toward the pylon. As I dropped back, I could tell they had Dimitrious defensed. They had cut him off. I looked down at Boston, and he was wide open. We won 20–17.

Being the Rose Bowl MVP, I couldn't describe a better ending. I will never forget standing up on that podium after the game with Orlando Pace and the seniors like Greg Bellisari, Luke Fickell, and Mike Vrabel. Those guys had always treated me well.

It was different to have the freedom in 1998, not to have to look over my shoulder. Stanley was gone and I was now the starting quarterback. I think it was good for the team, too. They could get used to my style of play and not worry about who was in the game.

The Michigan State game that year was the only real disappointment of my Ohio State career. We were ranked number one and we were leading them 24–9, when . . . I still don't know what happened. I think we just tried to run out the clock and sit on the ball. It was just one of those things. That [28–24] loss cost us a national championship. We had some big dreams that year, but we still beat Michigan.

I will never forget being announced and running through that tunnel of former players before the Michigan game. All my family was there to see it.

I honestly can't think of a better place to go to school and play football. Ohio State was second to none. Buckeye fans are the greatest in the world, and even though I came from Arizona, I am definitely a Buckeye.

Joe Germaine, the Big Ten's MVP in 1998, holds 12 Ohio State passing records, including most passing yards in a season (3,330), completions in a season (230), and 300-yard passing games in a season (seven). He has played for the St. Louis Rams, Kansas City Chiefs, and Cincinnati Bengals.

JASON SIMMONS

1990–1993

WHEN I WAS IN HIGH SCHOOL at St. Vincent St. Mary's in Akron, Ohio State was slow to recruit me. When they did, and they finally offered me a scholarship, it was one of the best days of my life—behind only the marriage to my wife and the births of our kids and, let me not forget, the day I received my diploma from The Ohio State University.

The experience of being a Buckeye will stay with me forever and will always be considered as the best years of my life. It has changed my life in so many ways that it is difficult to describe and to measure. I know I will forever be known as an Ohio State Buckeye and a former team captain. For that, people recognize me wherever I go in this great state. At Ohio State, I learned the importance of teamwork and leadership. I learned the value of hard work and having the will to never give up. How could you give up in front of the Ohio State fans—the best and most demanding fans in the country? I learned early to do whatever it took to make those fans happy.

The campus life was definitely one of the reasons I had such an enjoyable time at OSU. Some people always asked me, "Isn't it hard going to a big school?" To me, that was part of the fun, because I got a chance to meet new people every quarter.

I have so many great memories and funny stories. One time, during a road game at Iowa, the visitors' locker room was painted bubble-gum pink. As many people know, Iowa coach Hayden Fry was very much into gaining psychological edges any way he could. As we entered the locker room, there was a huge commotion a few lockers away. Suddenly, a bat came swooping down on our heads. People were diving for cover as this bat tried to find a quiet place to hide. Eventually, several players wielding their cleats chased it into the bathroom, where it landed above one of the stalls. We pushed the stall door open to finish off that poor bat, and there was Dave Monnot, sitting there listening to his headphones. He was reading the game day program and trying to get some peace and quiet.

The thing that you take from your playing days is the friendships with your teammates. I could mention dozens of them, but I want to mention Greg Smith and Brian Stablein. They both were deemed too small when they came out of high school, but that didn't stop them from accomplishing their goals. They entered as walk-ons, and the work ethic they displayed became contagious. They eventually earned scholarships and landed immense respect from their teammates.

I was one of coach Cooper's players, and I know that people find it easy to take shots at him now. Some of it may be deserved, but we need to keep in mind that he helped build the program into a national powerhouse. Although he never got us to the Promised Land, the players he recruited are the source of pride to thousands of Buckeyes everywhere.

I will never forget my position coaches—Bill Young, Fred Pagac, Bob Palcic, and Bill Conley. These men taught me as much about life and what it means to be a man as they taught me about football. Ohio State will always have great assistant coaches, and they fit in that category.

I am thankful for coach Tressel. He has brought back the pride and many of the traditions to Ohio State. I know that our ship will maintain its present course for greatness because coach Tressel is a winner, and I am glad he is a Buckeye.

Although playing football was a tremendous experience, it would have been for naught if not for getting my degree. That piece of paper validates everything I worked for while at Ohio State. I would not be as successful after Ohio State without it.

As I look back, I am truly thankful. I am thankful to all the coaches, trainers, equipment managers, and everybody else affiliated with the program. I am thankful for my teammates. And I am thankful for the Best Damn Band in the Land. Most of all, I want to thank the fans. Without them, the Shoe would be like any other stadium, and game day would be like any other

Jason Simmons celebrates a sack against Louisville in the 1992 season opener.

game. Now, I am just a fan, too. And like most Buckeyes, I bleed scarlet and gray. I live and die each Saturday afternoon during the fall. We past players regard the current players as part of our extended family. It is a brotherhood that we understand and treasure. I gained another family while playing at Ohio State, and there is no better surrogate family to have than the Buckeye family!

Jason Simmons was named All–Big Ten in 1991 and a team captain in '93. He holds the single-game sack record with four (at Washington State in 1991) and finished his career with 56.5 tackles for loss—third on Ohio State's all-time list.

The

NEW MILLENNIUM

JONATHAN WELLS

1998–2001

BEING FROM RIVER RIDGE, LOUISIANA, the SEC schools and Louisiana schools like LSU and Tulane wanted me to play football, but my mind was always elsewhere. I remember watching TV and seeing Eddie George running through holes at Ohio State, and that was the image that stuck with me. I remember in 1995 when the Buckeyes beat Notre Dame and Illinois and Eddie had huge games. That team had Terry Glenn and Orlando Pace, and they put up a lot of points and they made me an Ohio State fan.

I could have gone to Tulane and been the king of campus, or I could have gone to LSU and been a linebacker, but I didn't want to stay home—I wanted to go to Ohio State and be a running back.

When I first saw Ohio Stadium and the campus, I admit that I was in awe. I had never been away from home. That first day, I met Derek Ross and we became roommates for the next three years, and today, he is my best friend. My first real memory is coming up early before my freshman season and having [strength] coach Dave Kennedy put us through running and conditioning drills. I couldn't believe how tough it was. I stopped at one point, and he told me that if I ever stopped again, I may as well go home to New Orleans.

In that first game in '98, my first as a Buckeye, I scored a touchdown at West Virginia and it was a huge thrill. We had such a great season that year but lost in that fluke game to Michigan State. We capped that season off in the Sugar Bowl, and I did get to go home to New Orleans, but as a team member. I had about 50 friends and family there and got to carry seven times in the second half as we beat Texas A&M. That was a great thrill for a freshman.

Jonathan Wells looks for a hole against Purdue in 2001.

I remember when we got back to campus after that game, I was so excited because it was the first time I got to see snow. We had a few inches on the ground, and there were a few guys in my class who had never seen it before, either, so we went out and played "snow football" without our shirts on.

I didn't redshirt that season, and as it turned out, I would have been part of the 2002 national championship team if I had. But I have no regrets about that decision. I believe everything is done for a reason, and I was on the sideline at the Fiesta Bowl that night, and I felt just as tired and as drained after that game as if I had played. That is the thing I learned—that you sweat and bleed for the guys you played with.

The one thing that was special at Ohio State is that the running backs all stuck together, even though we were competing against each other in a way. We pulled for each other. I never started every game until my senior year, because of injuries or for not always doing things right off the field, and I understand that. That is part of the great tradition that we have, and that's why I went there in the first place.

When we had the transition of coaches [when John Cooper was fired in January 2001], the whole thing was made a breeze and made very simple for me because of one man: Jim Tressel. I am glad coach Tressel gave me the opportunity. He just told me straight up, "I'll give you an opportunity to do it, and it's up to you." It was all business with him, and I knew it was my last go-round. He just told me how to get it done. I really want to thank him for putting it on my shoulders.

I have to mention coach [Tim] Spencer. He was hard on me at times, but I really appreciate him today. He got on me pretty good, but I knew it was to make me better, and I never took it personal.

One of my best memories is that night game against Northwestern [139 yards rushing]. I had been benched the week before against Indiana, and after that, my season was totally different. Coach Spencer sat me down and asked me, "If the season ended now, where would you be drafted?"

I answered, "In the fifth or sixth round."

He said, "No, the scouts who come in here say you wouldn't be drafted—you would be a free agent."

I was under a little stress at that point, and I just decided to play hard every down. Then in the Northwestern game, I broke loose on that run [71 yards], and things worked out for me after that. Against Illinois, I had gained 192 yards, but we lost. It was our last day in the stadium, and after the game, I just sat there and cried for about 15 minutes. I couldn't believe it was coming to an end like that.

But the next week was nothing but a pleasant memory. Under coach Tressel, we had started preparing for the Michigan game back in the spring. When he was hired, we started watching tape on Michigan right away. He let us know that this was not a regular game, and it seemed like it was always on our mind. I liked the way he was confident about it, too. I think he knew he could come in and turn things around in the rivalry, and he put the pressure on himself by telling the crowd at the basketball game the day he was hired.

I took that game personal. I was a senior, it was my final game, and I considered myself a leader, so having three touchdowns in that first half up there was huge. Then my whole lower body cramped up and I couldn't play in the second half. The important thing was that we won the game, and my class ended up with two wins over Michigan.

You know, it took me until my senior year to get the whole tradition thing at Ohio State down. We learned the alma mater and the fight song, and we wrote letters to our parents, and everything seemed to come alive my senior year. I went to the spring game [in 2003], and I really feel like I am part of the big picture at Ohio State now. I have no regrets at all, and I wouldn't change a thing if I could.

I am from Louisiana, I am living in Texas, but I love Ohio State.

Jonathan Wells, who rushed for 1,294 yards and 16 touchdowns in earning team MVP honors in 2001, was selected in the fourth round of the 2002 NFL draft by the Houston Texans. He led the Texans in rushing during his rookie season.

CIE GRANT

1999–2002

M Y DREAM BEGAN WHEN I WAS A QUARTERBACK coming out of New Philadelphia High School, and I was considering going to either Michigan or Michigan State. Jim Roman was an assistant coach on my high school team, and he was a member of Ohio State's 1968 national championship team. He just told me, "No, no, you just take your visit to Ohio State . . . just go to one game." I said, "Why? I know I am not going there." But I went to the ['97] Illinois game and I had a real good feeling, and so did my parents.

Coach Cooper convinced me this was the best place for me.

I remember when I first got here, thinking how big this campus was. "Dang," I thought, "this is a lot of walking, especially in the wintertime." Then they showed us the bus system and I learned to get around.

I redshirted during that '98 season, and now as I look back at it, with or without the national championship, it was the best thing for me. I hated to waste a whole year just playing special teams, and as it turned out, I am really thankful for that decision.

I started practices as a safety and then went to linebacker in the spring of 2000. That year was a crazy time. We lost to Michigan and then at the Outback Bowl, and they decided to go in a different direction, firing coach Cooper. We had to get ready for winter conditioning, and we didn't know who the coach would be, but I remember [strength coach] Dave Kennedy working us out, telling us, "Don't worry, they'll bring a good coach in here. Just stay in shape."

We were coming off an 8–4 season, and we knew there was plenty of room for improvement.

After coach Tressel got the job, he really made a good impression in that first meeting. He had a certain confidence about himself, and he said right away, "We are going to work to be the best." We all left that meeting and said, "Let's give him a chance."

He had given us something called "The Block 'O' of Life," which outlined goals of family, football, and education. What struck me was that he wasn't just a football coach—he wanted to know everything about you.

Later, we each had one-on-one meetings with him, and I told him, "I am a junior, and most of my work has been on special teams. I just want a chance to play. I need the opportunity because my time is closing. I don't want you to give me anything, just the opportunity."

He promised me he would.

Late that summer, I had missed one of our senior's presentations in front of the team. The seniors give reports on themselves to the entire team, and I missed Mike Collins'. Coach Tressel asked me, "How are we going to punish you? I know, you have to sing 'Carmen, Ohio' in front of the team."

331

I had sung in the church choir a little, and he had made us learn all the school songs after he was hired. So I sang "Carmen, Ohio" in front of the team that day—and I ended up singing it each Friday night in front of the team before our next game.

That fall, I was behind Joe Cooper at linebacker, and I asked [defensive coordinator Mark] Dantonio if I could get a chance to get on the field with the nickel [coverage] package. He said, "We'll see how you do in the nickel in practice." So I did pretty well, and then I did pretty well in one-on-one coverage, and they pulled me aside. "We're going to try you at corner," he told me.

Now this is only a week or two before the opening game. I went to corner, played well, and started 10 out of those 12 games. I got beat some games, such as that touchdown pass in the Wisconsin game, and the media was on me some, but at the end of the season, I ended up playing pretty well.

When we beat Michigan at Ann Arbor, it was just one of the greatest feelings I had experienced. We celebrated down in that corner with all of our fans, and to see most of those 111,000 fans quiet and dumfounded, we were overwhelmed with emotion. Michigan had talked before the game about Michigan State being their rivalry now, not Ohio State.

332

Cie Grant wraps his hands around Miami quarterback Ken Dorsey on the final play of the 2003 Fiesta Bowl, which brought the Buckeyes their first national championship in 34 years.

In the locker room, coach Tressel told us, "Now this one feels good, but we got to do it again next year."

I think what happened in 2002 actually began in the second half of the Outback Bowl. We were getting embarrassed 28–0 by South Carolina, and I looked over at [linebacker] Courtland Bullard. He said, "It's not about the fans, it's not about the coaches . . . it's about us. We have to play for pride—starting now!"

We came back and tied it and had the opportunity to win, but something changed in that second half.

Then, leading up to the season opener against Texas Tech, we had a players-only meeting. I told everybody, "I've been on a really good Ohio State team (that '98 team when I redshirted was one game from winning the national championship) and then a 6–6 team that didn't go anywhere for a bowl. We came to Ohio State for one reason. We want to win the national championship. I feel like we have what it takes to do it."

Coach Dantonio and I had talked, and we agreed it would be best for the team if I switched back to linebacker. That way, we would be able to disguise coverages and do so many things.

We all decided from the beginning to take one game at a time. It sounds like a cliché, but that's what we really did very well. Once we won our first seven games, nobody expected us to go to Wisconsin and win. After that game, we thought, "Yes, now we're on to something." After beating Penn State at home, we said, "Yes, we can do this."

Then coach Tressel told us, "Champions go undefeated in the month of November." We had Minnesota, Purdue, Illinois, and Michigan left. In that Purdue game, we were facing fourth-and-1 with the game on the line, and we went for it all. Craig Krenzel to Michael Jenkins. That's the kind of team we had. We took chances. And then we beat Illinois in overtime and Michigan again when the stadium was as loud as ever.

What can I say about our defense? We just knew that anybody at any time could come up with the big play. We were all capable of it. One time it would be Mike Doss. The next would be Donnie Nickey, or Kenny Peterson, or Will Smith, or Matt Wilhelm . . . I could go on and on.

The week before the Fiesta Bowl, you would have thought Miami was out there just for the joy of it. It was a given that they would be crowned national champions again. But we didn't go out there to roll over. We practiced like we knew we had to dominate that game. We practiced all week at game speed. And we knew that Miami did not really know how good our defense was.

Before the game, in the locker room, coach Tressel told us, "Seize this opportunity. If you are a junior, sophomore, or a freshman, don't think you'll ever get here again and have another chance. This is it! Seize it! It has been 34 years since Ohio State last won a national championship. Know that you are playing for all of Ohio State's fans, alumni, and former players. Now go do it!"

I remember walking through that tunnel and the adrenaline was pumping so much. I came out of the tunnel, and it was just like a home game. It was overwhelming. There was scarlet and gray everywhere. In pregame, I got so worked up that I couldn't breathe. I saw Eddie George, David Boston, and Jonathan Wells on the sideline. As the game went on, I would look over at those guys and hear them yell, "Come on!" We may not know each other on a personal level, but we knew that anybody who had ever worn the scarlet and gray was rooting for us that night.

There were so many big plays during that game. . . . I remember Craig getting hit by their linebacker so hard, most quarterbacks wouldn't have gotten up . . . I remember Maurice Clarett stripping the ball on that interception . . . I remember Matt driving Ken Dorsey into the ground.

It came down to the final play, and when we got the call for our defense, I knew it was my play. I had stayed in the coaches' ears all night, "Bring me on the blitz, bring me on the blitz!" That was the call. I was thinking to myself, "This is big, this is big, this is really big." I remember seeing their tackle line up and thinking, "He can't stop me." Then they brought some short motion and I thought they might try to block me that way. There was a single back in the backfield, and I thought he might be the one assigned to me. I wondered why there was no tight end over there on my side. All these things were going through my head before the snap. I got the best jump on that snap that I ever had in my life. It was just me and Dorsey, and I told myself, "Don't miss him . . . just don't miss him." So many times you see a guy who has a kill shot at the quarterback, and he ends up missing him.

I grabbed him and got him to the ground, and I saw that he didn't have the ball, but I didn't know what happened. I couldn't hear anything, but then I saw all the coaches running toward me. It wasn't until coach [Mark] Snyder ran up to me that I realized it was over and we had won the national championship.

I just wanted to shout, "We are the champs! When we wake up tomorrow, we will be the champs! We will always be the champs!"

One of my fondest memories of the whole season will be our celebration in Ohio Stadium a few weeks later. On the bus ride over to the stadium, a few of the coaches asked me if I was going to sing "Carmen, Ohio." I said, "My last time singing in front of anybody was the night before the Miami game." Then Craig Krenzel came up and asked me again. He wanted to get it on tape. I really didn't want to do it. Finally, during the ceremony, Mr. [Andy] Geiger said, "Would Cie Grant come to the front, please?" I told the other seniors, "We've always had each other's backs, so you got my back today. Don't let me down." It was cold and I hadn't warmed up my voice, but the rest is history. I am very glad I did it.

This place means so much to me, I can't begin to put it into words. It's the winning tradition, the family, the teammates who I will remember until I am 70 years old. I will always be a big Buckeye fan. I think all of us will bleed scarlet and gray for the rest of our lives.

Cie Grant had 71 tackles in 2002, including 10 for loss of yardage. He finished his career with 146 tackles and the most important quarterback pressure in Ohio State history. He was drafted in the third round of the 2003 NFL draft by the New Orleans Saints.

ANDY GROOM

2000–2002

THIS IS VERY DIFFICULT TO WRITE, knowing that my time being a football player at Ohio State is now over, but I think to myself, "What a way to go out." From being a lonely walk-on, to a starter for the greatest team in college football, to All-American, to being on the 2002 national championship team, and to meeting the president of the United States . . . how could I have written a better script for myself?

My career will be something I will cherish for the rest of my life. I have met people that will be with me forever throughout life. Coaches, players, trainers, and academic counselors were some of the best people I have ever met.

The 2002 season was about the craziest season you could imagine. We had a few blowouts, but most of them were real nail-biters—from holding off Wisconsin on the road, to Chris Gamble scoring the only touchdown of the game to beat Penn State, to that gutsy throw from Craig Krenzel to Michael Jenkins on fourth down against Purdue, to the overtime win against Illinois, to the Michigan game everyone will remember . . .

There were so many big moments during the season, but I remember one especially. There were just a few minutes left against Penn State, and we were leading 13–7. We faced a fourth down from inside our 10-yard line, and the punt team was running onto the field. "Groom!" I heard coach Tressel's voice, "Come over here!" I went over and he told me, "Now you know the punt is the most important play in football. I want you to show me why it's the most important play in football." From five yards deep in our end zone, I hit a 60-yarder that got us out of trouble. On the next possession, there was only 1:13 left and we had to punt again. "Show me again," he told me. I hit a 58-yarder with negative return, backing up Penn State deep in their own territory. They didn't do anything offensively, and we won the game.

Then there was the national championship game that everyone said we would lose. I can honestly say that the one thing that this team possessed was that everyone cared for each other and loved one another. I would go to bat for anyone on that team. Whether it was a walk-on, freshman, nonstarter, or starter, I would always be there for them, and I knew they would be there for me.

We had something very special at Ohio State, something that not too many teams ever had.

The national championship game was truly unbelievable, as most fans know from watching it. But what people did not see was the behind-the-scenes things that the players got to see. The Fiesta Bowl treated us like kings in every way you could imagine. They had a hospitality room where we could all come together, relax, and play a number of different games. I can still see Darrion Scott sitting in there with his shirt off, playing cards with the guys, or Kenny Peterson talking junk all the way to the championship game of pool. These are the times I will miss most, the times that I will cherish forever. When you spend time with the fellas just being with each other and enjoying the camaraderie, there is nothing like it. Even though these times are over for me, I will never forget the good times I have had with all my teammates.

Before the Fiesta Bowl, I don't think there was one reporter who said we could win that game against Miami. The main thing was, everyone on that team knew we were going to shock the world. We had heard that we did not have enough team speed to beat Miami. We had plenty of that. Not to toot my own horn, but I'd like to race their punter and see if he ran a 4.4. All of that can be thrown out the window, because we came to Tempe to win, not to lose. We were just quiet about it, though, and didn't shoot off our mouths like some players from Miami.

At that final practice at the Fiesta Bowl, Mike Tomczak addressed the team this way: "I have never been this excited and pumped up since I played at Ohio State. I want each and every one of you to go back to the hotel tonight

Andy Groom, a former walk-on, became one of Ohio State's greatest all-time punters.

and write this down: '2002 national champions,' because if you don't write down your goals, they won't come true." I know I did it and others did it. I think Donnie Nickey even put his inside his helmet.

As I think back to that magical night, everything about the game was breathtaking, and I took it all in so I would remember it the rest of my life. Seeing the sea of scarlet in the Fiesta Bowl was a sight for sore eyes, and I felt like we were back at home in the "shoe." All I know is that when the silver bullets stopped Miami on fourth-and-goal on the game's final play, I just sat down and cried, because I knew what we had done was special.

At the same time, I was also saddened because I knew that my time at Ohio State was over and that there would be no more Buckeye football for me. It was a bittersweet feeling knowing that we had accomplished something that so many of the teams before us had tried to accomplish, and so many teams after us will try.

Weeks later, we had the celebration in the "shoe" allowing the seniors to be together one last time. It was a very emotional day to have all of us come together as a team for the last time. The seniors, as many know, got to dot the *I* in "Script Ohio" and then listen to linebacker Cie Grant sing "Carmen, Ohio."

All of that, and seeing my father cry for the first time in my life, was too much for me to absorb all at once, and I began to cry like a baby. It was so hard to say good-bye to something that I have known and loved for so much of my life. It was truly a day to remember, seeing more than fifty thousand fans sitting in freezing temperatures to see their beloved Buckeyes.

Our trip to the White House was something I'll never forget. About 30 minutes before we were supposed to meet President Bush, coach Tressel pulled me aside and said, "Groomy, you're my man."

I said, "What do you mean?"

He just said, "You're our guy who will present the helmet to the president. Don't screw it up. Don't talk politics. Just call him 'Mister President.'"

Now I knew I had come a long way from being a walk-on, but talking to the president of the United States was something I never could have imagined in my wildest dreams. I could not believe he picked me to do this, and I have to admit I was a little nervous—it's nothing like before a crucial punt.

Well, everything went well at the White House. I gave the commemorative helmet to President Bush, and when we were leaving, Ben Hartsock decided that he wanted to make a snow angel on the front lawn of the White

House. As he was doing this, the Secret Service popped out and screamed at the top of their lungs at Ben. Well, he didn't hear them and continued in his mission on the lawn. While this was happening, coach Tressel was dying with laughter, but Ben didn't understand what the fuss was about. He got scolded by the Secret Service and was a little red in the face. It capped off the day, making it one to remember for the rest of our lives.

I am very honored I am a Buckeye, and I will take these memories with me wherever I go in life. I truly think that winning the national championship will not sink in until sometime down the road. But I do know one thing—the 2002 national champion Ohio State Buckeyes did a lot of people around the country very proud, and we did something that many OSU teams before us could not do. My time at Ohio State honestly has been the best time of my life, and I am so proud to be a part of Buckeye history.

Andy Groom averaged 45.0 yards per punt in 2002 and was named to several All-American teams.

KENNY PETERSON

1999–2002

I GREW UP SORT OF UNUSUAL in the fact that I was never one of those guys who followed sports. I didn't follow college football or the NFL, so I never knew much about Ohio State. I am not ashamed to say that I was a big momma's boy, and when it came time to choose a college, I didn't want to go too far from my mom and family. I committed to Ohio State very early, at the end of my junior year in high school. I went to the football game at OSU, and coach Pagac and coach Cooper both told me, "Whenever you want to be a Buckeye, the invitation is open." Right then, I made my decision. In my senior season at Canton McKinley, I was a part of the team with Jamar Martin and Mike Doss that finished 14–0 and won the state and national championships.

When I arrived in Columbus, it was my first experience of living on my own, without my mom. It felt like freedom, but a scary kind of freedom. After the first few days of practice, I wanted to go home. I remember that after one afternoon practice, I was lying across the field inside at the Woody Hayes Athletic Center, and Jamar Martin was sitting on a bench with LeCharles Bentley. I looked up and said, "Man, Jamar, I am hurting!"

Jamar said, "My whole body hurts!"

LeCharles said, "I want to go home!"

We all wanted to go home. Then we all tried to figure out some injuries we had to get us out of practice . . . it was rough. We were ready to get right back on I-71 and head north to get back home.

When I redshirted that season [1998], it was like falling off the face of the earth. I went from a highly touted high school player and from being an All-American to feeling like a nobody. We would come off the practice field, and these reporters would be there, and they would walk right past me. Nobody wanted to talk to me.

I got very discouraged, because I wanted to contribute. I didn't want people back home saying, "I knew he wasn't good enough to play at Ohio State."

One thing that really picked me up was when I found out that Cie Grant was my cousin. I knew I had relatives in New Philadelphia, but I didn't know Cie. Our moms got to talking and we found out we were second cousins.

Anyway, by redshirting, I concentrated on my schoolwork and I had a 3.2 GPA after my first year. As it turned out, I valued that year so much, and I learned the game of football.

There is no doubt that our class had some real tough times—the whole process of Coop [being fired], and then we didn't know who our coach would be. But that period brought us together as a team. At that point, all we had was each other. I have always been a firm believer that everything happens for a reason.

When I heard the name Jim Tressel, I knew we would be OK. I had several friends in high school who had played for him [at Youngstown State]. They told me that he was a great guy, and they said, "He will kill you with kindness." When he came in that first day, he met with us and he didn't say one thing about football. It was kind of shocking to me—he came in and described what it took to be a champion and the importance of an education, our spiritual life, and how to be a good person. He hit on everything other than football, and that really impressed me. He said something like, "We want to be the class of college football, we want to be respected, and these people in this room will be a family."

He constantly stressed it was all about "we" and "team." It wasn't about "me" or "I." He had us read the book *Expanding Your Horizons*, about the 1942 national champion Ohio State team. He said, "This is part of the tradition." We always sang the fight song after games, and I knew we had an alma mater, but I never heard it until coach Tressel came here. I never knew the words. Do you know what goes through my mind now when I hear "Carmen, Ohio"? It almost brings tears to my eyes. Just thinking about it now, I am getting goose bumps on my arms.

Kenny Peterson sacks Miami quarterback Ken Dorsey during the 2003 Fiesta Bowl.

Coach Tressel's game plan was this: "All great teams have to be perfect at home. After that, our goal is to become Big Ten champions. Then, we will compete for the national championship."

Before games, coach Tressel wasn't the type to give rah–rah speeches. He would pace the floor back and forth like he was about to go out and play. And he was always encouraging. He would look at me before games and say, "Let's go, K.P.! Let's go, K.P.!" We would always say the Lord's Prayer and another prayer that got me so fired up. It went like this: "I am only one, but I am one. I can't do everything, but I can do something. What I can do, I ought to do. What I ought to do, by the grace of God, I shall do."

After the Washington State game, we knew what kind of caliber of team we had. I think we all realized that we had a good shot of doing what we did. We all believed that it wasn't about each individual—it was about us. Then we had so many nail-biters as the year went on. Mike Doss and I both talked about how it reminded us of Canton McKinley. We had so many close games and won the high school national championship.

In the past, bowl practices weren't the most crisp practices of them all. But at the Fiesta Bowl, we wanted to learn and improve every moment. We practiced at a fast pace, and we knew we had a group of guys that weren't going to be denied. When you get a group of guys willing to do whatever it takes, there is nothing else left but to succeed.

When we went out for warm-ups that night, we knew it was a home game. We were thousands of miles from home, but we felt like we were home. Everybody was so jacked up and ready to go. We were not being coached to come from behind, we were being coached to smack them in the mouth.

We didn't change anything about the way we played. We played physical and tried to dominate Miami from the start. I remember I got my first sack against [Miami center Brett] Romberg pretty early, and I knew right away we could play with them. Before that final play of the game, I was looking at everybody in the huddle, and I turned to Mike Doss, Donnie Nickey, and Dustin Fox. I said, "Let's go; this is what we've been waiting for." They were looking back through their face masks, and I could tell that they really wanted it. We had 11 heartbeats beating as one, and when it was over, I didn't know whether to cry or jump for joy. I didn't know my reaction until I watched the film—I started to walk off the field to the bench, but I turned around and saw David Thompson, and he had shouted, "We did it! We did it!" At that point, it started to sink in.

We all had been through so many ups and downs—to finish it like that is something you just can't describe. It seems like yesterday that I can reach out and touch the time I left my mom's house to head to Columbus.

That program means a lot to me. I can honestly say that if I had to do it all over again, I would do exactly the same thing. I have absolutely no regrets. Now I am so thankful that I did redshirt. I learned so much about myself in those five years. I learned how to be a man, and I matured so much. I don't know if I would have experienced those things at any other university.

I will always be a Buckeye.

Kenny Peterson, who had two quarterback sacks in the 2003 Fiesta Bowl, was drafted in the third round of the 2003 NFL draft by the Green Bay Packers.

M COUSINEAU · TIM FOX · EDDIE GEORGE · RANDY GRADIS

CHIE GRIFFIN · JOHN HICKS · JIM HOUSTON · REX KERN ·

HNSON · MARCUS MAREK · JIM MARSHALL · TOM MATTE ·

SIBAUGH · CHRIS SPIELMAN · JIM STILLWAGON · PAUL WAR

EITH BYARS · JIM OTIS · TOM SKLADANY · CORNELIUS GREE

AN BASCHNAGEL · CRIS CARTER · HOWARD "HOPALONG" CAS

M COUSINEAU · TIM FOX · EDDIE GEORGE · RANDY GRADIS

CHIE GRIFFIN · JOHN HICKS · JIM HOUSTON · REX KERN ·

HNSON · MARCUS MAREK · JIM MARSHALL · TOM MATTE ·

SIBAUGH · CHRIS SPIELMAN · JIM STILLWAGON · PAUL WAR

EITH BYARS · JIM OTIS · TOM SKLADANY · CORNELIUS GREE

AN BASCHNAGEL · CRIS CARTER · HOWARD "HOPALONG" CAS

M COUSINEAU · TIM FOX · EDDIE GEORGE · RANDY GRADIS

CHIE GRIFFIN · JOHN HICKS · JIM HOUSTON · REX KERN ·

HNSON · MARCUS MAREK · JIM MARSHALL · TOM MATTE ·

SIBAUGH · CHRIS SPIELMAN · JIM STILLWAGON · PAUL WAR

EITH BYARS · JIM OTIS · TOM SKLADANY · CORNELIUS GREE

AN BASCHNAGEL · CRIS CARTER · HOWARD "HOPALONG" CAS